£38.00

European Financial Reporting

Routledge, in association with the Institute of Chartered Accountants in England and Wales, is pleased to present a major new series in European accounting.

During the last decade many of Europe's largest companies have developed new approaches to financial reporting. In doing so they have sought to explain to the rapidly expanding international investment community not only their own financial results but also the complexities of the business environments in which they operate. Now, with the coming into force throughout the EC of a harmonized accounting framework, the scene is set for European companies to use a common approach to financial reporting. However, despite the moves towards standardization and harmonization, the underlying differences between Europe's various business environments are still far-reaching. Local accounting practices continue to reflect this.

The European Financial Reporting series provides the first detailed, authoritative, country-by-country guides to current accounting and financial reporting practices in Europe. Each volume also includes a comprehensive analysis of the current state of company law, taxation and other matters relevant to business activity.

The series aims to meet the needs of:

- Accountants, auditors and other business professionals, including those advising companies operating or intending to operate in the country in question.
- Analysts and investors wishing to interpret the financial statements of European companies.
- Students of international accounting at universities, business schools and other institutions of higher education.

The series editor **Stuart McLeay** and associate editor **Simon Archer** are, respectively, Professors in the School of Accounting, Banking and Economics at the University of Wales, Bangor and in the Department of Management Studies at the University of Surrey, Guildford. They are both internationally recognized as authorities in the field of financial reporting. In preparing the European Financial Reporting series, the principal editor has assembled a team of authors from among the leading figures in European accounting.

European Financial Reporting

Series editor: Professor Stuart McLeay
Associate editor: Professor Simon Archer

FRANCE
Jean-Claude Scheid and Peter Walton

SPAIN
José A. Gonzalo and José L. Gallizo

IRELAND
Niamh Brennan, Francis J. O'Brien and Aileen Pierce

GREECE
Anthony A. Papas

ITALY
Rosanna Ghirri and Angelo Riccaboni

DENMARK
Merete Christiansen and Jens O. Elling

GERMANY
Dieter Ordelheide and Dieter Pfaff

PORTUGAL
Leonor Fernandes Ferreira

LUXEMBOURG
Peter Clark

NETHERLANDS
Jan Dijksma and Martin Hoogendoorn

BELGIUM
Christian Lefebvre and John Flower

UNITED KINGDOM
Paul Gordon and Sidney Gray

Portugal

Leonor Fernandes Ferreira

London and New York

First published 1994
by Routledge
11 New Fetter Lane, London EC4P 4EE

Simultaneously published in the USA and Canada
by Routledge
29 West 35th Street, New York, NY 10001

© 1994 Maria Leonor Fernandes Ferreira

Typeset in 10/12½pt Times by Solidus (Bristol) Limited
Printed and bound in Great Britain by Clays Ltd, St. Ives PLC

British Library Cataloguing in Publication Data
A catalogue reference for this book is available from the British Library

ISBN 0–415–06200–4

Library of Congress Cataloging in Publication Data
has been applied for

ISBN 0–415–06200–4

To Luís
and our son, Pedro Manuel.

Contents

Figures

Tables

Examples

Series preface

During the last decade, many of Europe's largest companies have developed new and innovative approaches to financial reporting. One of their principal aims has been to explain the complexities of the business environments in which they operate to the rapidly expanding international investment community. Indeed, earnings and other reported figures are greatly influenced not only by the divergent accounting methods adopted in various European countries, but also by the specific application of local tax regulations, company laws and employment practices, as well as the considerable diversity of financial and commercial environments in which a European company may operate.

With the coming into force throughout the European Community of a harmonized accounting framework, the scene is now set for European companies to use a common approach to financial reporting. Nevertheless, the EC directives cover only a restricted subset of disclosure and measurement issues, and with respect to these, harmonization is sometimes at a fairly superficial level. For example, under the Fourth Directive alone, there are more than thirty optional areas of harmonization which provide for alternative ways of implementing the directive. In spite of this, the immediate impact of the European Commission's actions in the area of financial reporting will be to enhance considerably the level of corporate accountability throughout the EC. At the same time, the latest evidence suggests that International Accounting Standards are assuming an increasingly important role.

As a result, the 1990s will bear witness to an accounting revolution in Europe. In the next few years, the extent of financial disclosure will take a quantum leap forward in many countries, particularly with regard to the publication of consolidated financial statements and audit opinions. In some countries, the institutional and legal infrastructure of accounting is already undergoing rapid change.

These contemporary changes in European financial reporting are taking place in the context of a rich history of accounting development. Starting with the earliest record-keeping of the Ancient Greeks, accounting ideas spread rapidly throughout Europe in the Middle Ages in keeping with the commercialization of the trading ports of the Atlantic and the Mediterranean and Baltic seas. Throughout the entire continent the earliest books of account date back to this period. Subsequently, Napoleonic codification influenced the regulation of business activity throughout a large part of continental Europe, laying the basis for the later introduction of extensive uniformity and national accounting plans. At much the same time, the notion of direct accountability to owners and lenders and the establishment of an independent auditing profession occurred as a result of the creation of joint stock companies during the industrial revolutions which first took place in some of the north European countries.

More recently, Europe as a whole has experienced yet another era of cross-fertilization in accounting thought with regard not only to the development of financial accounting standards but also to broader issues such as social accountability. In this respect, the reader who consults the various books in this series will find that remarkable innovations have taken place in some of Europe's smallest countries, such as Greece, Luxembourg, Ireland and Belgium, where the very nature of the society and its economy and the narrowness of the capital market has led to original developments in financial accounting, such as the preparation of ECU accounts, concentration on accounting for financial institutions and investment trusts, innovative voluntary disclosures aimed at international investors and new solutions to the problems of reporting across different languages.

Harmonization may result in a common understanding of the scope of corporate financial reporting in Europe, but there still remain significant differences between Europe's various business environments. The authors of the first twelve volumes in the European Financial Reporting series have produced the most authoritative studies of European accounting to date, which chart the evolution of accounting thought through to its current position. In particular, considerable attention has been paid to the fiscal, legal and financial background, and each book contains a detailed examination of current trends and techniques in accounting practice.

Professor Stuart McLeay
University of Wales, Bangor

Preface

Since the book was written there have been a number of developments in the tax and accounting rules, some due to the implementation of EC directives.

Chapter 1

As a small open economy Portugal has not escaped the effects of international recession. Growth has not stopped, however, only slackened, and remains above the EC average.

Chapter 3

The most recent developments of note in the financial system are:

The law regulating banks and other financial institutions took effect on 1 January 1993.

Subject to certain conditions, companies may now issue commercial paper and use it as a source of financing (decree law 18/92 of 22 August 1992).

The government's privatization programme moved on apace.

Money markets saw interest rates decline, shares remained depressed and the volume of transactions did not expand as much as had been predicted.

The code of conduct regulating the securities market (*Código do mercado dos valores mobiliários*) came into force and the regulatory body met for the first time.

A major event of 1992 was the admission of Portugal to the European Monetary System, application having been made on 3 April and authorized on the 6th.

Legislation to introduce derivatives (e.g. futures, options) is being prepared.

Chapter 4

Since the reform of indirect taxes in 1986 and of direct taxation in 1988 most changes have been directed towards harmonization, particularly of value-added tax with the rest of the EC.

Income tax. Most of the percentage rates have changed. The following apply to income of the 1993 tax year:

Income (PTE)	Marginal rate (%)
Up to 860,000	15
860,001–2,010,000	25
2,010,001–5,160,000	35
Over 5,160,000	40

The deadline for submitting tax returns is 15 March if the income arises under category A or from a pension; by 30 April in all other cases. Tax is payable in the year after the income is earned, on or before 31 May in the former case, 30 June in the latter.

Combined income for the years 1992 and onward should be divided by 1.9 (rather than 1.85 as previously).

Turning to corporate income tax, tax credit on intra-group dividends when a participation is under 25 per cent was raised to 50 per cent.

Value-added tax. The bottom rate was raised from 0 per cent to 5 per cent, and the 17 per cent rate was reduced to 16 per cent. Electricity and hotel services were added to the lowest band. Goods and services (other than electricity and hotel services) formerly taxed at 8 per cent are now subject to 16 per cent.

Real property transfer tax. The percentage rates are now:

Basis (PTE million)	Rate (%) Marginal	Rate (%) Average
Up to 8.1	0	0
8.1–12.0	5	1.6667
12.0–16.2	11	4.0000
16.2–20.2	18	6.8000
20.2–24.2	26	–
Over 24.2	Single 10 per cent rate	

Vehicle tax. Up from 16 per cent to 17 per cent.

Double taxation. An agreement with Mozambique on the avoidance of double taxation was concluded on 30 December 1992.

Chapter 5

Directrizes contabilísticas. Further recommendations have been drafted, and some that were only in draft when Chapter 5 was written have since been approved by the CNC and published in the official journal:

1/91   *Accounting for Business Combinations*
2/91   *Accounting for Assets received as Donations*
3/91   *Accounting for Construction Contracts*

4/91   *Accounting for Concessions*

5/91   *Accounting for Liabilities arising from Bingo*

6   *Elimination of Gains and Losses resulting from Transactions between Under-takings in the same Group*

7   *Accounting for Research and Development Costs*

8   *Clarification of Extraordinary Items and Significant Prior-period Items*

9   *Accounting for Investments in Subsidiaries and Associated Companies in the Individual Accounts*

10   *Accounting for Leases*

11   *Intra-Community Value-added Tax*

12   *Accounting for Goodwill*

13   *The Concept of Fair Value* (in draft)

14   *Cash flow statements*

The accountancy profession. The provision of accounting services is no longer state-regulated. In contrast, statutory audit activity is supervised by the Ministry of Justice, through the Câmara dos Revisores Oficiais de Contas. The Eighth Directive is expected to be implemented soon, a draft is already in circulation.

Chapter 9

Decree law 36/92 of 28 March 1992 inaugurated consolidated accounting for banks and financial institutions, applicable to financial years beginning on or after 1 January 1992. Details of format and preparation are prescribed by the Bank of Portugal. The Bank also supervises the group auditing of banks and other financial institutions on the basis of regulations approved in 1992.

The Insurance Institute of Portugal is preparing the ground for the adoption of the EC directives affecting the group and individual accounts of insurance companies, and is expected to reach a conclusion before long.

It is obviously too soon to assess the impact of group accounting during the brief period in which Portuguese companies have had experience of it. All that can be said is that its implementation has been marked by a degree of flexibility so as to allow companies freedom of choice. This is very much what would be expected from the set of options in the EC directive adopted for enactment into Portuguese law.

July 1993

Acknowledgements

Part of Chapter 5 is adapted from the author's chapter in the *European Accounting Guide*. The substance of Chapter 9 was presented to the European Accounting Association meeting in Madrid, 22–4 April 1992.

Notes on the author

Leonor Fernandes Ferreira is a teacher of Financial Management at the Technical University of Lisbon. She previously taught Financial Accounting, Financial Management and Strategic Management Planning at various universities, and has also participated as a monitor on many professional national and international training courses organized by companies. She works as a consultant in corporate finance, financial statements analysis and taxation, and is a member of the Portuguese Association of Economists, the Portuguese Financial Executives Institute, the Portuguese Fiscal Association and the Portuguese Accounting Society. She obtained a degree in Business Administration from the Universidede Católice Portuguese in 1981 and a degree in Economics from the Instituto Superior de Economia e Gestão in 1982. She also has an MBA from the Faculdade de Economia de Universidede Nova de Lisboa, and is currently working on her Ph.D. in Equity Stock Valuation Methods at the Technical University of Lisbon.

Part I
The business environment

1

Portugal:
the country

1 AN INTRODUCTION TO FINANCIAL REPORTING IN PORTUGAL

Two fundamental events have shaped the recent history of Portugal which are crucial to an economic evaluation of the country and an understanding of the state of corporate financial reporting. One was the end of authoritarian rule in 1974 and the subsequent introduction of political democracy, the other Portugal's entry into the European Community in 1986, the culmination of a process of opening up its frontiers and stimulating free trade that had started nearly three decades earlier.

Portugal, the oldest sovereign state in Europe, is a constitutional parliamentary monarchy. Its capital is Lisbon and the language is Portuguese. The legal currency is the escudo (PTE).

In common with other countries in southern Europe, Portugal has a legal system based mainly on Roman law. The principal bodies of legal texts (the Civil Code, Penal Code and Commercial Code) date back to the Napoleonic era and are regularly amended to take account of changes in the social and business situation.

Portuguese law provides for various different kinds of corporate structure (see Chapter 2). The most significant are:

1   Corporations (*sociedade anónima*, SA for short).
2   Private limited company (*sociedades por quotas, Lda*).

The capital of a *sociedade anónima* is divided into shares, while the capital of a *sociedade por quotas* is divided into quotas that are not freely transferable by the owners.

Liability is not limited in a general partnership, and limited partnerships may contain partners with limited liability as well as others with unlimited liability. Neither type of partnership is common in practice.

Portugal's entry into the European Community led to a major reform of commercial and company law, and to the introduction of financial statement audits on a general basis. The key amending regulation in the field of company law was the Business Companies Code (Código das Sociedades Comerciais), published in November 1986, which superseded existing legislation and adapted it to EC Directives on Companies, including the Fourth and Seventh Directives.

The opportunity was taken when the Fourth and Seventh Directives were incorporated into Portuguese company law to introduce accounting regulations that would require Portuguese companies and traders to issue financial statements on a uniform basis. Until then, accounting obligations had been determined mainly by the tax regulations. Indeed, the 1977 Portuguese Official Accounting Plan (*Plano Oficial de Contabilidade*, POC) owed a good deal to the tax authorities; it was designed to facilitate tax inspections and to achieve equity in companies' income tax (because the basis for the calculation of the tax is the net income or profit from the accounting records) rather than to disclose information to shareholders or the public about a company's financial situation and operations.

Before the legislative reform, the corporate income tax regulations included a set of valuation and recording rules which were also applicable to the preparation of financial statements. After the Tax Reform Act (*Reforma Fiscal*) and the enactment of the new Accounting Plan in 1989, these recording obligations were repealed and the valuation rules were retained only for tax return purposes. (Although companies are free to set their own fiscal year, the customary practice is for it to run from 1 January to 31 December, and in this case the income tax return must be filed before the end of May the following year in accordance with tax regulations.)

A further influence on financial reporting is the stock exchange. Portugal's new law applicable to the stock exchange is the *Lei Sapateiro* of April 1991. There are two stock exchanges (in Lisbon and Oporto) on which corporate shares and bonds are traded, although their main activity is conducted on what is called the 'continuous market' in which trading takes place via computers linking the two exchanges as a single market. Stock exchange activity in Portugal is controlled by the Stock Exchange Market Commission (Comissão do Mercado de Valores Mobiliários), set up only in late 1991, which also stipulates the information to be provided by listed companies. However, the accounting obligations of Portuguese companies derive mainly from the Companies Act and from the Accounting Plan.

The required annual accounts are a balance sheet, a profit and loss account and the notes on the accounts. Companies below certain size criteria can present abridged financial statements. These annual accounts giving a true and fair view (*uma imagem verdadeira e apropriada*) of the company's situation and operations, together with the management's report and, where appropriate, the auditor's report, must be made public by depositing them with the Commercial Registry (Registo Comercial).

The layout of the accounts of certain kinds of companies differs from those in the Accounting Plan. This is the case with banks and other financial institutions whose accounting rules are issued by the Bank of Portugal and also with insurance companies whose accounting principles and procedures and financial reporting depend on the Insurance Institute of Portugal (Instituto de Seguros de Portugal).

With regard to consolidated accounts, the most recent amendment of the Accounting Plan, introduced on 2 July 1991, has made it mandatory for all groups controlled by a parent company to consolidate their accounts, although some are exempt for reasons of size or because they belong to larger groups with parent companies in EC member countries. However, all parent companies of listed groups must present consolidated annual accounts. The shareholders' meeting must approve the consolidated accounts at the same time as the parent's individual accounts, and the consolidated financial statements must be audited, presented together with a consolidated management report, and filed within the Commercial Registry.

The audit obligation affects all companies which exceed certain size limits, listed companies, credit institutions and insurance companies. Auditors are appointed by shareholders' meeting for a minimum of three years. In the case of companies not subject to compulsory audit, shareholders owning 5 per cent of the capital stock can demand the appointment of auditors. Auditors in Portugal are members of professional bodies and must be registered with the Official Auditors' Chamber (Câmara dos Revisores Oficiais de Contas), which is responsible for issuing standards and taking disciplinary measures.

The current state of accounting in Portugal has been influenced by a variety of factors, in particular, considerable recent change.

Since many of the measures have only been introduced over the last few years, the efficacy of the system will be determined in the next few years particularly with regard to the degree of harmonization that has been achieved with other EC countries.

This book presents a detailed description of the features of corporate financial reporting in Portugal, which should enable the reader to interpret company financial statements in the light of the economic background, and the legal and tax systems, and provide a broad general understanding of accounting and auditing in Portugal today.

Corporate financial reporting in Portugal – a profile

Companies
Most business in Portugal is conducted on the basis of sole proprietorship or limited companies, either private (*limitada* or *por quotas*) or public (*sociedades anónimas*), some of the latter having a stock exchange listing.

Accounting
The content and layout of the financial statements are prescribed by the *Plano Oficial de Contabilidade* (POC). The plan became law in 1977; it was amended in 1989 to conform with the Fourth Directive, on individual accounts, and in 1991 to comply with the Seventh, on consolidation, as from 1 January 1992. The Comissão de Normalização Contabilística (CNC) was responsible for both revisions. The CNC has issued *Normas Interpretativas* and more recently *Directrizes Contabilísticas* which are intended to round out the POC. The POC does not apply to banks, other financial institutions or insurance companies, which have sectoral Accounting Plans of their own, issued by the Bank of Portugal and the Portuguese Insurance Institute respectively.

The 1988 reforms abolished the requirement for state-registered *técnicos de contas* (chartered accountants) to sign company tax returns, and nowadays there is no single official body of authorized accountants, only a number of professional associations.

Auditing
The *Código das Sociedades Comerciais* requires *sociedades anónimas* and *limitada* companies over a certain size to be subject to an annual audit. Only auditors who have qualified as members of the professional auditing body, the Câmara dos Revisores Oficiais de Contas (Chamber of ROCs) may undertake such work. Auditing and ethical standards are specified by the Chamber in its periodically updated *Manual*, which embraces international auditing principles as well as the national *Recomendações técnicas*.

Company taxation
Corporate income tax (IRC) is levied on companies' world-wide earnings. Taxable income is calculated by reference to the rules of the *Código do IRC*, the *Estatuto dos Benefícios Fiscais* and the tax regulations and interpretations (*Circulares* and *Ofícios circulares*) issued by the tax authorities (Direcção-Geral das Contribuições e Impostos), a branch of the Ministry of Finance. IRC is assessed at a standard rate of 36 per cent. (Reduced rates apply to agricultural activities.) On top of this some local authorities levy a *derrama*, or local tax, of up to 10 per cent. Three payments on account fall due within six months of a company's financial year end, each reckoned as 25 per cent of the previous year's taxable income. The final instalment is paid the following year, no later than 31 May.

On the mainland value-added tax (*imposto sobre o valor acrescentado*, IVA for short) is levied at a standard rate of 17 per cent, with lower (zero or 8 per cent) and higher (30 per cent) rates on certain goods and services. Lower rates apply on the island of Madeira and the Azores.

The legal system
This is structured as a graduated hierarchy of laws, with the most important, the constitution (*Constituição da República Portuguesa*) as the basis. In descending order of priority the other sources of law are *leis* passed by Parliament (the Assembleia da República), *decretos-lei* of the government, *decretos-regulamentares* and *portarias* issued by Ministries, and *despachos normativos* and *despachos* signed by Secretaries of State. By the beginning of 1992 the first eight EC directives had been enacted in law, though it is too early as yet to assess their impact on the business community.

The currency
The monetary unit is the escudo (PTE or $), made up of 100 centavos. Unlike the dollar sign, the similar escudo symbol $ is often written after the number rather than before it. Decimals of the unit appear after the sign. Whereas a million dollars and fifty cents would be written $1,000,000.50 a million escudos and fifty centavos could be written 1 000 000$50. In everyday usage 1,000 escudos are commonly referred to as a *conto*.

The language
The official language is Portuguese, which is normally used in business. Accounts are always published in Portuguese, although some companies – mainly subsidiaries of foreign concerns – present bilingual financial reports.

2 GEOGRAPHY, CULTURE AND POPULATION

2.1 Geographical location, climate and natural resources

Portugal occupies an area slightly greater than 88,000 square km on the western side of the Iberian peninsula, between Spain and the Atlantic Ocean. The territory of Portugal also includes two autonomous island regions, the Azores and Madeira. The climate is temperate, without extreme temperatures or humidity. Winters are not excessively severe, nor are the summers particularly hot, the average annual temperature being 61°F (16°C).

Amongst the country's most valuable natural resources are various minerals such as iron ore, tungsten and uranium, many of which have yet to be fully exploited. Considering the country's geographical location and numerous rivers, it will be readily appreciated that fish are a particularly important natural resource. Portugal is also one of the leading producers of cork.

Table 1.1 Portugal: general data

Total area (km²)	88,500
Population	9,808,000
Inhabitants per square kilometre	110.8

Source: Bank of Portugal, *Main Economic Indicators, 1986–90*, Lisbon: Departamento de Estatística e Estudos Económicos, 1991.

2.2 Agricultural products, main industries and cities

Thanks to a diversity of soils and regional climates, the cultivation is unusually varied. The main agricultural products include potatoes, olives and viticulture, mostly in the north, cereals and rice in the centre and, in the south, citrus fruits and almonds. The major industries are principally related to the natural resources: textiles, wood products, paper, etc., based on traditionally run small-scale companies, with the exception of electronics and motor vehicle assembly.

Because of its long coastline, Portugal has always been orientated towards the sea. The most populous and important cities are near the mouths of two great rivers: Lisbon (population 2,126,400) on the Tagus and Oporto (population 1,670,400) on the Douro.

Table 1.2 Major industries, agricultural produce and natural resources

Natural resources	Agricultural products	Major industries
Fish	Cereals	Textiles
Cork	Potatoes	Footwear
Tungsten	Olives	Forest products
Iron ore	Wine	Paper
Copper	Rice	Cork

Table 1.3 Major cities and their population

Population	City
Over 2 million	Lisbon
Over 1 million	Oporto
Over 400,000	Setubal
	Coimbra
	Braga
	Aveiro
	Leiria

2.3 Currency, language and religion

The national currency is the Portuguese escudo (at October 1991, US$1 = 143.863 Portuguese escudos). The term *conto*, meaning 1,000 escudos, is used when referring to larger sums of money.

Portuguese is the official language spoken by over 160 million people from Brazil to Macao, near Hong Kong, and the former Portuguese territories in Africa: Angola, Mozambique, São Tomé e Principe, Cabo (Cape) Verde and Guinea-Bissau.

Although Portugal enjoys religious toleration, nearly all the population (97 per cent) are Roman Catholic.

2.4 Resident population

In 1989 the resident population was approximately 9.8 million, with a density of 111 inhabitants per square kilometre. The annual rate of population growth is 0.68 per cent. This figure reflects a birth rate (0.19 per cent) well above the European average. The population is relatively young, e.g. 32 per cent of the population are under 20, over half (51.1 per cent) are between 20 and 59, and only 16.9 per cent are 60 or over.

Table 1.4 Rate of population growth

Year	Population (000s)	Growth rate (%)
1986	9,716	
1987	9,755	0.40
1988	9,777	0.23
1989	9,797	0.20
1990	9,808	0.11

Source: Bank of Portugal, *Main Economic Indicators, 1986–90*, Lisbon: Departamento de Estatística e Estudos Económicos, 1991.

Table 1.5 Sex distribution of the population (000)

Sex	1986	1987	1988	1989	1990
Male	4,692	4,706	4,704	4,712	4,709
Female	5,024	5,049	5,073	5,085	5,099
Total	9,716	9,755	9,777	9,797	9,808

Source: Bank of Portugal, *Main Economic Indicators, 1986–90*, Lisbon: Departamento de Estatística e Estudos Económicos, 1991.

3 HISTORY, FORM OF GOVERNMENT AND INTERNATIONAL ORGANIZATIONS

3.1 Historical outline

The monarchy that had ruled the country since the eleventh century was overthrown in 1910 when the king was deposed in a bloodless revolution and a republic was proclaimed. In 1926 a military coup installed the regime of the Estado Novo (New State). Dr António de Oliveira Salazar became Minister of Finance in 1928 and Prime Minister in 1932, establishing a right-wing dictatorial regime. A constitution establishing a corporate state was adopted in 1933. Suffrage was limited and only one political party was authorized. Throughout the Salazar era Portugal maintained its overseas possessions, despite several rebellions.

Salazar remained in power until he was succeeded in 1968 by Dr Marcello Caetano. By October 1969 opposition parties had been legalized, though the government party remained in control until 1974.

In 1974 a group of army officers overthrew Caetano and formed a government that recognized the right of the overseas territories (*ultramar*) to self-determination but was divided with regard to Portugal's internal affairs.

The period 1974–76 was characterized by political unrest and upheaval, with six provisional governments in two years. Finally a general election based on universal suffrage was held in 1976.

Between 1976 and 1979 there were eleven governments.

3.2 Form of government

Portugal is a republic, governed by the constitution approved in 1976. The institutions of sovereignty are the President, the Assembly and the government.

The President, elected by popular vote for a five-year term, appoints the Prime Minister and, on the latter's recommendation, other members of the government. The President may also dissolve the Assembly, call elections and veto legislation. The President is head of state and commander-in-chief of the armed forces, while the Prime Minister actually leads the government.

The unicameral Assembly is the legislative body, comprising a minimum of 240 and a maximum of 250 members. The Assembly is elected by universal adult suffrage for four

Table 1.6 Government

Type
    Parliamentary democracy

Government leaders
    PRESIDENT Mário Alberto Soares (1986 and again 1991)
    PRIME MINISTER Aníbal Cavaco Silva (1985 and again 1987 and 1991)

Major political parties (in descending order of share of the vote)
    Social Democratic Party (PSD)
    Socialist Party (PS)
    Portuguese Communist Party (PCP)
    Centre Social Democratic Party (CDS)

---

years (though elections may be called at any time) and exercises all legislative power, approves annual state budgets, controls the actions of the government and ratifies international treaties. The overseas territory of Macao is governed by special statute, while the Azores and Madeira were granted political autonomy in 1976.

The constitution can be amended by a two-thirds majority in the Assembly. Certain amendments were enacted in 1982, the most notable of which included a reduction in the President's power of veto. The constitution was substantially revised in June 1989 to permit, among other things, full privatization of undertakings which had been nationalized in the 1970s.

3.3 The political situation in 1992

Since late 1985 Prime Minister Aníbal Cavaco Silva and the Social Democrats have been in power. In July 1987 the Social Democrats, led by Cavaco Silva, won a decisive electoral victory, establishing single-party majority rule for the first time and winning 148 parliamentary seats. The Social Democrats were re-elected in October 1991, and President Mário Soares was returned at the same time for a further term of five years.

3.4 International organizations

From the beginning Portugal has participated in the movement towards economic integration in Western Europe. In 1959 the country became one of the founding members of the European Free Trade Association (EFTA).

In 1972 a free-trade agreement was concluded with the European Economic Community. In 1986 Portugal became a member of the Community.

Portugal is also a member of the United Nations, the International Monetary Fund (IMF), the World Bank, the Organization for Economic Co-operation and Development (OECD) and the North Atlantic Treaty Organization (NATO), as well as being a party to the General Agreement on Tariffs and Trade (GATT).

4 THE ECONOMY

4.1 Main economic indicators

Events such as German reunification, the restructuring of Central and Eastern Europe, the Gulf crisis and the subsequent rise in oil prices changed the international economy significantly in 1990. With the exception of Germany, the economic growth of the EC countries slowed down. The Portuguese economy was amongst the most dynamic in 1990, with a 4.4 per cent growth (Table 1.7). Although the increase in GDP has been higher in Portugal than the European average, it suffered some diminution from the economically unfavourable international turn of events.

Since admission to the EC, Portugal has made considerable progress in bringing the national economy into convergence with those of the other European economies. With a 5.2 per cent growth rate in 1990, domestic demand, which rose faster than in the previous year, was stimulated particularly by investment and private consumption (see Table 1.8).

Table 1.7 Growth rate of gross domestic product compared with other EC countries

Country	1988	1989	1990
Total EC	3.8	3.3	2.9
Germany	3.7	3.9	4.2
France	3.8	3.6	2.5
Italy	4.2	3.2	2.6
UK	4.6	2.2	1.6
Spain	5.2	5.1	3.5
Portugal	4.0	5.5	4.4

Source: OECD; EC; Bank of Portugal.

Private consumption, which in 1989 registered some slowing down (2.8 per cent), expanded, mainly in respect of durable goods, particularly cars. The estimated growth rate for this variable (4.7 per cent) is also associated with the significant increase in disposable income, which rose 4.2 per cent (in real terms) in 1990. The increase in disposable family income, which resulted mainly from a combination of fuller employment and higher wages, contributed significantly to this development (Table 1.9).

Gross domestic investment, a key variable in a country's development and modernization strategy, increased to 6.6 per cent, which represents a slightly higher increase than that in 1989 (6.0 per cent). It is likely that the climb in interest rates, the prospect of economic activity declining and the uncertainty associated with the Gulf crisis led to the postponement of investment decisions and delay in implementing others.

The driving forces of economic expansion in 1990 were again investment and exports, accounting for a 12 per cent increase (in real terms), which represents a slight decline in the rate of increase in 1989 (16.5 per cent). Moreover, the estimated growth rate for imports (of goods and services), 12.4 per cent, presents a favourable trend relative to the year before (8.7 per cent) and reflects, basically, the important increase that occurred in import of finished goods.

PORTUGAL AND THE EUROPEAN ECONOMY

	Portugal	European Community
Population	9,828,000	344,735,000
Area (square kilometres)	92,100	2,363,000
GDP per capita (1992)[1]	56.3	100
	Averages 1981 – 92	
Imports as a % of GDP	43.3%	27.6%
Exports as a % of GDP	33.1%	28.3%
Unemployment rate	6.5%	9.5%
Increase in consumer prices	16.2%	6.3%

Source: EC Commission *(European Economy,* No 50, December 1991)
Note: [1]Estimated GDP at current market prices in ECU, expressed as a percentage of EC average (i.e. EC=100).

Prices and wages

	General inflation[1]		Consumer prices[2]	Labour costs[3]
	Annual % change	*Index 1980=100*	*Annual % change*	*Annual % change*
1980	20.9	100	21.6	25.6
1981	17.6	113	20.2	21.0
1982	20.7	142	20.3	21.6
1983	24.6	177	25.8	21.8
1984	24.7	221	28.5	21.2
1985	21.7	268	19.4	22.5
1986	20.5	323	13.8	21.6
1987	11.2	360	10.0	17.9
1988	11.6	401	10.0	13.4
1989	12.8	453	12.8	13.8
1990	15.0	521	13.6	17.8
1991	14.6	597	11.7	19.1
1992	11.4	665	9.5	14.4

Source: EC Commission *(European Economy,* No 50, December 1991)

Notes: [1]Price deflator, gross domestic product at market prices.
[2]Price deflator, private consumption.
[3]Nominal compensation per employee – total economy.

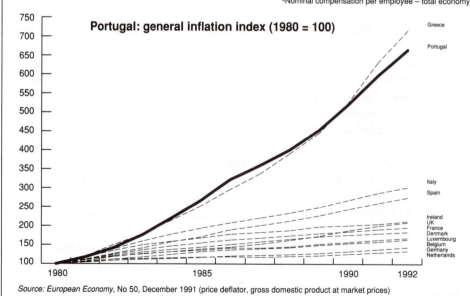

Portugal: general inflation index (1980 = 100)

Source: European Economy, No 50, December 1991 (price deflator, gross domestic product at market prices)

Gross Domestic Product per head of population (EC = 100)

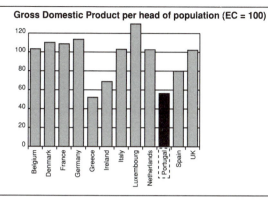

Population (in millions)

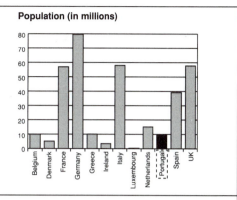

Exchange rates

	PTE/ECU	PTE/US$	
	Average rate[1]	Average rate[2]	Selected exchange rates for the Portuguese escudo at 31 December 1992
1980	69.5	50.06	1 ECU = PTE 176.9
1981	68.5	61.55	$1 = PTE 146.8
1982	77.6	79.47	DM1 = PTE 90.09
1983	98.2	110.78	£1 = PTE 222.3
1984	115.6	146.39	¥100 = PTE 117.6
1985	130.1	170.40	
1986	146.9	149.59	*Sources:* 1 EC Commission (*European Economy*, No 50, December 1991);
1987	162.5	140.88	2 International Monetary Fund (Datastream Economics Codes);
1988	170.1	143.59	3 Eurostatistic, No 11, 1992.
1989	173.4	157.46	
1990	181.1	142.56	
1991	178.1	144.48	
1992[3]	175.0	133.64	

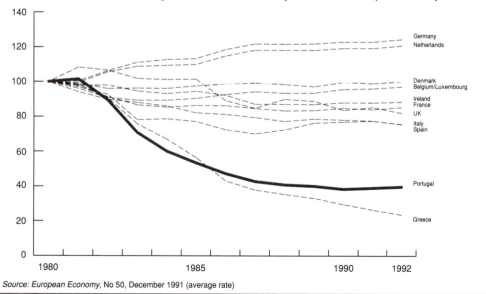

Variation of the Portuguese escudo with respect to the ECU (1980 = 100)

Source: *European Economy*, No 50, December 1991 (average rate)

Table 1.8 Domestic expenditure (PTE billion)

Measure	1987 Current price	1987 price	1988 Volume growth rate	1988 Price growth rate	1988 Current price	1988 price	1989 Volume growth rate	1989 Price growth rate	1989 Current price	1989 price	1990 Volume growth rate	1990 Price growth rate	1990 Current price
Private consumption	3,323.8	3,551.1	6.8	9.7	3,895.5	4,002.9	2.8	13	4,522.9	4,734.2	4.7	13.4	5,366.6
Public consumption	787.8	845.7	7.3	15.9	980.2	1,010.3	3.1	17	1,182	1,225.7	3.7	18.6	1,453.6
Investment	1,400.7	1,577.9	12.6	12.2	1,770.4	1,854.9	4.8	10	2,040.5	2,186.8	7.2	11.8	2,444.4
Gross fixed capital formation	1,250.8	1,441.2	15.2	11.8	1,611.2	1,707.7	6	10	1,878.6	2,003.4	6.6	11.8	2,239.4
Change in stocks	149.9	136.6	−0.3	0	159.2	147.2	−0.2	0	161.9	183.4	0.3	0	205
Domestic demand	5,512.3	5,974.6	8.4	11.2	6,646.1	6,868.1	3.3	12.8	7,745.3	8,146.7	5.2	13.7	9,264.6
Exports	1,777	1,905.7	7.2	10.3	2,102	2,448.5	16.5	8	2,643.5	2,959.9	12	4.9	3,105.4
Global demand	7,289.3	7,880.4	8.1	11	8,748.1	9,316.6	6.5	11.5	10,388	11,106	6.9	11.4	12,370
Imports	2,114.6	2,498.1	18.1	9.9	2,745.4	2,984.3	8.7	7.9	3,220.5	3,619.6	12.4	6.1	3,840.3
GDP	5,174.7	5,382.3	4	11.5	6,002.8	6,332.2	5.5	13.2	7,168.4	7,486.9	4.4	13.9	8,529.8

Source: Bank of Portugal.

Table 1.9 Disposable family income:
increase (%)

1986	1987	1988	1989	1990
1.1	3.6	3.2	2.3	4.2

Source: OECD; EC; Bank of Portugal.

The real growth rate of GDP (Table 1.10), which remained well above the EC average, was achieved mainly thanks to the contribution of manufacturing and mining (6.0 per cent) and services (5.2 per cent). As regards services, the rate of growth in GDP in 1990 was an estimated 5.2 per cent, boosted, in part, by a significant increase in tourism and financial activities. On the other hand, agriculture, forestry and fishing registered a decrease estimated at 3 per cent (contrasting with an expansion in 1989 of 12.5 per cent) which contributed to the slowing down of the GDP growth rate. The decrease was mainly a consequence of adverse weather conditions and poor harvests.

The increase in production capacity, which is quite strongly evident, is a result of the high level of investment in the past few years, which is now beginning to pay off. Production capacity utilization has remained at a high level, holding steady at around 81 per cent for manufacturing industry.

4.2 The labour market

The labour market registered no significant changes in 1990. Employment continued to increase and the unemployment rate, maintaining its downward tendency, reached the lowest levels for many years.

The total volume of employment presented a reasonable increase (2.3 per cent), especially women's participation in the economically active population, whereas the unemployment rate declined to 4.7 per cent. This development is related to the high level of economic activity and constitutes the background to the balance between the upward trend in real wages and the increases in productivity which, so far, have enabled pay rises to be absorbed.

This trend in the unemployment rate is accounted for by the growth in the economically active population (1.9 per cent) and the reduction in the numbers of unemployed. Credit should also be given to the government's efforts in 1990, with measures to encourage vocational training and the creation of job opportunities, heavily supported by the European Social Fund. As can be seen from Table 1.13, the average unemployment rate (4.7 per cent) is located below the EC average (8.0 per cent).

As regards employment by sector, the weight of agriculture, though declining, is still extremely high (787,800) when compared with the average for other European countries. The sector that employs the biggest proportion of the active population is services, with 2,120,000, followed by manufacturing, with 1,149,960. The increases were more significant in industries where there was a shortage of qualified workers, as was the case in construction, indicative of the need for training.

The percentage increase in nominal wages, reflecting the pressure of full employment,

Table 1.10 Gross domestic product at market prices (PTE billion)

Sector	1986	1987				1988				1989	1990
	Current prices	1986 prices	Volume growth rate	Price growth rate	Current prices	1987 prices	Volume growth rate	Price growth rate	Current prices	Volume growth rate	Volume growth rate
Agriculture, forestry and fishing	328.7	342.3	4.1	10.7	379.0	335.5	−11.5	8.8	365.1	12.5	−3.0
Manufacturing and mining	1,236.2	1,270.8	2.8	14.5	1,455.3	1,490.3	2.4	10.3	1,643.7	5.7	6.0
Electricity, gas and water	136.4	143.3	5.1	17.3	168.1	189.4	12.7	11.5	211.2	2.5	10.0
Construction	245.7	265.1	7.9	11.8	296.5	328.8	10.9	12.1	368.5	4.8	5.0
Services	2,360.0	2,536.7	7.5	9.1	2,768.5	2,889.7	4.4	12.7	3,256.9	5.5	5.2
Imputed banking services	222.8	277.5	24.6	10.2	305.8	324.9	6.2	17.8	382.6	–	–
Import taxes	54.8	–	–	–	80.0	–	–	–	117.1	–	–
VAT (tax)	281.4	–	–	–	333.3	–	–	–	422.7	–	–
Total	4,420.4	4,648.0	5.1	11.3	5,174.7	5,382.3	4.0	11.5	6,002.8	5.5	4.4

Source: Bank of Portugal.

Table 1.11 Production capacity utilization (%)

	Utilization rate[1]			
	1987	*1988*	*1989*	*1990*
Total manufacturing industry	82	81	82	81
Food and beverages	74	75	75	75
Textiles, clothing and footwear	87	80	83	83
Timber and cork	83	83	86	80
Paper	90	93	89	90
Chemicals	77	74	76	77
Non-metallic minerals	81	82	83	82
Base metallurgy	87	94	81	80
Metal products	72	77	76	75
Machinery other than electric	83	83	83	82
Electrical machinery and equipment	84	85	84	86
Transport equipment	86	88	90	88
Consumption goods	79	79	80	79
Intermediate goods	83	81	82	81
Investment goods	83	84	86	85

Source: INE.
Note:
[1] Based on quarterly averages.

moved from 10.3 per cent in 1989 to 13.6 per cent in 1990. Despite the aggregate increase of wages in manufacturing industry, company profit margins were maintained. In fact the increase in productivity observed in that sector exceeded the increase in real wages, as can be seen from Figure 1.1. The minimum national wage was updated in 1990, resulting in nominal increases of 18.2 per cent in 'Agriculture, forestry and fishing'

Table 1.12 The labour market (mainland Portugal)

	Homologous growth rate[1]				
Population/employment and unemployment	*1986*	*1987*	*1988*	*1989*	*1990*
1 Total resident population	0.7	0.4	0.2	0.2	0.1
2 Active population	0.1	1.0	1.1	1.5	1.9
3 Activity rate (%)					
3.1 Total	46.2	46.2	46.7	47.2	48.1
3.2 Aged 15–64 years	67.4	67.6	67.9	68.3	69.0
4 Total employment	0.2	2.6	2.6	2.2	2.3
4.1 Employees	1.5	2.2	4.3	3.5	2.9
% of employment by contract	15.8	17.6	19.2	19.1	18.0
5 Unemployment population	−0.8	−16.3	−17.9	−11.2	−5.5
5.1 First employment sectors	−2.9	−17.5	−26.5	−15.4	−12.9
5.2 New employment rate	0.3	−15.6	−13.8	−9.5	−2.6
6 Unemployment rate (%)	8.4	7.1	5.7	5.0	4.7

Source: INE, Employment Inquiry.
Note:
[1] Relating to annual averages (%).

Table 1.13 Average unemployment rates (%)

Country	1988	1989	1990
Total EC	6.9	8.5	8.0
Germany	6.2	5.6	5.0
France	10.0	9.4	8.9
Italy	12.1	12.1	11.1
UK	8.2	6.2	5.8
Spain	19.3	17.1	16.2
Greece	7.7	7.9	8.3
Portugal	5.7	5.0	4.7

Source: OECD; INE.

Table 1.14 Employment by sector (000)

	Total employment				Employees			
	1987	1988	1989	1990	1987	1988	1989	1990
Agriculture, forestry and fishing	925.9	885.4	829.0	787.8	146.0	146.9	139.2	144.3
Manufacturing	1,066.9	1,120.2	1,141.5	1,149.9	956.3	980.3	1,010.6	1,026.0
Electricity, gas and water	33.4	38.1	38.5	37.0	33.0	37.1	37.0	36.1
Construction	354.2	362.1	365.4	358.2	280.6	291.3	290.7	284.4
Services[1]	1,811.5	1,911.5	2,020.6	2,120.0	1,434.9	1,517.8	1,599.0	1,662.8
Total	4,191.9	4,317.3	4,395.0	4,452.9	2,850.8	2,973.4	3,076.5	3,153.6

Source: INE, Employment Inquiry.
Note:
[1] Includes those employed in the commercial sector and public sector. Public sector includes education and private health services.

and of 20.7 per cent in 'Domestic service', compared with 13.8 per cent on average for other activities.

Changes in legislation have enhanced the flexibility of the labour market, by way of work contracts and a framework for pay negotiations which are simultaneously a result and a condition of more competitiveness in this market.

Table 1.15 Percentage increase in nominal
wages, excluding public administration employees

1986	1987	1988	1989	1990
17.2	12.1	9.1	10.3	13.6

Source: Bank of Portugal.

Figure 1.1 Real wages and productivity (manufacturing industry base 1980 = 100): (1) real wages, (2) productivity

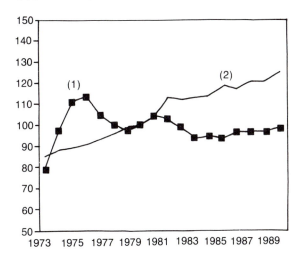

Source: Bank of Portugal.

Table 1.16 Minimum national wage increases (%)

Sector	1989		1990		1991
	Nominal growth rate	*Real growth rate*	*Nominal growth rate*	*Real growth rate*	*Nominal growth rate*
Agriculture, forestry and fishing	17.7	4.2	18.2	4.2	16.2
Domestic service	19.0	5.3	20.7	6.4	19.6
Other activities	13.1	0.1	13.8	0.4	14.6

Source: Bank of Portugal.

4.3 Inflation

Portugal exhibits an inflation rate much higher than any of its EC partners, as can be seen from Figure 1.2. Inflation again increased in 1990, worsening the differential in relation to the European average.

The similarity between the observed and the underlying inflation rates suggests that the inflationary pressures originated with internal factors (Table 1.17). Owing to the moderate levels of costs maintained in 1990, it seems that domestic demand was the main factor responsible for the increase in inflation, against a background of very high production capacity utilization.

Figure 1.2 Inflation rates (homologous growth, per cent). EMU = average rate for EC countries which were members of the European Monetary System

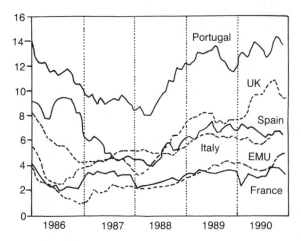

Source: Eurostat.

Comparing the differences between prices in various sectors of traded goods and services, we may conclude that those suffering external competition have a lower inflation rate. Other sectors that are largely locked into the internal market and protected from competition (e.g. transport and dairy products) experience higher costs and set higher prices.

In April 1992, Portugal joined the European Monetary System (EMS). Among the reasons were the balance of advantages and the need for Portuguese financial and

Table 1.17 Inflation indicators: variation rates of twelve-month averages (%)

Year	Inflation		
	Observed	*Underlying*	*Traded goods and services*
1980	16.6	21.4	14.8
1981	20.0	20.4	17.5
1982	22.4	22.7	24.1
1983	25.5	23.8	22.5
1984	29.3	29.2	29.7
1985	19.3	22.7	17.9
1986	11.7	15.2	11.6
1987	9.4	10.2	9.9
1988	9.7	9.7	9.5
1989	12.6	12.6	12.6
1990	13.4	13.2	0.0

Source: INE; Bank of Portugal.

Table 1.18 Exchange rates (annual averages)

Year	PTE/DM Nominal	Variation (%)	PTE/ECU Nominal	Variation (%)
1981	27.242	–	68.496	–
1982	32.693	20.00	77.846	13.65
1983	43.230	32.23	98.490	26.52
1984	51.384	18.86	115.697	17.47
1985	58.170	13.21	130.202	12.54
1986	69.206	18.97	147.005	12.90
1987	78.449	13.36	162.496	10.54
1988	81.967	4.48	170.019	4.63
1989	83.779	2.24	173.323	1.94
1990	88.240	5.30	181.429	4.68

economic policies to approximate those of the other EC member states as a necessary condition of successful Portuguese membership of the Economic and Monetary Union.

The inclusion of the *escudo* in the EMS requires Portuguese inflation rates to decrease, at least, to bring them into line with the EC average. As a consequence, escudo exchange rates against other EC members' currencies will vary between the upper and lower limits established by the system itself.

Thus it is envisaged that Portugal will have, in the medium term, a stable currency and lower interest rates by comparison with the present situation. However, the Portuguese economy is expected to grow at a more moderate rate than has been the case in recent years.

4.4 The public sector

The public sector's importance in the economy is still considerable. However, it will show a significant and continuous reduction in the next few years. This tendency became more visible with the beginning of the privatization programme in 1988. The government has made privatization a central plank of its agenda. The objective is not only the reduction

Table 1.19 Public sector share of the economy (percentage of GDP)

Measure	1988	1989	1990	1991
Total receipts	38.8	40.7	39.6	40.8
Total expenditure[1]	46.0	45.0	46.3	48.0
Financial needs	9.3	6.1	6.7	5.6
Public debt	74.2	70.9	68.2	–

Source: Bank of Portugal.
Note:
[1] Includes net expenditure on capital assets.

Table 1.20 Effective direct public debt

Debt	1988	1989	1990
1 In billions of escudos	4,455.2	5,081.8	5,817.8
Internal	3,571.1	4,212.0	5,145.3
External	884.1	869.8	672.5
2 As percentage of GDP			
Internal	59.5	58.8	60.3
External	14.2	12.1	7.9
Total	74.2	70.9	68.2
3 Structure (%)			
Internal	80.2	82.9	88.4
External	19.8	17.1	11.6

Source: Bank of Portugal.

of the public sector's role in the economy, potentially increasing economic efficiency, but also the development of the capital market and the reduction of public debt.

The most important sources of public revenue are taxation, social security contributions and the privatization programme. As a consequence of the tax reforms, revenue from direct taxes increased by 18.5 per cent and from indirect taxes by 15.0 per cent. Revenue from social security contributions increased more rapidly than GDP, reflecting in part the trend of wages.

Public spending increased by 22.4 per cent in 1990, hence its share of GDP rose from 45.0 per cent to 46.3 per cent. Current public spending was determined mainly by public consumption, borrowing interest rates and current transfers. Social security transfers registered a 28.2 per cent growth rate. This has to do partly with the fact that for the first time pensioners are now receiving an additional element of pension (known as the fourteenth month).

The financing of the public sector has been accomplished, for the most part, by internal non-monetary borrowing. In 1990 gross public debt was 5,817.8 billion escudos, equal to 68.2 per cent of GDP.

The Treasury continues to pursue its aim of reducing total external debt from 17.1 per cent to 11.6 per cent of GDP. By the end of 1990 the external public debt represented 7.9 per cent of GDP.

Also important was the fact that interest on public debt registered a significant increase in 1990, from 7 per cent to 8 per cent of GDP.

4.5 Foreign trade

Exports of goods have continued to rise rapidly. The more modern industries continued to strengthen their position in total exports. However, traditional sectors, such as textiles, clothing and footwear, maintained a healthy level (Table 1.21). This pattern may seem contrary to the tendency to deterioration revealed by traditional competitive indicators: the real exchange rate (Table 1.22) and unit labour costs.

It is worth pointing out, however, that, on the one hand, the real exchange rate is calculated from the consumer price index (CPI), which overestimates the loss of competi-

Table 1.21 Foreign trade: growth rates in imports and exports

Sector	1989 weighting (%)	1986	1987	1988	1989	1990
Total imports	(100.0)	18.5	27.6	22.4	8.4	15.1
Agricultural products and food (1)	(12.4)	4.1	19.4	15.2	2.7	15.7
Energy products (2)	(10.5)	19.7	−0.6	8.6	22.0	7.3
Chemical products	(11.2)	14.5	22.0	16.3	6.3	19.3
Hides, timber, cork and paper	(5.2)	28.0	24.8	20.1	2.3	22.2
Textiles, clothing and footwear	(10.1)	23.4	43.0	17.4	13.7	20.5
Metals and minerals	(8.9)	11.0	30.2	8.9	9.7	12.2
Machinery	(23.0)	25.5	42.1	26.6	10.6	13.5
Transport equipment	(13.8)	23.2	45.7	54.8	1.3	11.2
Other	(4.9)	45.2	29.2	25.0	7.9	23.7
Total, excluding (1) and (2)	(76.1)	21.9	35.2	25.4	7.8	15.8
Total exports	(100.0)	8.4	11.2	10.2	19.9	12.8
Agricultural products and food (1)	(7.6)	2.9	6.1	7.2	4.2	6.5
Energy products (2)	(3.3)	32.9	−21.4	80.2	39.9	9.6
Chemical products	(6.6)	21.3	7.3	10.4	13.1	13.9
Timber, cork and paper	(14.0)	2.9	7.0	4.9	1.6	3.6
Hides, leather and textiles	(9.3)	−1.5	7.7	7.5	11.5	7.6
Clothing and footwear	(27.9)	19.5	19.5	6.6	20.3	12.9
Metals and minerals	(6.4)	−6.5	0.7	9.5	42.3	28.0
Machinery	(11.9)	−4.6	19.3	9.6	31.1	20.1
Transport equipment	(7.2)	20.1	19.7	26.4	56.2	8.4
Other	(5.8)	3.6	7.2	15.5	18.2	25.8

Source: Bank of Portugal, *Relatório*, 1990.

tiveness of exports, owing to the fact that the price index of traded goods increased at rates significantly lower than the global CPI in 1990 (13.4 per cent in average terms, while the index for traded goods did not exceed 9 per cent). On the other, the modernization and restructuring of the economy during the last few years with the help of EC funds and foreign investment, have brought about significant changes in relative productivity.

The encouraging performance of exports in recent years can also be explained by the effect of EC membership, which affords foreign capital the opportunity of entering a small economy where labour costs are still low, yet producing for a market with over 300 million consumers. The prospect of a single market in 1993 only added to that attraction. It is likely that the influence of foreign capital in Portuguese industry will increase.

After having slowed down in 1989 (8.4 per cent) the growth of imports increased in 1990, reaching 15.1 per cent, almost certainly driven by domestic demand. The growth in imports of certain consumer goods whose penetration of the national market was rapid, is particularly striking, and readily explained in terms of their greater price-competitiveness and what might be called their 'novelty value' and the 'me too' effect.

In 1990 the most noticeable feature of the geographical pattern of foreign trade was the increased share of trade with the European Community, basically resulting from the increase in trade with Germany (imports up 14.4 per cent, exports up 16.7 per cent),

Figure 1.3 Portugal: main trading partners. FPTA former Portuguese territories in Africa

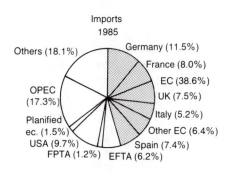

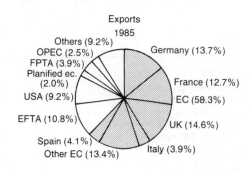

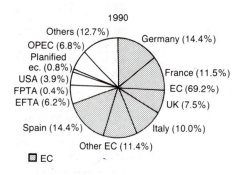

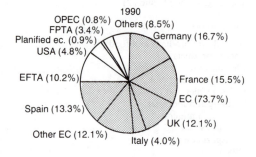

Source: Bank of Portugal.

Table 1.22 Real exchange rate (1985 = 100)

Year	Consumer price index	Homologous variation rate	Unit labour costs	Homologous variation rate
1980	95.9		111.8	
1981	100.8	5.1	117.9	5.5
1982	100.1	−0.7	109.1	−7.5
1983	95.1	−5.0	99.1	−9.1
1984	97.9	2.9	93.4	−5.7
1985	100.0	2.2	100	7.0
1986	102.3	2.3	99.1	−0.9
1987	102.1	−0.2	103.8	4.8
1988	103.2	1.1	106.7	2.8
1989	107.7	4.4	115	7.8
1990	114.2	5.9	118.5[1]	3.1

Source: Bank of Portugal.
Note:
[1] Estimated.

France (imports up 11.5 per cent, exports up 15.5 per cent) and Spain (imports up 14.4 per cent, exports up 13.3 per cent).

In relation to other economic areas, the share of trade with EFTA countries continued stable, the share of trade with the United States and Eastern Bloc countries continued to decline and the share of imports from OPEC (Organization of Petroleum Exporting Countries) decreased.

4.6 The balance of payments and direct foreign investment

In the external market, the current account at the end of 1990 showed a small deficit of 10 billion escudos, compared with a small surplus of 25.9 billion escudos in 1989. This success in avoiding a sizeable deficit is a result of an extremely favourable trend in services and investment income, which alone almost compensated for the increase in the trade deficit. Free invisible transfers also played an important role (Table 1.23).

Capital inflows were maintained at a very high level, especially those from external credit received by the private sector and from direct foreign investment. Even though direct foreign investment was affected by the uncertainty that persisted in financial markets during the second half of 1990, it once again contributed the biggest slice of the balance of payments on capital account. Direct foreign investment tripled as a percentage of GDP from 1985 to 1990 (1 per cent against 3 per cent).

Capital transactions related to direct foreign investment registered a surplus of US$1,832 million in 1990. This development of direct foreign investment (an increase of 22 per cent from 1989 to 1990) continued to be associated with certain positive factors, such as the opportunities opened to Portugal by joining the European Community and the favourable political and economic situation (Table 1.24).

Table 1.23 Balance of payments (PTE million)

Measure	Values			Homologous variations		
	1988	*1989*	*1990[1]*	*1988*	*1989*	*1990[1]*
A Current account	−145.5	25.9	−10.0	–	–	–
1 Goods (f.o.b.)	−793.5	−767.5	−934.0	57.4	−3.3	21.7
Imports	2,358.8	2,769.8	3,269.6	30.5	17.4	18.0
Exports	1,565.3	2,002.3	2,335.6	20.0	27.9	16.6
2 Services and income	24.3	77.4	145.0	−31.7	218.5	87.3
Tourism	272.1	332.5	384.4	12.0	22.2	15.6
Transport	83.9	−104.3	−131.5	60.3	24.3	26.1
Investment income	125.8	−113.1	−54.2	−3.8	−10.1	−52.1
Other services	38.1	−37.7	−53.7	57.6	−1.2	42.4
3 Free invisible transfers	623.7	716.0	779.0	17.3	14.8	8.8
of which: emigrants' remittances	488.9	561.9	604.9	6.5	14.9	7.6
B Medium and long-term capital	118.8	414.6	390.6	262.6	249.0	−5.8
C Basic balance (A + B)	−26.7	440.5	380.6	–	–	−13.6
D Short-term capital	270.6	176.6	177.0	48.2	−34.7	0.2
E Balance of non-monetary transactions	243.9	617.1	557.6	−12.5	153.0	−9.6

Source: Bank of Portugal.
Note:
[1] 1990 estimated.

Table 1.24 Balance of payments – capital account (US $ million)

Measure	1986	1987	1988	1989	1990
Current account balance	1,150	444	−1,064	139	−61
CAB without EC transfers	983	131	−1,649	−585	−909
EC transfers	167	313	585	724	848
Capital operations in the non-monetary sector	−1,372	1,467	2,669	3,709	3,954
Organized debt flows	−1,510	207	−249	−365	−1,213
Medium and long-term external credit	−234	−214	20	−182	−925
Short-term external credit	−1,276	421	−269	−183	−288
Autonomous capital flows	138	1,260	2,918	4,074	5,167
Non-organized debt	−251	−123	334	1,293	78
Medium and long-term external credit	−282	−347	−108	637	399
Short-term external credit	31	224	442	656	−321
Direct foreign investment	155	316	659	1,504	1,832
Foreigner investment in real estate	89	153	265	231	288
Bonds and stock	6	299	239	878	1,429
Other operations	139	615	1,421	168	1,540
Medium and long-term	−27	−13	−232	−270	−323
Short-term (including errors and omissions)	166	628	1,653	438	1,863

Source: Bank of Portugal.

Direct foreign investment by industry continued to reveal financial services and the property sector as preferred by foreign investors (reaching 55.7 per cent of the total in 1990, against 47 per cent in 1989). Meanwhile manufacturing investment was maintained at around 21 per cent (Table 1.25).

Analysing direct foreign investment in Portugal by country of origin reveals that the relative importance of countries that constitute the main source of foreign investment has hardly altered (Table 1.26). The EC countries continued to register the greatest

Table 1.25 Direct foreign investment, by sector (US $ million)

Sector	1986	1987	1988	1989	1990
Overall total	166	367	692	1,577	2,171
Paid-up capital	146	318	622	1,414	2,003
Reinvestments	12	41	48	70	112
Credit and subsidies	8	8	22	93	56
Agriculture, forestry, hunting and fishing	3	14	24	22	24
Mining	7	12	20	25	12
Manufacturing	76	108	226	344	456
Electricity, gas and water				1	
Construction and government building	2	4	30	113	197
Commerce, restaurants and hotels	48	69	122	279	214
Transport, storage and communications		13	6	17	8
Banks and other financial institutions, insurance, real property and services rendered to firms	29	144	248	741	1,209
Services rendered to public; social services; personal services	1	3	16	35	27
Roughly defined activities				0	24

Source: Bank of Portugal.

Table 1.26 Direct foreign investment in Portugal, by country of origin (US $ million)

	1986	1987	1988	1989	1990
Total	166	367	692	1,577	2,171
OECD	160	340	642	1,387	1,900
EC countries	127	241	478	1,149	1,579
Germany	18	26	51	115	141
Spain	14	57	63	184	238
France	17	36	74	270	395
Italy	5	2	6	22	32
UK	64	80	174	364	491
Other	9	40	110	194	282
Switzerland	15	31	46	94	91
Other European countries					
belonging to OECD	2	7	3,131	60	105
USA	15	52	81	71	81
Canada	89	1	265	1	1
Japan	1	8	6	12	43
Non-OECD countries	6	27	50	190	271

Source: Bank of Portugal.

importance, with almost 73 per cent, especially the United Kingdom and France with 22.6 per cent and 18.2 per cent of investment respectively. With 11 per cent, Spain has maintained its importance relative to 1989.

4.7 The financial system

Financial institutions in Portugal may be classified into three large groups: banking institutions, non-bank credit institutions and other non-monetary institutions.

With the opening up of the banking sector to private enterprise in 1984 and entry into the European Community in 1986, the financial system has undergone major liberalization and deregulation of capital, financial and money markets, and has become much more dynamic. The authorities have recognized the need to liberalize and integrate the money market (under the supervision of the Bank of Portugal) and the capital market (under the supervision of the Ministry of Finance).

To sum up, the increase in the number and type of institutions operating in the market, together with the development of secondary banking activities, has accelerated the whole process of change, stimulating competition.

From the rapid expansion of investment companies, leasing companies, and others, via the creation of new financial instruments which allow both enterprises and individuals to increase their savings, to the remarkable recovery of the capital market, starting in 1986, what is evident is a progressive liberalization of the system. For more information about the financial market see Chapter 3.

4.8 Trends

In accordance with the objectives established by the government budget plan for 1991, the pace of economic activity should slow down, bringing the GDP growth rate down to 3.5 per cent (still above the EC average). This decrease is a consequence of the reduction in investment and consumption, the goal being a 4 per cent growth rate for domestic demand.

Exports are expected to be less dynamic in the immediate future, owing to the fact that the rate of international economic activity is forecast to decrease. Thus a deficit on current account was foreseen for 1991; this was presumed to be not too significant, and financing it should not give rise to problems because of the expected inflow of external capital.

To some extent the increases in productivity which have offset the upward trend in real wages have been due to favourable exogenous conditions resulting from Portugal's entry into the European Community, and may not persist.

As for monetary policy, apart from the entry of the escudo into the ERM, the main novelty has been the complete liberalization of credit growth and a change in the means of controlling liquidity, to be achieved indirectly through open-market operations and the fixing of the liquidity ratio. This system will make the market more transparent. With the disappearance of quantity restrictions, the availability of credit will start to conform basically to cost and risk criteria. The absorption of liquidity should, however, continue to be a major concern.

As for interest rates, it is forecast that:

1   The range of active rates will broaden, offering more flexibility with regard to operating risk.
2   Passive rates will change, owing to the increased competition for deposits and other sources of capital.

This situation will reduce the spreads from banking intermediation, drawing them nearer to the European level.

Despite the economic boom, most economists believe the country cannot repeat the past five years' achievements, which were helped by favourable circumstances and the initial impetus that came from joining the European Community in 1986. As a distinguished Portuguese economist has said, 'We've had a good ride since we joined the European Community, but now we have to be in the driving seat. Everything will depend on our own policies.'

5 SOURCES OF COMPANY DATA

The Economic Press in Portugal only became important a few years ago, some twelve to fourteen years after the establishment of democracy, when it became possible to study the country's development. In recent years, as a result of generally increasing interest in the subject, have seen a mushrooming of economic data with the introduction of several magazines and financial sections of newspapers. Nowadays, corporate financial information is included in the following publications:

Daily newspaper:

Diário Económico

Weekly newspapers:

Independente
Semanário
Expresso
Vida Económica
Comércio de Lisboa
Semanário Económico
Diário de Notícias

Magazines:

Cadernos de Economia
Comércio de Lisboa
Exame
Fortuna
JTCE
Expansão
Informador Fiscal
Revista das Empresas
Pequena e média empresa
Valor

Journals:

Fisco
APOTEC
Revista de Contebilidade e Comércio

Financial data sources:

Boletim de Coíações
Boletim da Câmara dos ROC

6 SUMMARY AND STRUCTURE OF THE BOOK

The book is in three parts. Part I, on the conditions and context in which business operates, outlines the recent history of the country and its economic situation (Chapter 1), the forms of business organization (Chapter 2) and the financial system (Chapter 3), tending as it is towards liberalization and deregulation, together with the way the system of taxation works (Chapter 4). Value-added tax, income tax on companies and on individuals, and other taxes, with the rates and main exemptions, are described.

Part II deals with the financial reporting system. Recent reforms are connected with tax law and changes in company law; auditing requirements depend upon both. The first Accounting Plan prescribed by law, in 1977, was heavily indebted to the French *plan comptable*. In 1989 it was superseded by a new set of requirements based on the Fourth EC Directive and amended in 1991 in the light of the Seventh Directive. Chapter 5 sketches the basic contours of the accounting and auditing professions. After noting the recent history of accounting in Portugal, the generally accepted principles and standards are described and the structure of the current Accounting Plan, the POC, is outlined. The next two chapters, 6 and 7, deal with the main rules to be followed in valuing the items in the balance sheet, and the reporting of expenses and revenues, with some actual examples of disclosure from company accounts. The aim of these chapters is to help the reader understand the relation between taxation and accounting in Portugal, and the procedures that have to be followed in the case of such special items as leasing contracts, foreign exchange differences, building contracts, depreciation, provisions and reserves. Chapter 8 deals with the presentation of annual accounts and other financial statements: the possible layouts are shown and explained. Finally, Chapter 9 looks at consolidation and accounting for mergers.

Part III offers supplementary material, beginning, in Appendix A, with the financial statements of an actual company. It includes (in Appendix C) a listing of the options in the Fourth and Seventh Directives adopted by Portugal, and in Appendix B reference to other accounting standards.

Appendix D lists addresses and telephone numbers of organizations connected with financial reporting and the business community more generally, as well as public institutions, professional associations, government Ministries, etc. It also indicates the most useful periodicals; a bibliography suggests books and articles, while the glossary lists an extensive range of accounting terminology in English and Portuguese.

2

Business organization

1 FORMS OF BUSINESS ORGANIZATION

Portuguese law recognizes several types of legal entities. The most significant are:

1 *Sociedade anónima* (abbreviated to 'SA'), designated in English by the term 'corporation'.
2 *Sociedade por quotas de responsabilidade limitada* (abbreviated to *Lda*), in English a private limited liability company, so that a *Lda* approximates a 'Ltd'.
3 *Sociedades em nome colectivo* (abbreviated to 'SNC'), in English a general partnership.
4 *Sociedades em comandita*, in English a limited partnership.

All these forms of business organization are governed primarily by the Companies Act, the *Código das Sociedades Comerciais* (abbreviated 'CSC'), published in 1986 and in

Table 2.1 Incidence of different forms of
business organization

Corporations	3,288
Private limited liability companies	139,894
General partnerships	742
Limited partnerships	7
Co-operatives	3,896
State-owned companies	92

Source: Registo Nacional das Pessoas Colectivas, February
    1988.

force since 1 November 1986. The ones most frequently encountered are the *sociedade anónima* and the *sociedade por quotas*. The *Lda* form is most commonly used for smaller companies, according to its characteristics (Table 2.1).

The SA is a form of company in which the liability of the shareholders is limited to the amount of capital they have contributed. The minimum capital is PTE 5 million. The minimum number of shareholders is five, and they may be individuals or enterprises of any nationality or residence.

The *Lda* is a type of company in which the liability of the quotaholders is limited to the amount of capital subscribed by each one. The capital is divided into quotas and the minimum capital may not be less than PTE 400,000. The minimum number of members is two, and they may be individuals or enterprises.

A *sociedade em comandita* is a partnership that has one or more general partners whose liability to the partnership's creditors is unlimited and which also has one or more special partners whose liability is limited to their capital contribution. Capital contributions may be in the form of shares (partnership with stockholders). Directors may be elected only from among partners with unlimited liability.

Nowadays SNCs and *sociedades em comandita* are very uncommon forms of business organization because the liability of its members is not limited.

2 COMPANY LAW: SA COMPANIES AND *Lda* COMPANIES

Table 2.2 sets out the main characteristics that distinguish an SA from a *Lda* company.

2.1 Formation

The *sociedade anónima* must be incorporated with at least five shareholders, who must subscribe the entire share capital. A deed of incorporation must be signed before a public notary, containing the statutes relating to the operations of the company. It would normally include the following:

1   Name and address of the company.
2   Operating locations.
3   Main purpose or activity.
4   The date of commencement of operations and the company's expected life span.
5   The share capital of the company and details thereof.

Table 2.2 Limitada companies and *sociedades anónimas* compared

Feature	Lda	SA
Minimum no. of quotaholders/shareholders	Two quotaholders	Five shareholders
Minimum capital	PTE 400,000, of which 100% must be paid before the notarial deed of foundation	PTE 5 million, of which 30% must be paid before the notarial deed of the incorporation
Quotas/shares	Capital is divided into *quotas* which cannot be used as collateral for bank financing	Capital is represented by *shares* which can be deposited as collateral for bank financing
Quotaholders'/shareholders' liability	Limited to the nominal value of their quotas, unless the statutes state otherwise	Limited to the nominal value of their shares
Minority rights	Any quotaholder can consult the company documents	Shareholders with at least 1% of shares can consult the company documents
Formal social bodies	Board of management. Quotaholders' general meeting. Audit board[1]	Board of management. Shareholders' general meeting. Audit board
Board of management's members	Appointed for an unlimited period the number of directors can be one or more	Appointed for a period of up to four years (re-election is allowed). The number of directors must be an odd number
Supplementary capital (*prestacoes suplementares*)	Supplementary (refundable equity[2]) capital is permitted as a means of equity financing if the statutes of the company allow it	Supplementary (refundable equity) capital is not allowed
Transfer of quotas/shares	Transfer of quotas always means notarial modification of the statutes, as partners are identified in the statutes	Transfer of shares does not mean notarial modification of the statutes, as shareholders are not identified. (Bearer shares may be sold freely)
Going public	Quotas may not be listed on stock exchange	Shares may be listed on stock exchange

Notes:
[1] Only for companies which in two successive years exceed at least two of the following indicators: turnover PTE 370 million; total assets PTE 180 million; fifty employees.
[2] Supplementary capital carries no dividend rights.

The *sociedade por quotas* is also formed by notarial deed executed by the founding members (a minimum of two) which must include the company's statutes. The number of members of the company may not be reduced to less than two for more than six months.

In both forms, none of the members needs to be a Portuguese citizen.

2.2 Capital structure

A *corporation* (SA) requires a minimum capital of PTE 5 million. Its capital is divided into shares, which may be either bearer or registered. All the shares must have the same nominal value (of at least PTE 1,000 each). Only 30 per cent needs to be paid-up at the time of subscription.

The shares of certain categories of company must be registered if the company is governed by specific regulations, namely banks and other financial institutions.

The capital of a *private limited company* (*Lda*) may not be less than PTE 400,000. Each *quota* cannot be lower than PTE 20,000 and is subdivided into amounts of PTE 250 for voting and similar purposes. At least half the nominal capital must be contributed in cash before the notarial deed is executed, but the minimum capital of PTE 400,000 must be paid up before the notarial deed of foundation.

With regard to capital contributions not made at the time of the establishment of a company, these may be postponed only to fixed or determinable future dates. The amounts ultimately fall due on the expiry of five years from the day of signature of the company's statutes.

2.3 Rights of shareholders and quotaholders

Shareholders and quotaholders have the following rights, among others: the right to vote, to information, to profit and capital.

Resolutions are normally carried by a simple majority of votes. The company's statutes may require a higher voting majority for specific resolutions. Unless the statutes provide otherwise, each share carries one vote.

Each PTE 250 of the nominal capital of a *Lda* company is entitled to one vote, unless the company's statutes state otherwise. Except when the law or the company's statutes provide otherwise, the decisions are to be taken by a majority of votes cast, ignoring any abstentions.

Quotaholders are usually shown in the company's statutes and are not identified by share certificates. Quotas can be transferred only by notarial deed, and this requires changes in the statutes. In contrast, transfers of shares are not formalized before a public notary but may be effected through a stockbroker, bank or other authorized financial institution.

The statutes of an SA may establish rules or limits on the transfer of shares (both registered and bearer), but the rules may not be such as to render transfers impossible. The shares should first be offered to existing shareholders. Registered shares must be transferred by endorsement. They must be registered in the company's books or deposited in a special account in a credit institution. In the first case, the transfer will include the cancellation of the prior registration and its replacement by a new registration in the name of the buyer (register conditions). In the case of the deposit system, the institution where the shares are deposited will transfer the shares to a new account in the name of the buyer, informing the company of the alterations effected.

The liability of quotaholders is limited to the total capital of the company until it is fully paid up. From that moment the liability is limited to the amount of the holders' quotas, except when the company is reduced to one quotaholder, in which case the sole quotaholder assumes unlimited liability towards creditors.

In general, quotaholders can hold a meeting with a quorum of at least 50 per cent of the voting rights. Nevertheless, some decisions require higher percentages. Such is the case with mergers, transformation from SA to *Lda* status and vice versa, and dissolution, where it is necessary to control three-quarters of the votes.

So far as profit allocation is concerned, at least 5 per cent of net profits for the year have to be allocated to a legal reserve until the reserve reaches 20 per cent of share or quota capital. The remainder can be paid out as dividends without restriction by decision of the annual general meeting, if the statutes so permit. Otherwise, at least 50 per cent of the remainder must be paid out as dividends.

SAs and *Lda*s alike may acquire their own shares only in certain circumstances. The *sociedade anónima* may acquire its own shares only in very limited circumstances (normally, up to 10 per cent of the total shares of the company and only if the statutes allow it). Own quotas can be acquired only up to 10 per cent of a *Lda*'s issued capital. For both types of company, there must be a balance of free reserves equal to at least double the amount payable for the shares. An amount of free reserves equal to the amount paid for the shares then becomes non-distributable pending resale of the shares.

2.4 Management structure

Under company law a company is managed by two distinct bodies:

1 The general shareholders'/quotaholders' meeting.
2 The board of directors/managers.

The functions of these two bodies are dealt with separately below for SA and *Lda* companies respectively.

In an SA company the general shareholders' meeting may be either ordinary or extraordinary. The ordinary meeting must be held at least once a year, within the first three months of the year, to approve the financial statements, the proposed distribution of profits, the board of directors' report (which resumes the main management decisions during the year), and to appoint the auditors of the company. An extraordinary meeting of shareholders may be called by the board of directors or by any shareholder holding at least 5 per cent of the total share capital. The statutes of the company may also set out conditions which require an extraordinary meeting.

The issue of debentures is normally approved by a resolution of the shareholders at a general meeting. In some cases, it depends also on the case-by-case authorization of the Ministry of Finance. Also, the issue of the debentures must be recorded at the Commercial Registry prior to the issue taking place. The relevant document must record certain details concerning the company and the terms of the issue.

The directors are appointed and may be removed at any time by the general shareholders' meeting. The shareholders of the larger *sociedades anónimas* normally elect a board of directors to manage the company. The shareholders of the smaller *sociedades anónimas* may appoint one or a small number of directors rather than electing a formal board of directors.

The board of directors normally has a chairman. Certain powers are often delegated to one or more directors or other personnel. The board of directors of a company is responsible for its management and represents the company in dealings with third parties. It is also responsible for the preparation of the annual accounts, which must be presented, together with the annual report and statement of distribution of profits, and that of the statutory audit board, for approval by the general shareholders' meeting, as mentioned above.

The *sociedade por quotas* is run much less formally, since it is required to have only one director and the audit board is optional. (A statutory auditor must be appointed in circumstances defined by law.)

At general meetings, among other matters stipulated by law or by the company's statutes, quotaholders may decide upon:

1   Supplementary provision of capital.
2   The redemption of quotas, the acquisition, disposal or purchase of its own quotas, and the division or cancellation of quotas.
3   The expulsion of members.
4   Approval of the directors' report and of the accounts for the period, the distribution of profits and the treatment of losses.
5   The merger, demerger, transformation or dissolution of the company, or the return of a dissolved company to business activity.

Unless the company's statutes provide otherwise, the meetings of the quotaholders must also appoint the managers and members of the audit board of the company, among other matters. Decisions of the members are to be taken either by written ballot or in general meeting, the rules being the same as those governing corporations (*sociedades anónimas*), with appropriate modifications. Any member of the management may call a general meeting.

Sociedades por quotas may be managed by one or more managers (*gerentes*) who must be individuals, either Portuguese nationals or foreigners, having been nominated by the general meeting of quotaholders. If the duration of the appointment of the managers is not fixed by the company's statutes, it continues until one of the managers is dismissed or resigns from his post. Managers are competent to carry out all acts necessary for the attainment of the company's objectives, and can bind the company in contracts with third parties. These powers exist regardless of any obstacles or limits imposed by the company's statutes or by decisions of the quotaholders. However, a company may not be bound in dealings with third parties in contravention of limitations on the powers arising from its objects, if it can be proved that the third party was aware or could not have been unaware in the circumstances that the act in question was *ultra vires*, and that it did not have the express or tacit approval of the members. This constituted an important innovation in the 1986 companies code.

Managers may not pursue activities in competition with their company without the consent of its members. A competing activity is regarded as an activity falling within the objects of the company as set out in its statutes.

2.5 Audit

The financial statements of an SA company must be audited by a registered statutory auditor (*revisor oficial de contas*). In the *sociedade por quotas* a statutory audit is required when two of the following three limits have been exceeded for two successive years:

1   Total assets: PTE 180 million.
2   Turnover: PTE 370 million.
3   Average number of employees: fifty.

An SA is required to have a statutory audit board (*conselho fiscal*) in order to keep watch over management and the undertaking's observance of the law and of company statutes, to ensure the satisfactory auditing of the financial statements, and to convene the shareholders' general meeting if the body responsible for that procedure fails to do so.

A statutory audit board consists of three or five members or, in special cases, one, depending on the share capital (less than PTE 20 million). One member of this body must be an individual certified auditor (*revisor oficial de contas*, ROC) or an audit firm responsible for auditing the financial statements. The statutory audit board must meet at least once a quarter, the findings and conclusions being set down in a minute book.

In respect of the annual financial statements, the audit board must report to the general meeting of shareholders on the company's general performance, and especially on the report of the board of directors and the financial statements. The statutory audit board is empowered to inspect all transactions entered into by the company and may examine the books, accounting records, correspondence, minutes and, generally, all documents belonging to the company. Statutory and certified auditors have to comply with independence and secrecy requirements established in the Companies Act and in the professional rules of certified auditors.

3 STEP-BY-STEP APPROACH TO THE INCORPORATION OF A COMPANY

Figure 2.1 resumes the legal requirements for setting up a company, and indicates the timetable affecting each step. In the case of foreign investments, additional requirements have to be complied with. These are indicated in Figure 2.2.

4 THE LAW RELATING TO BRANCHES AND SUBSIDIARIES OF FOREIGN COMPANIES

Inward foreign investment may be effected through the establishment of a branch, the constitution of a subsidiary company or by the acquisition of shares or quotas in existing companies.

A foreign company may operate in Portugal through forming a subsidiary, instead of acquiring a participation in a separate legal entity. A branch is a legal representative of the parent company, empowered by the head office to administer its affairs. There are no requirements with regard to the minimum amount of capital or the formal bodies – committees, boards, etc. – of the branch.

The choice between this form and those mentioned earlier depends essentially on commercial reasons, some exchange control considerations or tax differences. There are no specific advantages or disadvantages in forming a subsidiary or buying shares or quotas except that in the latter case formation costs do not come into it.

Setting up a branch involves some formalities. The most important requirements are the presentation of a translation of the minute that records the decision of the board of directors to create a branch in Portugal and the appointment of a legal representative empowered by head office to administer the affairs of the branch. The translation should be duly legalized and published in the Portuguese official gazette. A certificate approving

Figure 2.1 Legal requirements for setting up a company in Portugal

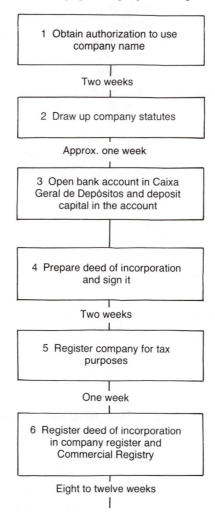

```
┌────────────────────────────────┐
│ 1  Obtain authorization to use │
│        company name            │
└────────────────────────────────┘
              │
          Two weeks
              │
┌────────────────────────────────┐
│ 2  Draw up company statutes     │
└────────────────────────────────┘
              │
        Approx. one week
              │
┌────────────────────────────────┐
│ 3  Open bank account in Caixa   │
│ Geral de Depósitos and deposit  │
│      capital in the account     │
└────────────────────────────────┘
              │
┌────────────────────────────────┐
│ 4  Prepare deed of incorporation│
│        and sign it              │
└────────────────────────────────┘
              │
          Two weeks
              │
┌────────────────────────────────┐
│ 5  Register company for tax      │
│        purposes                  │
└────────────────────────────────┘
              │
          One week
              │
┌────────────────────────────────┐
│ 6  Register deed of incorporation│
│    in company register and       │
│      Commercial Registry          │
└────────────────────────────────┘
              │
      Eight to twelve weeks
              │
```

the company's name is also required. When all the necessary documents are assembled, the branch office must be registered at the Commercial Registry. Except for the company's legal representative, mentioned above, the branch is not required to have other formal administrative or management bodies. Apart from its internal structure and organization, a branch operates much like a corporation in its dealings with third parties.

5 IMPACT OF EC DIRECTIVES ON COMPANY STRUCTURE

It is still too early to give any definite opinion about the impact of the EC directives on companies' structure, as, despite membership of the Community since 1 January 1986 Portugal is still in a transitional phase and not all the directives have been incorporated into Portuguese law, while others have recently been amended.

Figure 2.2 Additional requirements in the case of foreign investments

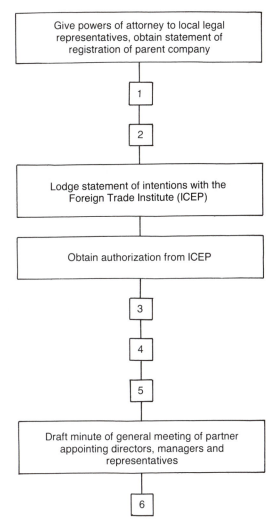

The new Companies Act contains some clauses that seek to bring Portuguese legislation more into line with that of other EC countries. In particular the First, Second, Third, Fourth and Seventh Directives have already been enacted into Portuguese law. Some effects of progress to date in integrating EC directives into the Portuguese setting may be outlined as follows.

First Directive

1   Obstacles to limiting the company's legal capacity through contractual clauses.
2   The clarification of certain grey areas of the law in respect of companies whose formation contained irregularities.
3   Liability of managers to their companies, in particular by virtue of their actions

performed in the name of the company. Obviously managers who disregard the terms of the company's statutes or the decisions of the annual general meeting are to be held responsible for the harm they may cause.

4   Inclusion of matters concerning disclosure, spelled out in more detail in the Commercial Register Act.

Second Directive

1   Alteration of the contract in general, and especially as regards the increase or reduction of the corporation's capital extending to private limited liability companies, creating a legal right of preference in the subscription of quotas and shares.
2   Continuing of the dissolution according to traditional way.
3   Authorization of the shareholders' preferred rights in capital increases.
4   Stipulating the limitations on a company acquiring its own shares, thus better guaranteeing creditors' rights.

Third and Eighth Directives

1   Adapt the company law with respect to mergers and demergers.

Fourth Directive. As the 1977 version of the Accounting Plan (POC) anticipated many requirements of the Fourth Directive, and the 1989 plan was designed to differ as little as possible from its predecessor, the implementation of the Fourth Directive via the 1989 plan did not introduce any major changes.

1   Protection of minority rights and requirement that the financial statements should provide a 'true and fair view' of a company's assets, liabilities, costs and revenues.
2   Requirements regarding accounting disclosure (profit and loss account, balance sheet and notes to the accounts).
3   Auditing of the accounts is compulsory where the company's size justifies it (ascertainable by the indicators mentioned in section 2.5 above).

Furthermore, in 1991 new legislation (decree law 83/91, dated 10 April) enacted into Portuguese law Directives 88/627/EEC (dated 12 December 1988) and 1989/298/ EEC (dated 17 April 1989), setting out the information required concerning public offers and tenders, and the listing of securities on the stock exchange. The Seventh Directive on group accounts, introduced through decree law 238/91, dated 2 July, is discussed in a later section.

6 THE FORM AND CAPITAL STRUCTURE OF OTHER TYPES OF ORGANIZATION

In addition to the above forms of organization, laid down by the Companies Act, businesses can also carry on their activities as:

1   Co-operative societies.
2   Government-owned companies.
3   Individual entrepreneurship.

The following sections look at these forms of organization in turn.

6.1 Co-operative societies

In Portuguese law a co-operative is a society, enjoying considerable measure of freedom as to its constitution, capital and organization, that seeks, through the co-operation of its members, and through the observance of its co-operative principles, the satisfaction of its economic, social and cultural purposes. It differentiates itself from a business company essentially by virtue of the fact that the latter's object is to make a profit, while the co-operative's concern is the community of its members' interests (which may or may not include the commercial profit motive).

The Co-operatives Act distinguishes the following types: consumption, trade, worker's production, agricultural, credit, construction and housing, craft, fishing, culture, services and education.

The co-operative may be constituted by notarial deed (if its members are individuals or societies), or by some other instrument whose basic elements must be published in the official gazette.

The liability of the members of the co-operative may be unlimited, limited to the subscribed capital, or both.

The number of members is variable, but it must not be less than ten in the case of some co-operatives and three in others (whose members are themselves co-operatives: unions, federations and confederations).

The management structure is to consist of the following:

1   Annual general meeting.
2   Board of directors.
3   Audit board

The annual general meeting is to be formed of all the rightful members of the co-operative. The board of directors, an administrative body, is to consist at least of a president, a treasurer and a secretary. As for the audit board, it is a control and audit organ, consisting of a minimum of three members.

It is a requirement not only to constitute legal reserves until the total amount equals the issued capital, but also to set aside reserves for co-operative education and training. In law the mandatory reserves are not normally susceptible of distribution to members. The annual net surplus, after allocations to reserves, may be distributed to the members.

6.2 Government-owned (nationalized) companies

Government-owned companies owe their existence mainly to the nationalizations of 1975, when the state acquired the capital of certain companies or the capital of their parents. Their main objective is not so much financial profit as other aims such as employment, income redistribution or the specific objectives of the National Budget Plan. Owing to the privatization programme nationalized companies are now disappearing. Those which have not yet been returned to the private sector (becoming corporations) are either in an advanced stage of privatization or awaiting their turn.

6.3 Sole proprietorship

Sole proprietorship is very common in the case of small businesses. They have unlimited liability. It is, however, possible to limit liability through a commercial establishment called an *estabelecimento individual de responsabilidade limitada* (EIRL). The minimum capital is PTE 400,000 and two-thirds of it must be in cash. In the case of an EIRL the business is liable only for the debts the entrepreneur incurs in the pursuit of his business activities. Hence creditors cannot appropriate the entrepreneur's non-business assets to meet debts arising from the business activity. Despite this advantage, the EIRL is not widely encountered.

3

The financial system

---

1 BACKGROUND

The financial system reflects the recent reforms as well as the role of the stock exchange in the light of European economic integration in general and the single market for financial services in particular. In the last few years it has undergone a rapid process of transformation amounting to a financial revolution.

1.1 The recent past

Prior to 1974 the banking system was based on private commercial banks linked with economic groups. There were two other institutions:

1   Caixa Geral de Depósitos, a state institution dating back to the previous century and, even today, the biggest in the system.
2   Crédito Predial Português, originally a construction credit institution which now operates as a bank.

Foreign banking was represented by the agencies of only three different banks, which did not have much effect on the system as a whole. The banking system was strictly regulated, capital and exchange movements depending on the authorization of the Bank of Portugal.

    Monetary policy was based on:

1   The observance of minimum treasury reserves by banks.
2   The Bank of Portugal's rate.
3   'Moral persuasion' exerted by the central bank upon other banks.

Interest rates were fixed administratively for the various terms of deposits and credit (as a minimum for deposits and as a maximum for loans). In practice the banks did not compete on rates but simply applied the minimum and maximum rates.

    Lending consisted mainly of short-term credit. Noting the inadequacy of credit for company investment needs, in the late 1950s the government decided to create a specialized institution that would precisely offer medium and long-term credit for:

1   Company investment projects, i.e. for industrial investment.
2   Transport, production, energy and other infrastructure projects.
3   Financing exports of equipment produced by firms based in Portugal.

Hence the Banco de Fomento Nacional (now the Banco de Fomento e Exterior) opened its doors in 1960.

    In 1974–5 all banks, except Banco do Brasil, the Bank of London & South America (now the Bilbao e Viscaya Bank) and Crédit Franco-Portugais, were nationalized. External and internal factors led to a breakdown of economic equilibrium:

1   Inflation accelerated.
2   The deficit on the external balance became more significant.
3   The excess of state expenditure, with Bank of Portugal financing, became a permanent source of liquidity for the economy.

Interest rates on deposits had at least to compensate for inflation, otherwise there might have been an outflow of capital and the escudo would have come under pressure.

Long-term deposits and, in the course of time, state bond issues (risk-free), were practically the only financial assets available to individuals and firms.

State-controlled banks had to increase the liquidity that continued to be generated by the need to finance the state deficit. Government monetary policy had no supporting instruments at its disposal in the money markets to deal with this situation – it was essential that liquidity should not transform itself into excess demand, and thence into rising inflation, so increasing the deficit and entailing further devaluation.

The only option open to the monetary authorities was 'quantitative credit control'. Banks were periodically given credit limits which they could not exceed. (The quantitative control framework began in 1977 and still remains in force.)

There was a fundamental change of policy in 1984, when new legislation allowed competition from the private sector and enabled a limited number of foreign banks to open branches. State-owned banks still dominate the industry, however.

1.2 The present

The Bank of Portugal (established in 1846) is nowadays a public institution and performs the role of central bank. It is responsible for monetary policy (as set by the government). It also acts as depository for the government with regard to Portugal's membership of the IMF. The bank manages the country's gold and foreign currency reserves and is responsible for the remaining exchange controls. It provides credit and rediscount facilities to the country's lending institutions and regulates domestic interest rates and legal reserve requirements. The bank is also charged with overseeing the liquidation of the foreign currency trade payments and controlling the settlement of international payments.

Following EC membership, the bank has introduced several new financial instruments aimed at progressive liberalization.

In August 1987 various term deposits were introduced. In November 1987 the bank introduced medium-term treasury bills with maturities ranging from eighteen to thirty-six months and fixed interest rates set by market auction. In July 1988 legislation was passed authorizing the creation of closed-end funds, bonds with warrants, no-paper share registration and portfolio management companies, in addition to the regulation of broking houses.

Capital movements within the European Community had to be completely liberalized by the end of 1993, but with the possibility, in the Portuguese case, of a postponement until 1995 not only for 'pure' financial credits (those not related to commercial transactions) but also for short-term flows of monetary bonds and the opening of short and long-term accounts in foreign exchange credits of another member state.

So far liberalization has been extended to:

1   Short and medium-term credit related to commercial transactions.
2   The acquisition by non-residents of Portuguese listed securities.
3   Direct foreign investment in companies outside the financial sector.

The number of banks practicaliy doubled between 1982 and 1989. The number of *caixas económicas agrícolas* (agricultural credit banks) rose by two-thirds in the same period and dozens of other financial institutions were created.

Substantial liberalization of the regulations governing the financial system took place: liberalization of interest rates, simplified rules applying to exchange rate operations and decontrol of most financial operations were considered amongst the most important.

This spectacular transformation of the financial system will reach completion in the near future. It results, essentially, from the following factors:

1   *Increased competition* resulting from the establishment of new banks and other financial institutions, bringing with it economic benefits such as greater efficiency and productivity in the financial sector, reduced intermediation margins from financial institutions, reduced financial risks, etc.
2   *The consequences of EC financial integration* which, amongst other things means the liberalization of financial services and of capital circulation.
3   *A wider, international trend towards structural transformation* in the financial sector, observable in all other industrialized countries, from which Portugal cannot escape. It translates into innovation, liberalization, deregulation, etc.
4   The privatization of banks and insurance companies, already initiated, with the exception of two state groups recently created (Caixa Geral de Depósitos group and Banco de Fomento e Exterior group).

To sum up, the increase in the number and types of institutions operating in the market, together with the development of securities activities, has accelerated the whole process of change, stimulating competition. From the rapid expansion of investment companies and leasing companies, via the creation of new financial instruments which allow both enterprises and individuals to put their savings to work, to the remarkable recovery of the capital market, starting in 1986, the benefits of progressive liberalization of the system are beginning to show through.

So far as the foreign exchange market is concerned, with the introduction of the quotation of spot and forward rates, the gradual internationalization of the escudo and the imminent introduction of new products such as options, the key concepts are flexibility and liberalization, and these are among the government's main concerns.

A description of the capital market in Portugal concerns the role and performance of stock exchanges in the light of European economic integration.

Financial institutions are corporations and as such are subject to the Companies Act (*Codigo das Sociedades Comerciais*). Moreover, as financial institutions they are under the supervision of the Bank of Portugal, which clarifies and details the existing legislation for financial institutions, including their own specific chart of accounts, since the Chart of Accounts for the Banking System differs from the POC.

Specifications, details, adaptations, clarifications and some valuation rules are governed by instructions of the Bank of Portugal, which are published from time to time. Reporting requirements are strict, and credit institutions must provide the bank with detailed accounting and statistical information on a regular basis.

The Bank of Portugal is also responsible for the inspection of financial institutions, and regularly inspects banks (at least once a year).

2 CAPITAL MARKETS

2.1 The primary market

In the primary market the following securities may be offered: shares, bonds, participatory bonds and warrants.

2.1.1 Securities

Shares can be issued in registered or bearer form. A company may issue both types of shares simultaneously, although they may have different prices.

Bearer certificates can be converted into registered certificates, and vice versa, upon request. Such changes are usually made at the shareholder's expense.

In certain cases the shares must be registered, in particular whilst they are still not completely paid up or when there is some restriction in the company's statutes regarding the transfer of ownership. The registered shares have to be registered either in the company's books or with a credit institution in an account which must identify the account holders.

The company's statutes may authorize the issue of shares without certificates, in whole or in part, and can also state the convertibility rate between the former and the share certificates. Shares without certificates are not numbered and are registered in accounts

Table 3.1 Some types of shares

Type of share	Capital	Voting rights	Dividends
Ordinary (*acções ordinárias*)	Represent a portion of the capital	Yes	The owner is entitled to dividends
Preference (*acções preferenciais*)	Represent a portion of the capital	No	The owner is entitled to a preferred dividend[1]
Redeemable preference (*acções remíveis*)	Represent a portion of the capital	Yes	Special reimbursed shares to be paid out must have been completely paid in previously
			Redemption made at par value unless the acts of the company state differently

Note:
[1] The owner is entitled to a prior claim on the assets of the company if the company goes into liquidation.
   In the case of liquidation the reimbursement of preference shares has priority over ordinary shares.
   Issue of preference shares may be authorized up to one half of the paid-in capital stock.
   The owner is entitled to a minimum dividend of 5 per cent on the nominal value.

Table 3.2 Some credit instruments

Security	Features
Bond (*obrigação*)[1]	Debt security, usually issued with long-term securities (over one year)
Floating rate bond (*obrigação de taxa variável*)	Issued with indexed interest rates. The most usual indexations are a reference rate fixed by the central bank for that purpose, the average treasury bill rate over one year, etc.
Zero coupon bond (*obrigação sem cupão*)[1]	Issued without coupon to be redeemed at a specified date in the future and at a certain value
Cash bond (*obrigação de caixa*)[1]	Short-term bond which can be issued on a continuous basis, redeemable on request from the holder
Medium-term treasury note (*bilhete de Tesouro*)[1]	Bond with a term of eighteen to thirty-six months, at a fixed rate of interest, sold in the primary market at a discount in the auction system and reimbursed on maturity
Convertible bond (*obrigação convertível*)[2]	Carries the right to convert into shares, according to the issue conditions
Warrant bond ('*warrant*')[2]	Entitles the holder to subscribe for one or more shares. The price, period and other conditions are specified at the time of issue
Participating certificate (*título de participação*)[1]	May be issued by public companies in which the state has a controlling interest for an unlimited period of time but with no voting rights. The income includes a fixed element and a variable element

Notes:
[1] Can be traded on the stock exchange.
[2] Can be issued only by companies listed on one of the Portuguese stock exchanges.

opened in the name of the respective account holders. The legal regime of 'dematerialized' shares, which was only established in 1988, is applicable, with the proper alterations, to bonds and other securities issued by share capital companies.

Before the definitive issue of shares, the issuer may distribute provisional registered shares (allotment letters). These are not tradable on the exchanges.

As regards interest rate variability, bonds can be participating (consisting of a fixed element and a variable element indexed to an indicator of the firm's performance) or with variable interest rate and reimbursement premium.

According to the form of the reimbursement, bonds can either be convertible or with a warrant (the right to subscribe to shares).

Participatory bonds can be issued by government-owned firms. Thus, private capital was raised as an alternative to financing by the government, whose budget deficits during the last few years have reached significant levels. These bonds allow the issuer great financing stability (ten years' minimum). Participatory bonds can be classified as a mix of shares and bonds because in their composition they present some typical aspects of both. They carry a minimum fixed income (about 70 per cent) and a variable income component (generally 30 per cent of the bond's global income) related to performance indicators such as a company's profit, cash flow or sales. The redemption of those bonds can take place only in the event of liquidation or after the requisite ten years. In the first case, redemption takes place only after payments to all the other creditors of the firm. However, the firm may choose not to redeem the bonds and they can then be integrated into the issued capital.

2.1.2 Funds, unit trusts, etc.

A unit trust certificate is one of the units into which the assets of a mutual fund are equally divided. There are two types of unit trust: securities or real estate trusts. Unit trusts can be open-ended or closed-ended, depending on whether or not the capital to invest is fixed at the time of constitution. The funds must be run by a fund management company, which may in turn be managed by a bank or banks.

2.1.3 Money market instruments

Treasury bills are issued by the treasury for a term of less than one year in book entry form and are placed on the primary market by the central bank by auction at a discount. Access to the primary market is reserved to financial institutions which are authorized to deal in treasury bills with the public (with or without repurchase agreements).

Certificates of deposit are registered certificates representing banking deposits in Portuguese escudos for periods between 181 days and five years. The interest can be paid periodically or on maturity, and the interest rate can be fixed or variable. The minimum amount is PTE 5 million. Certificates of deposit can be traded in the secondary market following endorsement.

The sources of corporate finance above are those most commonly used by companies. Others exist, but without such general application.

2.2 The stock exchange

A reform of the Portuguese stock exchange is currently in progress. Two markets already exist: the official one and the over-the-counter market. The creation of two additional markets is planned, namely a secondary market and an unlisted securities market. As a result securities already deposited with a financial intermediary or shares without certificates registered by a financial intermediary will be negotiated in the secondary markets.

With the aim of guaranteeing not only transparency in all the markets but also stability and homogeneity in the prices posted, an interconnected system has been set up between the various secondary markets which is designed to ensure the timely flow of information between them about transactions in 'sensitive' securities.

The management of the exchanges is the responsibility of the respective broker and dealer associations. However, ownership and management are in the hand of non-profit-making associations. The associates of the exchanges comprise individual brokers, broker companies and authorized dealers as well as financial institutions and undertakings (see section 3 for details).

The official market will be national, unlike the present situation, where there are two exchanges, one in Lisbon and one in Oporto. These will merge through a common computerized dealing system with the aim of bringing liquidity to the market through global supply and demand.

The secondary market is meant for small and medium-size firms, the admission of which to the market needs only a resolution of the stock exchange.

Securities that do not meet the conditions of admission to the official market or the secondary market may be quoted on the unlisted securities market. The admission decision is up to the stock exchange.

Negotiable securities in the over-the-counter market must be registered or deposited with a financial intermediary. It is possible to trade any security direct with any financial institution without going through the stock exchange markets, in fact this represents the most important percentage of the traded volumes.

As regards trading volumes on the stock exchanges, during 1990 the combined trading volume on both Lisbon and Oporto exchanges was PTE 826 billion (55 per cent up on the previous year). Of the total amount in question, PTE 169 billion was made on special stock market trading sessions connected with public offers and privatizations. Participa-

Table 3.3 Financial institutions in Portugal

Type of institution	No. of institutions extant at end of:			Total assets at 31 December 1989 (PTE billion)
	1985	*1989*	*1990*	
Investment banks	3	3	3	3,028
Savings banks	16	11	11	59
Saving and loan institutions (building societies)	195	218	224	360
Agricultural savings and loan institutions	6	18	16	222
Investment companies	7	16	21	355
Leasing companies	2	4	5	23
Factoring companies	–	1	9	0.6
Regional development companies	0	1	1	0.5
Investment fund management companies	–	18	23	5
Portfolio management companies	–	8	11	0.4
Money market/exchange dealer companies	–	6	5	0.4
Dealers	–	1	6	1.7
Brokers	–	6	8	2.1
Group holding companies	–	26	25[1]	58
Venture capital companies	n.a.	21	25	17.5[2]
Entrepreneurship development companies	–	n.a.	approx. 3	n.a.
Pension fund management companies	0	12	12	2.9[3]
Property investment companies	n.a.	n.a.	approx. 42	87.3[4]
Loans with mortgage guarantee companies	n.a.	n.a.	n.a.	n.a.
Other	7	6	6	38.0[5]
Insurance companies	50	65	104	470
Pension funds	0	178	190	108
Investment funds	n.a.	31	60	244.5[6]
Representative offices	18	17	20	–

Source: Ministry of Finance, 'As instituições de credito', *Livro branco sobre o sistema financeiro, 1992*, I, *Relatório principal*, Lisbon, 1991, pp. 14–15.
Notes:
[1] Of the twenty-five, only ten were effectively operating by 31 December 1990.
[2] The figure refers to eleven only of the twenty-five companies mentioned.
[3] Total assets of nine companies only.
[4] The figure refers only to the thirty-one companies that were in operation at 31 December 1989.
[5] IFADAP (agriculture), ParaEmpresa (financial clearing company), SIBS (stock exchange information system), UNICRE (credit card company) and COBRIMPE.
[6] The value of the portfolios of medium and long-term securities of twenty-three of the non-property investment funds (excluding securities, bonds and participatory bonds as well as other securities, including repurchase agreements) amounted to PTE 107.3 billion at 31 December 1989.

tion bonds and unit trust transactions accounted for only a small proportion of total business on the stock exchanges.

3 FINANCIAL INSTITUTIONS

Financial institutions in Portugal may be classified into three large groups:

1   Banking institutions, those legally authorized to create means of payment, including the central bank (the Bank of Portugal), the commercial banks and the specialist credit institutions.
2   Non-bank credit institutions, which include leasing companies, factoring companies, investment companies and securities houses which are not authorized to receive deposits and thus cannot create means of payment.
3   Other non-monetary institutions, which, although having no credit function, attract savings to be applied in financial activities, as in the case of insurance companies, investment funds, pension funds and asset management companies. The latter manage both real estate and financial assets on behalf of individuals and corporate entities, and are incorporated under a specific legal form which authorizes them to do so.

Opposite and below we present each of the most important types of financial institutions, in some detail. Table 3.3 shows the range of existing financial institutions in Portugal.

Table 3.4 Minimum issued capital of financial institutions (PTE million)

Activities		*Minimum capital*
Banking institutions	Commercial banks	3,500
	Investment banks	3,500
Non-bank credit institutions	Regional development companies	400
	Venture capital companies	600
	Factoring companies	200
	Leasing companies	
	Other	750
	Real estate	1,500
	Investment companies	1,500
	Group buying consortia	50
	Real estate investment management companies	1,500
Other non-monetary institutions	Insurance companies	
	Life branch	1,500
	Mutual	750
	Other[1]	500
	Pension fund management companies	200
	Holding companies[2]	5
	Dealer companies	500
	Broker companies	10

Source: *Diário da República*, decree law No. 28/89, 23 January.
Notes:
[1] If only one type of insurance is offered, excluding life insurance, legal protection, medical assistance.
[2] *Sociedades gestoras de participações sociais.*

Most of these companies are subject to legal minimum capital requirements, as indicated in Table 3.4.

3.1 Banking institutions

3.1.1 Types of banks

There are three types of banks in Portugal: savings, investment and commercial banks, as shown in Table 3.5. Thus the main banks are adopting an all-round approach as 'universal' banks, constituting or participating in other financial institutions and activities such as investment, leasing and investment fund management.

Table 3.5 Types of banks in Portugal and their size

Banks operating in Portugal on 31 December 1990	Number	Total assets (PTE million)
Commercial banks	26	6,640
Investment banks	4	476
Savings banks	3	3,028
Caixas económicas (housing loan institutions)	19	59
Caixas de crédito agrícola mútuo (mutual agricultural credit institutions)	224	360
Total	276	10,563

Source: Ministry of Finance, *Livro branco sobre o sistema financeiro*, 1991.

3.1.2 Main banking operations

Any purchase of securities is likely to involve calling upon the services of a bank. Banking intermediation is necessary to acquire, amongst other things, treasury bills (*bilhetes do Tesouro*), auction credit and stock investment treasury bills (FIP) issued by the state, and certificates of deposit, commercial paper and participatory investment fund units. Banks also act as intermediaries in the acquisition of bonds, shares and participatory bonds.

With regard to the internal market, banks offer their clients such facilities as payment by cheque and bank transfers – where the client instructs the bank to debit his or her account in favour of another – and standing orders. Bank intermediation enables firms to transact business safely with overseas customers. Above and beyond straightforward settlements in which the bank confines itself to receipts and payments, documentary operations are particularly important, such as one-way transfers and letters of credit.

Bank lending continues to be the main source of the banks' revenue. In Portugal, the main forms of credit banks grant are:

1   *Overdrafts*: a very short-term operation permitting the client to overdraw the existing balance, up to a certain limit. This negative balance will have to be repaid.
2   *Discounting commercial paper*: a short-term operation in which a client endorses to

the bank a credit security (bill or note) before the expiry date, receiving the respective value and paying the interest by way of discount. This type of operation usually involves promissory notes, which are the most widely used credit security.

3   *Credit facility*: a short to medium-term operation involving a contract by which the bank commits itself to put at the client's disposal a certain amount of funding over a certain period of time. In this situation the interest rates paid are in proportion to the amount drawn. However, if the line of credit is not fully used up, the client is obliged to pay an additional commission.

4   *Loan account*: a medium to long-term operation where a predetermined contract exists between the bank and the client concerning the amount and the term of the credit.

3.2 Non-bank credit institutions

3.2.1 Leasing companies

Leasing companies (*sociedades de locação financeira*) are business enterprises which concentrate on a single activity, leasing. A lease is a contract by which one of the parties (the *lessor*) places at the disposal of another (the *lessee*) land or other property for a specified period in return for an agreed rent. The land or property can be acquired at the lessee's discretion and the purchase may be completed, totally or partially, in an agreed period of time (usually, within the term of the contract) against a stipulated rent between the parties.

It should be noted that a leasing company can engage in transactions involving marketable commodities *or* transactions involving real estate, but not both. The legal requirements mean sticking to one line of business or the other.

A leasing company must be constituted in the form of a corporation, with an authorized capital equal to or greater than PTE 750 million (for the leasing of non-real estate assets) or PTE 1,500 million (for real estate assets), depending on which activity it engages in.

No one shareholder may own more than 20 per cent of the authorized capital, except by authority of the Ministry of Finance.

3.2.2 Factoring companies

Factoring is a business activity in which a company takes over the responsibility for collecting the debts of another. It is a service primarily intended to meet the needs of small and medium-size firms.

Typically, the client debits all his sales to the factor. The factor takes over the entire responsibility for retrieving the debts due from the client's customers, so protecting the client from bad debts. This is known as 'contract recourse factoring'. All the credits that are ceded under the cover of this contract must be supported by invoices or by other equivalent documentation.

A factoring company (*sociedade de factoring*) must be incorporated as a corporation with an authorized capital not less than PTE 200 billion. At least 80 per cent of the capital must consist of registered shares. No shareholder can have more than 20 per cent of the authorized capital, unless authorized by the Ministry of Finance.

3.2.3 Investment companies

Financial institutions of this type (*sociedades de investimento*) have the sole aim of performing financial operations, namely the acquisition or conveyance of participations in companies' capital, the granting of medium-term and long-term credit, the promotion of new enterprises, or the organizational and financial restructuring or reconstruction of viable enterprises in which they take a holding.

They must be formed as corporations, with an authorized capital at least equal to PTE 1,500 billion. The participations they undertake may not exceed the capital value plus the reserves. No single shareholder can have more than 20 per cent of the authorized capital, unless so authorized by the Ministry of Finance.

3.2.4 Venture capital companies

Venture capital companies (*sociedades de capital de risco*, SCRs) support and promote investment and technological research in projects or companies through temporary participation in their capital.

The participation of such concerns in other companies may not individually exceed 20 per cent of their own capital and reserves, and in totality such participations must not exceed three times their capital and reserves. At any given point in time, at least 75 per cent of their participations should have been held for not more than twelve years. A participation held by an SCR in a venture must not exceed 50 per cent of the total capital of the venture.

With regard to their legal form, such institutions must take the form of a corporation, with an authorized capital of at least PTE 600 million.

3.2.5 Regional development companies

Regional development companies (*sociedades de desenvolvimento regional*) are special credit institutions whose object is to promote regionally located productive investments, through financing transactions and rendering related services. Their activities are directed exclusively to the region where they are located.

Their form must be that of a corporation with an authorized capital of at least PTE 400 million, represented by registered, ordinary or preference shares. Preference shares can be subscribed only by certain types of entity, for example local authorities, welfare institutions and non-profit-making associations, as well as private individuals normally resident in the region. Usually, none of the shareholders may have a participation exceeding 10 per cent of the authorized capital of the company.

3.2.6 Property investment management companies

The main object of such companies (*sociedades de gestão e investimento imobiliário*) is to let dwelling houses (either built or acquired by them). The incorporation of these companies is intended to stimulate the property sector, particularly as regards rented property, for which they are the chosen instrument.

With regard to their legal form, they must be corporations with an authorized capital of at least PTE 1.5 billion, in the form of registered shares. Up to 75 per cent of the capital may be subscribed in kind (i.e. in the form of buildings). None of the shareholders may have more than 25 per cent of the authorized capital of the company, except by official authorization. Companies of this type must have their registered office in Portugal.

3.2.7 Entrepreneurship development companies

Sociedades de desenvolvimento regional in Portuguese, these are similar to the venture capital companies but with the special role of promoting dynamic management, particularly with reference to young entrepreneurs (aged not over 35). So their objective is to help them in the building up or acquiring of companies. Entrepreneurship development companies cannot normally undertake transactions that are not directed towards young entrepreneurs and to small or medium-size companies. However, exceptions are envisaged in the law. Entrepreneurship development companies are subject to the same rules as venture capital companies with regard to their constitution, registered office, etc.

3.2.8 Consumer credit companies

Consumer credit companies (*sociedades de financiamento de aquisição a crédito*) have as their object the financing of purchases of goods and services through the grant of direct credit, discounts or other forms of lending. They also render services directly connected with the above-mentioned means of financing (e.g. the provision of warranties). They must be formed as corporations, with an authorized capital not less than PTE 500 billion.

3.2.9 Securities dealing and broking companies

The number of dealer and broker companies operating on each stock exchange is set by the Minister of Finance. Dealer companies (*sociedades financeiras de corretagem*) buy and sell securities on behalf of clients and may also act as principal. They may manage portfolios, receive securities on deposit, subscribe, underwrite and place new issues, grant loans to clients in order to buy securities, as well as lend securities through margin accounts.

Existing individual stockbrokers were appointed by the Minister of Finance. They carry out transactions in their own name, although they deal only on behalf of clients and are not allowed to deal on their own account.

Dealers may take the form of a corporation or a private limited company with an authorized capital of at least PTE 500 million. If the former form is chosen, the shares must be registered and cannot be listed on the stock exchange.

In relation to their participations in other companies, no participation may exceed 10 per cent of the issued capital of the company. Banks are not allowed to deal on the stock exchange floor. However, banks as well as finance companies and brokers can match the orders of their clients on the over-the-counter market.

3.2.10 Group buying consortia

Since the first Act setting up *sociedades de aquisição de compras em grupo* (SAGECs) in December 1987, the group purchasing system has undergone rapid implementation and significant growth. Group buying, as the name implies, is a joint system of acquiring goods and services. A group of people constitute a common fund, making periodic payments into it, with the object of acquiring, for each participant, goods and services over a previously determined period of time. The order in which participants receive their goods or services is determined by periodic random drawing, weighted by the amounts contributed.

It is an activity which can be engaged in only by commercial companies constituted in the form of a corporation and having the activity as their exclusive object. Group buying companies must have a minimum issued capital of PTE 50 million. The shares are registered.

3.3 Other non-monetary institutions

3.3.1 Securities brokerage companies

Securities brokerage companies (*sociedades de corretagem*) are similar to dealers except that they purchase and sell securities only on the account of third parties. Their exclusive object is intermediation in the money and exchange markets and in the rendering of related services.

This activity can be pursued only by unlisted corporations and by private limited companies with a capital not less than PTE 10 million or over PTE 100 million, according to whether they operate only in the money market or simultaneously in both markets.

Members of the managing bodies of securities brokers may not invest in or exercise any function in any securities brokerage company other than their own.

3.3.2 Portfolio management companies

Sociedades gestoras de patrimónios have as their exclusive object the management of real estate and securities and underwriting issues of securities. Such companies must be corporations with an authorized capital of at least PTE 25 million. However, at any time it can be established by the competent authority (the Ministry of Finance) that the minimum required value of the company's capital and reserves should be a percentage of the total value of the managed portfolios. It is illegal for any partner, manager or employee to undertake investments or to exercise functions in other portfolio management companies.

3.3.3 Holding companies

The main activity of holding companies (*sociedades gestoras de participações sociais*) is the management of groups of other companies. Beyond their main activity such companies can also render technical, administrative and management services to the companies in which they participate. As regards legal form, an SGPS may be either a corporation or a private limited company. Its authorized capital must be at least PTE 5 million.

3.3.4 Unit trust management companies

Unit trust management companies (*sociedades gestoras de fundos de investimento*) have as their exclusive object the administration, management and representation of one or more investment funds (handling securities or property but not both together). A unit trust must be constituted as a corporation, with an authorized capital not less than PTE 50 million or PTE 75 million, according to whether it manages securities funds or property funds. Either way, the total issued capital and reserves must not fall below a certain percentage of the value of the whole fund, the percentage being set by the Ministry of Finance.

3.3.5 Life and non-life insurance companies

The importance of life insurance companies (*seguradoras*) in the non-banking sector has been tending to increase. The life insurance companies have emerged as competitors of the banks in stimulating savings by means of a cluster of financial products involving a pension element. Their presence is increasingly felt in mortgage lending and capital markets, too. The relationship between banking and insurance has traditionally been close, since almost every insurance company has links with the banks in the fields of life insurance and pension funds. Some indeed are bank subsidiaries.

As in other countries, there are legal requirements on insurance companies to maintain technical reserves (based on statistical calculations of current risks, unreported claims, etc.), so that future pay-out obligations are covered.

Table 3.6 Insurance companies in Portugal (PTE million)

Insurance group	Total premiums	Market share (%)	Financial investments	Types of insurance
Império	35,776	12.3	85,958	All
Fidelidade	32,769	11.3	55,056	All
Mundial Confiança	32,749	11.3	69,641	All
Tranquilidade	27,943	9.6	86,086	All
Bonança	25,123	8.7	54,034	All

Source: *Suplemento Exame*, No. 28A, July 1991.

3.3.6 Pension fund management companies

Pension funds, which have been regulated since the end of 1985, are assets, not legal entities, that are managed by specialist bodies (*sociedades gestoras de fundos de pensões*) whose purpose is to receive contributions and deliver them to the insured on retirement or to the appointed beneficiaries if the insured dies. Pension funds are the materialization of pension plans.

In Portugal pension plans and funds are instruments for routeing savings and investments. Pension plans may be promoted by companies (employee plans), by associations or by financial entities (insurance companies or unit trust management companies) for their customers (individual plans). The contributions to pension funds are a tax-deductible expense for the contributors, subject to certain quantitative limits. Accordingly, the tax on the amounts contributed can be deferred until the benefits are collected.

Depending on the type of plan, a control commission to ensure compliance with the plan's purposes and its proper administration may be set up with varying members representative of the participants, the beneficiaries and the promoter companies (for example, in employee plans the company financing the pension plan participates in the plan). Pension funds are under the supervision of the Bank of Portugal or the Portuguese Insurance Institution and their share prices must be published monthly in the stock exchange journal.

The investments of pension funds are regulated; a certain percentage of their assets must be state risk-free bonds with a maturity longer than one year (at least 50 per cent) or bank deposits and cash (limited to 2 per cent), property or loans to other entities (no more than 20 per cent). However, the total investment in any one entity must not exceed a certain percentage of the fund's assets.

4 OTHER SOURCES OF FINANCE: EC PROGRAMMES

Portugal's recent accession to the European Communities has given it access to European aid programmes. These have offered the following incentives among others:

1   Specific Programme for the Development of Portuguese Industry (*Programa Específico para o Desenvolvimento da Indústria Portuguesa*, PEDIP), a programme due to run till the end of 1992, aiming not only to modernize industry but also to reinforce competitiveness in the light of the European single market. Through this programme powerful financial resources, that will support the industrial objectives similar to the PEDIP's general objectives, are being channelled to Portuguese companies. PEDIP has two sources of financial aid: 1,350 million ECUs from the EC (not refundable) and a loan from IEB in the amount of 1,000 million ECUs.

2   System of Regionally Based Financial Incentives (*Sistema de Incentivos de Base Regional*, SIBR). SIBR contributes to the balanced development of the regions of Portugal, with an emphasis on the less favoured regions. It stimulates industrial activity, fostering the creation, innovation and modernization of businesses. There are grants (limited to PTE 220 million per project) that can be extended further by joint decision of three government Ministries upon consultation with the Directorate General of Regional Development and the Directorate General of Industry. These authorities have to evaluate the regional and job creation components.

3   System of Incentives to Investment in Tourism (*Sistema de Incentivos para Financiamento de Investimentos Turísticos*, SIFIT). The aim of SIFIT is to stimulate invest-

ment in tourism projects, again with the emphasis on the less favoured regions. The amount of the grant (a maximum of PTE 220 million) is determined in each case by two components, one linked with the geographical location and the other with the location and number of jobs created.

The European Community offers other general incentives such as: employee training, financial aid to special industries, agriculture and craft work co-financed aid, energy investment, general loans, European Investment Bank loans, European Coal and Steel Community loans, European Social Fund grants, research and development funding, the European agricultural guidance and guarantee fund and the European regional development fund.

4
Taxation

1 BACKGROUND

There have been a number of attempts at tax reform in Portugal over the years. The first tax, introduced in 1641, was called the 'military tenth': it taxed the whole income at a single rate of 10 per cent. In the present century, in 1922, a reform attempted to create a whole-income tax taking account of the payer's personal situation. This reform was based on a set of partial taxes not related to ability to pay. The system was modified by the introduction of a new tax (complementary tax), the taxable basis of which was the whole income. Various difficulties led in 1929 to income tax based on 'normal' values which remained in force until 1988.

Then a major overhaul of individual and corporate income taxation saw the abolition of the previous scheduled-based system, on 1 January 1989. This reform brought the Portuguese taxation system up to the standards accepted in the rest of Europe. At the same time it adjusted the taxation of individuals' income to the constitutional (basic) law. This implies that the tax should be the only tax on income, and should be progressive, and should take account of needs as well as income.

In order to comply with the principles of social justice and equity foreseen in the constitutional law, this recent tax reform brought about the enlargement of the tax base by extending it to cases that were not included in the old regime and also by reducing the applicable rates of tax (the 'broadening basis, reducing rates' principle, as it is known).

Under the constitutional law Parliament has the sole power to levy individual taxes and to establish the overall tax system. However, Parliament may delegate its powers to the government under the terms of article 201(b) of the constitution. The taxes are created by a law which determines the incidence of the tax, exemptions, taxable income, percentages, returns, payment and the taxpayer's rights and remedies. The basic instrument is the state budget.

The proportion of GDP taken by the main direct and indirect taxes increased from about 14 per cent in 1986 to 21.3 per cent in 1988. Marginal tax rates on individual incomes range from 15 per cent to 40 per cent. In general, companies are taxed at a rate of 36 per cent plus a municipal tax (which does not exceed 3.6 per cent).

2 CORPORATE INCOME TAX

2.1 Scope

Generally, corporate income tax (*imposto sobre o rendimento das pessoas colectivas, IRC*) is applied to the worldwide profits of companies domiciled in Portugal whose principal activity is within the commercial, industrial or agricultural sphere, to the income of non-domiciled (i.e. branches of foreign) companies from permanent Portuguese establishments and to the specific earnings from Portuguese sources of a non-resident without a permanent establishment.

A legal or other entity is considered to be domiciled if it has its registered office or effective place of management in Portugal.

2.2 Taxable basis

Taxable income is defined in balance-sheet or 'comprehensive income' terms as representing the difference between the net equity at the beginning and end of the financial year, adjusted in accordance with the IRC code. If the company's records are not regarded as acceptable, tax liability is estimated.

This definition clearly embraces capital gains, but, to eliminate doubt, the code develops the concept of taxable gains further, to include the worldwide revenues of domiciliary companies and a detailed list of taxable gains of non-domiciliary entities. For non-Portuguese entities these are of particular relevance.

In addition to the income and capital gains directly earned by a permanent Portuguese establishment, non-domiciled companies are also liable to tax on income or gains, of whatever character, which are obtained through the activity of the permanent establishment, or through the conduct in Portugal of activities identical or similar to those of the permanent establishment.

If a non-domiciliary entity has no permanent establishment in Portugal, it will be taxed there in respect of:

1   Gains arising from the sale of securities or quotas issued by entities with their head office or place of management in Portuguese territory, even when their issuer is non-domiciled, wherever the dividends or interest on the shares or securities arose from a permanent establishment in Portugal.
2   Certain types of income such as: income from intellectual or industrial property and from the provision of information derived from experience acquired in the industrial, commercial or scientific sectors; other income from the application of capital, income from the use, or from granting the use, of agricultural, industrial, commercial or scientific equipment; income arising from office-holding or from membership of the statutory boards of legal entities; winnings from gambling, lotteries or sweepstakes.

2.3 Exemptions

The following institutions and activities are exempt from corporate income tax in respect of gains from capital investments:

1   State bodies, autonomous regions, town halls, municipal associations and social security institutions.
2   Legal entities of a social, charitable or similar nature.
3   Cultural, entertainment and sporting activities.
4   Co-operatives, in certain circumstances.
5   Corporations and other entities under the 'fiscal transparency' regulation.
6   Legal entities and other entities involved in marine or aeronautical navigation.

2.4 Taxable income

Taxable income consists of the sum of the net profit of the fiscal year and the difference, whether positive or negative, between the value of the net equity at the beginning and at the end of the tax period, after adjusting for the net profit and excluding share issues and dividends. This is similar to the concept of 'comprehensive income' explained in the US Financial Standards Board's Statement of Financial Accounting Concepts No. 3, namely the net change in the owner's equity during the period after adjustments for capital paid in (excluded) and dividends paid out (added back). However, revaluation surpluses are not included in taxable income, and there are other exceptions.

Table 4.1 Assessment of corporate income tax

Net income of the year

plus

Equity increases (excluding share issues) not included
in the accounting income of the year

less

Equity decreases not included
in the accounting income of the year

plus or less

Income corrections for fiscal purposes

equal to

Income for fiscal purposes

less

Fiscal losses

less

Tax benefits

equal to

Taxable basis

multiplied by

Companies income tax percentage

equal to

Calculated tax

2.5 Rates

Corporate income tax is levied on taxable profits (accounting profits adjusted to comply with tax law) at a rate of 36 per cent. It is levied on a calendar year basis. Specific authority to use a different annual period may be granted by the Ministry of Finance (it is valid for a period of three years), but branches or subsidiaries of foreign companies need only inform the Tax Authority.

Special reduced rates apply to companies whose income from agricultural activities exceeds 60 per cent of the total income earned in the year. In such cases income tax rates are as shown in Table 4.2.

Table 4.2 Corporate income tax rates on
agricultural activities

Year	Tax rate (%)
1990	16
1991	20
1992	25
1993	31
1994	36

Income relating to branches of foreign companies is taxed at a rate of 36 per cent.

Non-domiciliary companies are taxed at the rate of 25 per cent but there are some exceptions:

1   Dividends, interest, royalties, rentals and technical assistance fees are taxed at a 15 per cent rate. (If paid by SA companies, inheritance tax also applies at a rate of 5 per cent.)
2   Income from dividends, bond interest and other income from financial assets is taxed at a rate of 20 per cent.
3   Capital gains from transfers of shares by companies are taxed at a rate of 10 per cent.

The rate of municipal tax (*derrama*) is set by the local authority at a rate not exceeding 10 per cent of the IRC percentage.

2.6 Intra-group dividends

The treatment of intra-group dividends aims at avoiding or reducing the effective double taxation of such dividends (as income to both payer and payee). Hence the treatment has some of the features of an 'imputation' tax system whereby tax withheld on dividends at source may be treated as a tax credit by the recipient of the dividend.

2.6.1 Participations of at least 25 per cent

In the case of domiciliary companies, 95 per cent of intra-group dividends received are excluded from taxable profits and the 20 per cent tax withheld by the paying company constitutes a recoverable tax credit if the shares have been held for more than two years (or with an undertaking to hold them for such a period if the company was formed later). The tax withheld is considered as a payment on account of the tax due by the recipient company. By way of illustration Example 4.1 sets out a sample calculation.

Example 4.1 **Rule if company A owns between 25 per cent and 100 per cent of company B's equity, e.g. A owns 100 per cent of B's shares**

1 Profit before income tax of company B	1,000
2 = (1) × 36% Income tax paid by B (36%)	360
3 = (1) − (2) Profit of B after tax	640
Suppose this profit all goes to company A as dividends:	
4 Gross dividend received by A from B	640
5 Deduction from A's taxable income (95%)	608
6 = (4) − (5) Portion of dividends received from B that is taxed in A's hands	32
7 = (6) × 36% Income tax on dividends to be paid by A (36%)	12
8 = (4) − (7) Dividend after income tax	628
9 = (2) + (7) Total income tax paid by companies A and B	372
10 = (9) ÷ (1) Effective tax rate on dividend	37.2%
11 = (2) + (4) × (3) Tax that would arise if the deduction did not exist	590
12 = (1) ÷ (11) × 100 Effective tax rate if the deduction did not exist	59.0%

2.6.2 Participations of less than 25 per cent

As from 1991, there is also a tax credit corresponding to 35 per cent of the corporate income tax, currently at the rate of 36 per cent, attributable to the grossed-up dividend. Example 4.2 illustrates this.

Example 4.2 **Rule if company A owns less than 25 per cent of company B's equity, e.g. A owns 10 per cent of B's shares**

1 Ten per cent of company B's profit before tax	1,000
2 = (1) × 36% Income tax paid by B (36%)	360
3 = (1) − (2) Profit of B after tax	640
Suppose this profit all goes to company A as dividends:	
4 Gross dividend received by A from B	640
5 = (4) × 36% Income tax on dividend before tax credit calculation	230
6 = 35% × (2) Tax credit on dividends (35%)	126
7 = (5) − (6) Income tax on dividends to be paid by A (36%)	104
8 = (4) − (7) Dividend after income tax	536
9 = (2) + (7) Total income tax paid by companies A and B	464
10 = (9) ÷ (1) Effective tax rate on dividend	46.4%
11 = (2) + (4) × (3) Tax that would arise if the tax credit did not exist	590
12 = (1) ÷ (11) × 100 Effective tax rate if the tax credit did not exist	59.0%

2.7 Returns and payment of tax

Corporate income tax due is paid in four instalments. Three advance payments on account are required, each based on 25 per cent, calculated on the basis of the previous year's corporate income tax assessment. They fall due during the months of June, September and December of the year in which taxable income arises. The fourth instalment will be paid (or received, if a credit) on or before 31 May the following year with the submission of the annual tax return.

2.8 Tax benefits

The Tax Benefits Act grants several tax benefits to corporate income tax payers, such as exemptions on some portions of the income or on the whole, or taxation at reduced rates. In addition the following may be mentioned:

1   Only 60 per cent of the dividends received from privatized companies are included in income for tax purposes.
2   Investment projects with a value above PTE 10 billion may qualify for a special tax regime. This can be negotiated direct with the tax authorities. Investments in exporting industries which improve the balance of payments are favoured.

2.9 Tax incentives to company investment

The recent performance of the economy has attracted the interest of Portuguese and foreign business investors. In order to respond to investment expectations and the need to maintain and promote growth, the government has introduced a system of regionally based aids to stimulate the creation of new jobs in industry and tourism with particular emphasis on the less developed areas of the country:

1 *Investment tax credit* (CFI). Under CFI (*crédito fiscal ao investimento*) companies can deduct, as a credit against corporate income tax, a specified percentage of the escudo value of new investment in certain categories of assets. Not all assets are eligible, only those directly involved in the conduct of the company's business. Unused credits can be carried forward for five years, after which they expire and cannot be claimed if an equal incentive is being obtained under other legislation.
2 *Deduction for reinvestment of retained earnings* (DLRR). Under DLRR (*dedução por lucros retidos e reinvestidos*) profits retained or transferred to reserves and reinvested in the company within the subsequent three years can be deducted from the taxable profit during the three years immediately after the conclusion of the investment. The investment must be in tangible fixed assets used in the business. The deduction is spread in equal portions over a period of three years. Any portion not used in one year because of insufficient taxable profits may be deducted in subsequent years. (1991 is still a year of deduction, but this incentive is not expected to apply in the following years.)

3 OTHER TAXES
3.1 Individuals' income tax

The fiscal year for individuals ends on 31 December.

If the contributor is married, both the wife's and the husband's income will be subject to income tax (*imposto sobre o rendimento das pessoas singulares*, IRS) after the authorized deductions and allowances (depending on actual earnings and circumstances) against the combined income.

For tax purposes, income (including capital gains) is computed under the following eight categories:

A Income from employment.
B Income from self-employment.
C Commercial or industrial profits.
D Income from agriculture.
E Investment income.
F Income from rent and property.
G Capital gains.
H Pensions.
I Other income.

Individuals are taxed under IRS if they are resident in Portugal, and on income arising in Portugal if they are not. For those resident in Portugal IRS is calculated on total income, including the portion earned abroad. Foreign individuals resident in Portugal are taxed in the same way as Portuguese nationals.

For IRS purposes, a resident is anyone who spends more than 183 days in Portugal during the fiscal year or who within the year to which the income is related has a permanent residence (owned or rented) in Portugal even if he or she has not stayed in the country for more than 183 days (successive or not). Non-resident individuals, whether Portuguese or foreign, are liable only in respect of income derived from Portuguese sources.

The scope of taxable income, allowable expenses, the rates of taxation and permitted deductions from the resulting liability are outlined below. Factors such as the marital status of the taxpayer and the age and number of his dependants are to be taken into account. Conditions and limits related to health care, education and other expenses are also established. Provision is also made for special treatment of windfall gains, for the allocation of income to years other than the one in which it was received and for the carrying forward within income categories of losses or excess deductions.

Certain deductions are allowed under each category of income which take into account the costs of generating income either on an actual or on a percentage basis. Others are allowed by reference to the personal expenditure or family circumstances of the resident taxpayers. Deductions allowable by reference to personal expenditure or the family circumstances of the resident taxpayer include, *inter alia* (within certain limits) the following:

1   Unreimbursed expenses.
2   Education expenses.
3   Premiums for life, health and personal accident insurance.
4   Payments to voluntary social security systems.
5   Alimony and similar obligations.

After the assessment calculations there are several deductions in connection with the taxpayer, his or her family circumstances and dependent relatives. Other deductions result from payments on account, withholding, municipal tax (autarchic tax).

The tax rates applied vary between 15 per cent and 40 per cent in accordance with the scale shown in Table 4.3.

In the case of a married couple living together (in the legal sense) income tax is levied on the couple's combined income. However, the applicable tax rates are determined after dividing the combined income by two. The tax payable (subject to any further tax allowances mentioned below) is thus equal to that which would be payable on two

Table 4.3 Individuals' income tax: marginal rates (%)

Tax band	Marginal rate
Up to PTE 750 million	15
From PTE 750 million to PTE 1,750 million	25
From PTE 1,750 million to PTE 4,500 million	35
Over PTE 4,500 million	40

Example 4.3 Individual income tax of a married couple when neither taxpayer's income is equal to or greater than 95 per cent of their combined income

1	Income of taxpayer A	900,000	
2	Income of taxpayer B	900,000	
3	Combined income, (1) + (2)		1,800,000
4	Splitting coefficient		2
5	Income to apply maximum marginal tax rate, (3) ÷ (4)		900,000
6	Tax calculation per family member:		
	15% × 750,000 =	112,500	
	25% × (900,000 − 750,000) =	37,500	150,000
7	Family income tax, (6) × (2)		300,000
8	Average tax rate, (7) ÷ (3)		16.7%

separate incomes each equal to 50 per cent of the combined income (Example 4.3).

However, when one taxpayer's income is equal to or greater than 95 per cent of the combined income, the applicable tax rates are determined by dividing the combined income by 1.85. The tax payable is calculated as twice the amount which would have been payable on an income equal to $1/1.85$ plus the combined income (Example 4.4).

For some income categories, income tax is deducted at source by the payer. Such are the following cases, with the corresponding rates:

Winnings from gambling, lottery and mutual bets: 25 per cent.
Categories A and H income obtained by non-residents: 25 per cent.
Income from royalties, patents, etc. (rights in intellectual or industrial property) from non-residents in Portugal: 15 per cent.
Capital gains, interest on current deposits and bonds, dividends received by non-residents in Portugal: 20 per cent.

Example 4.4 Individual income tax of a married couple when one of the taxpayers' income is equal to or greater than 95 per cent of their combined income

1	Income of taxpayer A	1,800,000	
2	Income of taxpayer B	0	
3	Combined income, (1) + (2)		1,800,000
4	Splitting coefficient		1.85
5	Income to apply maximum marginal tax rate, (3) ÷ (4)		973,000
6	Tax calculation per family member:		
	15% × 750,000 =	112,500	
	25% × (973,000 − 750,000) =	55,700	168,200
7	Family income tax, (6) × (2)		336,500
8	Average tax rate, (7) ÷ (3)		18.7%

Example 4.5 **Individual income tax of a single person**

1 Individual's taxable income			1,800,000
2 Tax calculation:			
15% × 750,000 =		112,500	
25% × 1,000,000 =		250,000	
35% × 50,000 =		17,500	380,000
4 Average tax rate, (3) ÷ (1)			21.11%

To date, Portugal has signed treaties with twelve countries to avoid or reduce international double taxation, and these laws override the IRS code (see section 5 below).

Whenever the taxpayer receives a wage or salary as an employee or has income to be taxed at the special rates outlined above, the employer has to withhold IRS from the wage packet.

Those in receipt of income classified as category B, C or D (non-salaried workers) have to make three payments on account, each reckoned as 25 per cent of the previous year's tax.

Income tax returns have to be submitted to the tax authorities by the following dates:

- 28 February when the income arises only from category A and pension (category H), or
- 10 May in the other situations.

Tax payments have to be made on or before 10 May in the former case and on or before 10 July in the latter one.

3.2 **Value-added tax**

Value-added tax (*imposto sobre o valor acrescentado*, IVA) was introduced to Portugal in January 1986. In concept and form it closely resembles the value-added tax (VAT) system of the European Community (based on the Sixth Directive, on VAT, dated 19 June 1977). The tax applies to a wide range of goods and services. Imports and local supplies are liable to it, but not exports. The standard rate applicable to most goods and services is 17 per cent. The rates vary according to the goods and services concerned. The

Table 4.4 Value-added tax rates (%)

Operations from	Mainland	Madeira and Azores
List I of the VAT code	0	0
List II of the VAT code	8	6
List III of the VAT code	30	21
Other	17	12

Table 4.5 Items not subject to the standard value-added tax rate

List I	List II	List III
Exports	Hotel and restaurant bills	Perfumes
Seeds	Telephone, electricity charges	Aircraft
Agricultural machinery	Petrol	Alcoholic liquor
Vegetables	Certain kinds of food, wines and services	
Bread		
Fish and meat		
Pharmaceutical products		
Books		

rates that apply in mainland Portugal are higher than those in the Islands (Madeira and the Azores), see Table 4.4. Comprehensive lists of goods subject to zero rating, 8 per cent and 30 per cent are attached to the VAT code. The lists include, among other things, the goods and services shown in Table 4.5.

A registered VAT taxpayer is entitled to recover input VAT (paid on purchases of goods and services) by deducting it from output VAT (calculated on any sales of goods and services).

There are two kinds of exempt transactions. Full exemption is granted to exports. Limited exemption is granted to a number of activities or transactions, among them health care, education, cultural activities and sport, financial and insurance transactions, certain property transactions and certain technical transactions.

The VAT on certain inputs is not deductible (e.g. the acquisition of vehicles, travel expenses, the acquisition of imported products subject to the higher rates, the acquisition of goods or services as gifts to customers, employees or third parties).

When the taxpayer carries on simultaneously activities which carry the right to deduction and activities which do not, a special rule (*pro rata*) has to be applied to calculate the VAT.

3.3 Real estate transfer tax

Property transfer tax (*imposto municipal da Sisa*, SISA) is imposed on conveyancing. The basis of the tax is usually the value of the transaction and it is paid by the purchaser. The rate is 10 per cent on urban property or land with planning permission to build on it. On other kinds of property the rate is 8 per cent.

Some reduction in the rate of tax is available on the purchase of the individual's personal home, as shown in Table 4.6. (Under PTE 7,000,000 no SISA payment is due.)

Tax is also assessed on beneficiaries or purchasers of 75 per cent or more of the capital of private companies (*sociedades por quotas*) holding real estate.

Some exemptions are provided by law. One involves the case of property acquired for resale. To benefit from exemption the purchaser must prove his right by the production of a certificate. The certificate will state that the purchaser has been engaged in the activity of buying and selling property, and it must confirm that the purchaser was already involved in real estate activity the previous year. The purchaser is considered to

Table 4.6 Property conveyance tax rates

Basis (PTE million)	Rates (%)	
	Marginal	Average
Up to 7	0	0
Over 7 to 10.5	5	1.6667
Over 10.5 to 14	11	4.0000
Over 14 to 17.5	18	6.8000
Over 17.5 to 21	26	–
Over 21	Flat rate 10%	

Note: The percentages are the rates for 1991.

have been involved in real estate activity only if during the previous year he acquired property for resale or if he sold property that had been acquired previously for resale.

It is important to note that if there is no certificate or it cannot be produced the tax has to be paid and there will be no exemption. However, if a property is resold within three years after the payment of SISA upon its acquisition, the tax may be recovered. In that event the taxpayer must prove that the transaction took place and the fiscal authorities will refund the tax.

Property companies have to pay attention to their VAT situation, which has to be dealt with alongside the SISA. The VAT code states that transactions which are subject to SISA are exempted from VAT.

3.4 Stamp duty

Certain documents and transactions, including negotiable securities, bills of exchange and deeds, are subject to stamp duty (*imposto do selo*). The rates payable vary according to the nature of the article or document as well as the amount involved. The largest source of revenue from this tax is bills of exchange, on which is paid 0.005 per cent of face value.

3.5 Vehicle tax

Vehicle tax (*imposto automóvel*) is payable on the purchase of new vehicles. The rate of tax is based on engine size. Vehicle tax is included in the price of the vehicle for VAT purposes, and VAT at 17 per cent is charged. Vehicle tax is also payable on the purchase of used vehicles.

3.6 Tobacco and beer duties

Duty is applied to the consumption of tobacco manufactured or for public consumption on the mainland and in the self-governing islands of Madeira and the Azores (whether home-produced or imported) in two cumulative ways:

1   Specific, that is, PTE 596 per thousand cigarettes.
2   *Ad valorem,* that is, as a percentage (54 per cent) of the retail price of all types of tobacco.

The 30 per cent duty on alcoholic liquor shown in Table 4.5 was recently abolished. At the same time the special tax on the consumption of alcoholic beverages was increased from PTE 500 to PTE 1,000.

The rate of duty on beer has recently been adjusted to PTE 21 per litre. Beer with an alcoholic content less than 0.5 per cent is exempt.

3.7 Local taxes

The municipal tax on income (called the *derrama*) may be levied on companies' income tax, in an amount up to 10 per cent of the corporate income tax due. Whenever local authorities decide to exercise this option the total rate of the corporate income tax will be (at 1991 rates): 36 per cent + 3.6 per cent = 39.6 per cent, of which 36 per cent is due to national and 3.6 per cent to local taxation.

Municipal income tax is not levied on individuals' income.

Another municipal tax, municipal property tax (*contribuição autárquica*), was introduced in 1989 and is levied on the registered value of property. The value is based on the Valuation Code. The tax authorities are entitled to revalue property for the purposes of assessing the tax. The rates in 1991 were 8 per cent on rural and 1.1 per cent to 1.3 per cent on urban property. There is a temporary exemption for low-value buildings to protect purchases deemed desirable for social and economic reasons.

3.8 Death duty and gift tax

The gratuitous transfer of property situated in Portugal is taxed at progressive rates, varying with the value of the property and the nearness of the relationship of the recipient to the deceased or donor. Foreign nationals are also subject to estate and gift tax on property situated in Portugal.

The tax is applicable to the voluntary transfer of any goods. It is progressive, from 4 per cent to 50 per cent, depending on the amount involved and the family links with the donor or deceased.

Transfers not exceeding PTE 250,000 to the spouse and to descendants under 18 years of age are exempt.

The maximum tax rate (where property worth more than PTE 50 million passes to a non-relative) is 50 per cent.

4 SOCIAL SECURITY CONTRIBUTIONS

In general, under the social security regulations, all the Portuguese employees of a Portuguese entity must be registered with, and both the employee and employer must make the corresponding contributions to, the social security authorities.

Social security contributions of 24.5 per cent for employers and 11 per cent for employees are payable on almost all wages and salaries, with no ceiling. However, a deduction limit applies to members of the board, managers and directors. The employees' contributions are deductible by them for income tax purposes.

Foreign employees working in Portugal temporarily may obtain exemption from social security contributions for up to two years if they are covered by comparable social security schemes in their home country.

Social security basically covers medical care, retirement benefits, family allowances, illness and unemployment benefit. Accidents at work are also insured.

5 TREATIES TO AVOID DOUBLE TAXATION

The purpose of these treaties is to avoid or reduce the incidence of the same income being taxable (or fully taxable) in the hands of the same person by more than one state. Such treaties will become more important in the future as the volume of commercial transactions, capital transactions and labour mobility between Portugal and other countries increases. They also have to be taken carefully into account and applied when transactions between two different countries take place.

Table 4.7 Treaty agreements on double taxation

| Country | Applied since | Maximum tax rates (%) applied to | | |
		Dividends	Interest	Royalties
UK	1 January 1970	10–15	10	5
Spain	1 January 1971	10–15	15	5
Finland	1 January 1972	10–15	15	10
Norway	1 January 1972	10–15	15	10
Belgium	1 January 1972	15	15	5
Austria	1 January 1973	15	10	10–15
France	1 January 1973	15	10–12	5
Brazil	1 January 1972	15	15	10–15
Denmark	1 January 1974	10–15	15	10
Switzerland	1 January 1976	10–15	10	5
Italy	15 January 1983	15	15	12
Germany	8 October 1982	15	10–15	10

According to the IRC code any income obtained by non-resident companies without a permanent establishment is subject to tax of 20 per cent. However, under tax treaties this rate may be reduced in connection with the payment of royalties, dividends and interest. In addition, income not expressly mentioned in the treaties (e.g. head office expense allocations) can be taxed only in the domiciliary country of the receiver. Table 4.7 shows the limits on taxes paid in Portugal which apply under the existing twelve treaty agreements. Resident individuals of the twelve countries listed are normally exempted from income tax (IRS) in Portugal on income from an employer domiciled in the treaty country, provided they spend no more than 183 days in Portugal during the fiscal year.

Part II
Accounting, auditing and financial reporting

5

The accounting and auditing background

1 HISTORY OF PORTUGUESE ACCOUNTING

1.1 The past

According to the noted scholar Fernando Gonçalves da Silva, Portuguese accounting history may be divided into four periods. The first lasted from the foundation of the Portuguese nation in 1143 to the end of the fifteenth century. By that time Portugal had become a leading maritime and trading country. However, it would seem that the accounting techniques in use remained primitive.

The second may be considered to include the sixteenth and seventeenth centuries and the first half of the eighteenth. It was during this period that the use of Venetian-style double-entry bookkeeping first made its appearance in Portugal. However, little is known about the extent to which such methods were used at the time. There are no books on accounting in Portuguese dating from this period, either original works or translations, nor were any legal requirements for accounting introduced.

According to Professor Lopes Amorim, double-entry accounting was introduced to Portugal, probably in the early sixteenth century, during the reign of King Manuel I, who authorized foreign merchants worth at least twenty-five ducados (a currency of the time) to establish themselves in the Portuguese kingdom.

The third period began when Sebastião José de Carvalho e Melo (the future Marquis of Pombal) became Minister of Finance in 1750, and lasted until the early twentieth century. Under Pombal efforts were made to lay down a legal framework for trade and commerce, including accounting. In 1755 a trade association (the Junta de Comércio) was set up by royal decree which was to play a lasting role in the teaching of accounting and business methods. The first accounting texts in Portuguese appeared in 1758 (*Mercador exacto nos seus livros de contas*, edited by João Baptista Bonavie) and 1764 (*Tratado das partidas dobradas*, by an unknown writer). However, Gonçalves da Silva comments that the lack of education and inertia of the businessmen of the day was such that Pombal's reforms were not as rapid, as profound or as lasting as the Marquis had intended.

Accounting for the governmental activities of the kingdom was first imposed by Royal Decree on 22 December 1761. In the following century commercial codes were introduced by the liberal politician Ferreira Borges (1786–1838) in 1833 and by the politician and academic lawyer Veiga Beirão (1841–1916) in 1888, under the influence of the nineteenth-century French commercial codes. These included requirements for the keeping of books of accounts and other records. Some of the provisions of the 1888 codes are still in force today. Such provisions include the obligation to keep a journal, a ledger and a balance sheet book (inventory), which must be written up within ninety days and retained for ten years. The pages of these books must bear the official stamp of the fiscal authorities.

The fourth period may be considered to have begun in the late 1920s. At that time accounting acquired recognition in Portugal as a body of knowledge having a relationship with business economics and the theory of the firm. Several influential books on accounting were written by Portuguese authors, and foreign classics by authors such as Schmalenbach, Zappa and Dumarchey were translated. An accounting journal, *Revista de contabilidade e comércio* (Review of Accounting and Commerce), started in 1933 and continues today. A scientific and cultural association, the Sociedade Portuguesa de Contabilidade, was founded, and while specialized accounting in university curricula was slower to gain acceptance, in due course it began to make its appearance in economics faculties and in some law faculties.

To Gonçalves da Silva's four periods one is tempted to add a fifth, since certain developments during the last twenty years have had particular significance not only for the economic and political life of the country but also for accounting. During this latter period, Portugal relinquished its overseas territories in Africa, notably those in Angola and Mozambique, putting an end to the colonial administration and wars which had taken such a heavy toll of its resources. Turning its face towards Europe, Portugal has become established among the Western European democracies, and since January 1986 has been a member state of the European Community, with all that such membership implies for the country's economic orientation and its accounting and financial reporting practices. In particular, the influence of French ideas, already important in the commercial codes of the nineteenth century, have been significant in the field of accounting. However, French influence is starting to lose its dominance as international standards, derived mainly from the English-speaking countries, gain more and more supporters.

Prior to EC membership Portugal had already embarked on the modernization of its financial accounting practices under the influence of French ideas. In fact during the period 1970–73, that is to say before the 1974 revolution, studies had begun under the aegis of the Directorate General of Taxes in the Ministry of Finance, aimed at defining proposals for accounting modernization with a view to greater equity in the taxation of company profits. The study group identified the French 1957 *Plan Comptable Général* (General Accounting Plan) as a suitable model.

The political and economic history of Portugal since the 1950s has had important implications for accounting, which began to be recognized in the early 1970s, although the various endeavours to introduce reforms kept being overtaken by political events until the early 1980s.

1.2 The present

On one hand, the process of modernizing accounting regulation took a step forward in 1976 with the law establishing the Comissão de Normalização Contabilística (CNC, the Accounting Standardization Committee), and with the issuing of the first *Plano Oficial de Contabilidade* (POC), the Official Accounting Plan, in the decree law of 7 February 1977. This signified official adoption of the institutional model for accounting regulation suggested by the Finance Ministry study group mentioned above, namely the French model. This model involves a standard-setting body attached administratively to the Ministry of Finance, with powers to lay down a national accounting plan the provisions of which are given legal force in the form of decrees or decree laws (see p. 6).

On the other hand, although the law creating the CNC was passed in 1976, the decree specifying its structure and powers did not appear until October 1980, and the members of the committee were not appointed until June 1983. Thus the political and economic vicissitudes of the 1970s and early 1980s have made the creation of a modern framework for accounting regulation in Portugal a protracted affair, spread over some twelve or thirteen years. They have also resulted in the temporary demise of private-sector industrial and financial groups (which were broken up after the 1974 revolution), so that consolidated accounts were hardly called for until new ones emerged. This helps to explain the delay in implementing the Seventh Directive.

In November 1989 a revised version of the POC was issued to give effect to the EC

Table 5.1 Opinions (*Normas Interpretativas*) originally published by the Accounting Standardization Committee (1987 and 1989)

1/87	Accounting for assets received through donation (corresponds to DC 2/91)
2/87	Accounting for concession contracts (corresponds to DC 4/91)
3/87	Accounting for the costs and revenues of bingo (corresponds to DC 5/91)
4/87	Time-sharing accounting
5/87	Accounting for financial and tax benefits
6/87	Accounting for subsidies
7/87	Acquisition of fixed assets through the payment of a perpetual rent
8/87	Accounting for the incorporation of reserves into the capital stock as an asset in the participating company (corresponds to DC 6/91)
9/87	Accounting for the relations between parent companies and affiliated companies
1/89	Accounting for provisions according to tax rules
2/89	Accounting for corporate income tax
3/89	Accounting for withholding tax

Fourth Directive. Some time later, proposals for implementing the Seventh Directive, on consolidated accounts, and for revising the POC accordingly, were produced in draft form, and in July 1991 a revised version of the POC was issued to give effect to the Seventh Directive. This latter is to apply to annual and group accounts for financial years beginning in 1991 onward.

Accounting principles are promulgated in the official Accounting Plan. Given the tax orientation of Portuguese financial accounting, however, tax rules also have a considerable bearing on certain areas of accounting, such as fixed assets and provisions. The basic bookkeeping requirements are laid down in the Commercial Code.

The main document produced by the CNC has been the POC, whose content is outlined in section 4. The CNC has also produced Opinions, which were known at first as *Normas Interpretativas* (Interpretations of Standards) and are now called *Directrizes Contabilisticas* (Accounting Guidelines) abbreviated to DC. Accountants are not sure whether or not the Opinions are compulsory. This is mainly because they are not law,

Table 5.2 Draft Opinions (*Directrizes Contabilisticas*) of the Accounting Standardization Committee (1991)

1/91	Accounting for mergers and acquisitions
2/91	Accounting for assets received as donations
3/91	Accounting for long-term contracts (corresponds to NI 1/87)
4/91	Accounting for concession contracts (corresponds to NI 2/87)
5/91	Accounting for the costs and revenues of bingo (corresponds to NI 3/87)
6/91	Accounting for the incorporation of reserves in the capital stock as an asset in the participating company (corresponds to NI 8/87)

Note: At the time of writing, these proposals exist in draft only for discussion. If approved, they will be published in the *Diário da República* (official journal) (second series).

unlike the POC. In effect, the Opinions are published in the *Official Journal* (second series) and are signed only by a Secretary of the Executive Committee of the CNC (whereas the POC was approved by the Council of Ministers as a sign of its importance). The first set of Opinions appeared in 1987 and were related to the 1977 version of the POC. With the enactment of the new POC they ceased to be relevant. Table 5.1 shows a list of these original Opinions. At the time of writing, proposals for Opinions (now known as Accounting Guidelines) exist in draft form. Some of them are simply a copy or a modified version of the previous *Normas Interpretativas* which appeared in 1977. Table 5.2 lists the proposed new Opinions.

Banks and other financial institutions, as well as insurance companies, are subject to a separate set of accounting requirements. The POC was drawn up in the light of the EC Fourth Directive, which does not apply to banks and financial institutions. The latter are subject to the 1986 directive on the financial statements of credit and financial institutions, and an Accounting Plan applicable to the financial sector, drawn up in the light of the 1986 directive, exists and has been applied since 1 January 1990. This accounting plan is the responsibility not of the CNC but of the Banco de Portugal, the central bank.

In addition, insurance companies are subject not to the POC but to a sectoral national accounting plan drawn up by the Instituto de Seguros de Portugal (Insurance Institute of Portugal).

These changes will need to be digested before any substantial further developments can be expected. In general, the separation between tax accounting and financial accounting will tend to increase.

Nowadays, the tax rules still affect financial accounting, specifically in the following areas:

1   Inventory valuation.
2   The revaluation of fixed assets.
3   Depreciation of fixed assets.
4   Provision for reductions in the value of assets.
5   Confidential expenses.

2 THE ACCOUNTING STANDARDIZATION COMMITTEE
2.1 Powers of the committee

According to the Ministry of Finance regulation dated 3 April 1987 (article 1), which set out the current powers of the CNC, the committee's remit is to oversee the process of improving national accounting standardization, specifically:

1   To promote the requisite studies to establish accounting principles and procedures which can be considered generally acceptable.
2   To undertake projects concerned with updating, amending and interpreting the POC.
3   To steer the development of accounting plans for the various sectors of industry or to comment on and approve those developed by other bodies.
4   To comment on draft laws that would have repercussions on company accounting.

5   To respond to enquiries from companies concerning the implementation or inter-
    pretation of the POC.
6   To participate in international meetings where matters relating to accounting
    standardization are discussed, with the object of issuing a technical opinion.

2.2 Structure of the committee

The CNC has a president, a general council and an executive committee (article 2). The
president is appointed by the Minister of Finance and must be someone whose
professional and intellectual competence is widely recognized (article 3). The general
council is the deliberative body which represents, at national level, the various groups
with an interest in accounting standardization (article 6). In addition to the president, the
committee consists of thirty-three members, drawn from the following constituencies
(article 7):

1   Ministry of Finance, National Statistical Institute, Bank of Portugal, Portuguese
    Institute of Insurance and the Department of Trade: six members.
2   Professional associations: seven members.
3   Academic institutions: eight members.
4   Nationalized industries: four members.
5   Employers' organizations: eight members.

The executive committee has eleven members drawn from the membership of the general
council for a renewable period of three years (article 10). The chairman of the committee
is elected by the general council in a secret ballot. The other ten members are chosen so
as to represent the various constituencies listed above.

2.3 Functions of the committee

The president has the power to represent the CNC in its relations with the government
and international bodies, and he may delegate that power to other CNC members or may
be accompanied by them. He or she also chairs the general council and attends meetings
of the executive committee at the request of the latter or its chairman.

The powers of the general council of the CNC are set out in the law (article 8). They
are:

1   To advise the Minister of Finance on accounting principles, concepts and procedures
    as set out in section 2.1 above.
2   To approve the annual plan of activity and the programme of research to be carried
    out by the executive committee or by working groups.

The general council normally meets once a quarter; in order for it to be quorate at least
twelve members must be present. The chairman of the executive committee may act as
vice-president of the CNC (article 9). Decisions are reached by a simple majority of those
present, with the president having a casting vote (article 9).

The executive committee carries out work laid down by the general council. It sets up
working groups and co-ordinates their activities, decides on the submission of draft

proposals from the working groups to the general council, prepares annual activity programmes and budgets for submission annually to the general council, and arranges the publication of periodic reports the preparation of which is entrusted to a working group (article 11). The executive committee meets regularly four times a month, and also at the special request of its chairman. The required quorum is six, including the chairman (or his deputy), who has a casting vote (article 12).

Working groups are composed of a member of the executive committee, who acts as co-ordinator, plus other members of the executive committee or of the general council, plus external assessors chosen for their particular qualifications in order to ensure the quality or appropriateness of the work (article 13). The members of working groups are selected by the executive committee (article 14).

3 THE ACCOUNTING AND AUDITING PROFESSIONS

In common with certain other European countries (e.g. Belgium), Portugal has separate professions, not just separate professional bodies, for accounting and for auditing. However, the major international accounting firms are now well established in Portugal.

3.1 The accountancy profession

The accountancy profession consists of *técnicos de contas* (registered accountants), who are registered with the Ministry of Finance. To be eligible for registration, they must hold a relevant degree (including approval in financial accounting, cost accounting and taxation courses). It is also possible to be registered on the basis of five years' experience without a relevant degree if the person concerned has passed a professional examination previously.

Under Portuguese tax law before the reforms in 1988, company accounts prepared for tax purposes had to be signed by a registered accountant who was also responsible for keeping the company's financial records in one central location. As a result of the 1989 fiscal reforms, it is no longer necessary for an accountant to be registered in order to sign a company's tax return, provided he or she is named as the company's official accountant in its statutory declaration of the commencement of its activities.

There is no officially recognized professional organization of accountants, but there are several professional, scientific and cultural associations, the oldest of which is the Sociedade Portuguesa de Contabilidade (SPC), founded in 1930. Nowadays the most

Table 5.3 Membership of accounting associations (approximate figures)

Association	No. of members
Sociedade Portuguesa de Contabilidade (SPC)	500
Associação Portuguesa Técnicos de Contas (APOTEC)	7,000
Associação Portuguesa de Contabilistas (APC)	2,500
Câmara dos Técnicos de Contas	3,000

influential of them is the Associação Portuguesa de Técnicos de Contas (APOTEC). Other bodies are the Associação Portuguesa de Contabilistas (APC) and the Câmara dos Técnicos de Contas. Table 5.3 indicates the number of members of the four associations. The associations publish journals; in the case of APOTEC there is a regular monthly journal which contains a useful technical section as well as theoretical articles.

In addition, accounting firms have their association, the Associação de Empresas de Contabilidade e Administração (APECA), which also issues a periodical bulletin.

3.2 The auditing profession

The auditing profession consists of *revisores oficiais de contas*, usually known as ROCs, statutory auditors registered with the Ministry of Justice and belonging to the Câmara dos Revisores Oficiais de Contas (Chamber of Registered Statutory Auditors). The latter is the officially recognized professional body for auditors. It has approved technical standards for the auditing of Portuguese companies, and publishes a periodical bulletin for its members. Individuals and professional associations of persons meeting the conditions listed below may undertake official auditing work only after being admitted to the Câmara de Revisores Oficiais de Contas and registered on the list of ROC.

The main bodies, government-owned, public or private entities, whose members have powers to carry out legal and statutory audits of the annual financial statements are:

1   Câmara de Revisores Oficiais de Contas (Chamber of ROCs).
2   Inspecção Geral de Finanças, Inspectorate General of Finance, part of the Ministry of Finance.
3   Private Portuguese auditing firms.
4   International auditing firms.

The Câmara dos Revisores Oficiais de Contas was established in 1974 (Ministerial Order 83/74, dated 6 February), under the Ministry of Justice, as the representative body of ROCs and partnerships of ROCs. At the end of 1990 there were 599 registered members. Of these 599 members, 203 carry on their profession as partners in one of the eighty-three partnerships of statutory audit companies. Some 12 per cent of registered members did not engage in statutory audit activity.

Upon the enactment of decree law 519-L2/79, dated 29 December 1979, the require-

Table 5.4 Technical recommendations of the Chamber of Registered Statutory Auditors for legal auditing

---

1 The auditing of the financial statements and other published reports
2 Influence of initial balances on the final balances to be verified
3 Verifying the application of the consistency principle
4 Influence of tax rules on the statutory audit
5 The auditing of interim financial statements
6 Annual report on statutory auditing carried out
7 Auditing of non-monetary paid-up capital
8 The auditing of accounts which include comparative figures relating to the previous year
9 Statutory audit of consolidated accounts

---

ments for access to professional audit practice were defined. The prerequisites for registration and practice as an auditor are, *inter alia*:

1   Portuguese nationality.
2   A university degree in law, economics, management or accounting.
3   Age at least 25 years and no more than 65.
4   At least three years (minimum 700 hours) of practical experience in financial and accounting work under the supervision of a statutory official auditor (ROC), who must have been a member of the chamber of ROCs for more than five years.
5   Successful completion of the official professional qualifying examination.

Since 1977 the Inspecção Geral de Finanças – a department of the Ministry of Finance, has performed the specialized service of auditing the non-financial government-owned companies. The audit reports issued by the auditing department of the Inspecção Geral de Finanças replace the statutory audit report issued by a statutory auditor.

The services offered by the indigenous private auditing firms usually include auditing, accounting, software, taxation and consultancy. The same services are available from the multinational auditing and accounting companies.

Portuguese corporations (SAs) and private limited companies (*Ldas*) must also appoint a statutory board of auditors (*conselho fiscal*), the size of which is usually three people, but in some cases may be one or five. The appointment is for a period of not more than three years. It is made by the shareholders' meeting.

All SAs must have a three-member audit board (see Chapter 2), one member of which is the company's *revisor oficial de contas*, unless the share capital is under PTE 20 million, in which case a single ROC may constitute the audit board. For private companies above a certain size as specified in the Código das Sociedades Comerciais (fifty employees, net assets of PTE 180 million and sales turnover of PTE 370 million), the same applies in the case of an SA. No statutory audit is required of smaller *Lda* companies. Although only one member of the statutory board of auditors need be professionally qualified, the following restrictions apply to all members. No member of the statutory board of auditors may:

1   Be a director or employee of the company or receive any special benefits from it.
2   Be a director, employee or member of the audit board of the company's parent or subsidiary companies or of any company which is in a position to control or be controlled by the company because of any special contractual obligations.
3   Be a shareholder, owner or employee of any company carrying out in its own name any of the functions or subject to the restrictions described above.
4   Perform any functions in a competitor company.
5   Have a close family relationship with persons in any of the preceding categories.
6   Be legally disqualified from carrying out public duties.

According to the central register of companies kept by the Ministry of Justice, the number of entities among Portuguese companies subject to the statutory audit requirement is as shown in Table 5.5. At present, the types of companies which are subject to the statutory audit system are:

1   All government-owned companies.

Table 5.5 Organizations subject to the statutory
audit requirement

Legal form	No. of registered entities
Government-owned companies	54
Corporations	6,456
Partnerships	198,416
One-man businesses	1,165,017
Other entities[1]	32,760

Source: Ministry of Justice statistics, July 1991.
Note:
[1] Co-operatives, limited partnerships, general partnerships, etc.

2   All public limited liability companies.
3   Some private limited liability companies (all those that have an audit board and those
which meet two of the three size criteria).

In addition to the statutory audit, which must be carried out subject to the conditions
just described, a number of the largest companies employ international accounting firms
to carry out an independent audit in accordance with international auditing standards. In
a number of cases the statutory auditor may be a partner in an international firm, and in
that case he or she may also act as the audit partner responsible for the independent
audit.

Auditors' fees are calculated in terms of the number and size of an individual ROC's
customer's companies, determined by a points system. Each company is attributed a
certain number of points (from 0 to 8) calculated on the basis of their total assets and
revenue. Each individual ROC has an allocation of forty-eight points, which may not be
exceeded. This system was designed to ensure independence.

4 THE OFFICIAL ACCOUNTING PLAN (POC)
4.1 List of contents

The current version of the POC was published in October 1989 and was modified and
amended in July 1991 to take account of the requirements of the Seventh EC Directive
on group accounts. It is perhaps noteworthy that publication took the form of a
document annexed to a decree law approved by the Council of Ministers and not simply
by the Finance Ministry, a fact which may indicate the national importance attributed to
the document.

The POC does not deal with cost accounting. As far as cost accounting is concerned, it
is expected that individual industry accounting plans will be prepared but nothing has
been decided as yet.

The POC is arranged in fourteen sections:

1   Introduction.
2   General considerations.

3 Objectives and qualitative characteristics of financial information.
4 Accounting principles.
5 Accounting rules for specific classes of items.
6 Balance sheet layout and content.
7 Profit and loss statement layout and content.
8 Notes on the balance sheet and the profit and loss statements.
9 Statement of sources and application of funds.
10 Overall chart of accounts.
11 Detailed code of accounts.
12 Explanatory notes on the operation of certain accounts.
13 Group accounting methods and procedures.
14 Group financial statement layout and content.

Section 1 of the POC makes it clear that the November 1989 POC is a revision of the original 1977 version. The reasons for the revision were:

1 The implementation of EC directives, i.e. the Fourth Directive, on annual accounts, and the Seventh Directive, on group accounts.
2 To take the opportunity to introduce improvements and clarifications in the light of twelve years' experience, e.g. as regards the titles of accounts.
3 To remove some minor differences between Portuguese accounting and internationally accepted principles (IASC), e.g. accounting for leased assets.

The CNC decided to keep the changes to a minimum in order to facilitate matters for both accountants and users.

Section 2 of the POC seeks to explain the reasons for the changes and to justify the options exercised under the Fourth Directive as regards the layout of the financial statements, notes on the accounts, related companies (subsidiaries and associates), accruals, provisions, bills of exchange and promissory notes. It also provides a number of legal definitions regarding related companies and provisions.

Portuguese law draws the following distinctions between different categories of related companies:

1 *Group companies*, where one company holds a majority of the voting capital of another, either directly or indirectly, or over which it exercises control by other means.
2 *Associated companies*, where one company holds at least 20 per cent of the voting capital of another and may not be considered a mother company.
3 *Other companies*, not fitting into the above categories.

These definitions are important in connection with group accounts, because each can be roughly identified with one of the three methods envisaged by the POC (see Chapter 9).

Section 3 of the POC sets out certain general ideas which are essentially a very brief summary of those expressed in the US Financial Accounting Standards Board's (FASB) Statements of Financial Accounting Concepts (SFAC) Nos. 1 and 2, regarding the objectives and qualitative characteristics of financial statements.

The contents of sections 3 and 4 of the POC are described in more detail in sections 4.2 and 4.3 below, and section 4.4 includes the overall Chart of Accounts presented in section 10 of the POC. The other sections of the POC are covered in much more detail in Chapters 6–9 below. Appendices A–C complete them.

4.2 Objectives and qualitative characteristics of financial information

Financial statements should be useful for making rational economic decisions and hence should contribute to the functioning of efficient capital markets and the accountability of management. The user groups which are specifically cited are: investors, lenders, workers, creditors, government and other official authorities, and the public in general. It is worth mentioning that managers are not referred to, as they are mainly interested in cost accounting and this is not yet standardized by law. The responsibility of preparing and presenting financial statements is laid upon management and in particular on the board of directors. (These responsibilities are set out in detail in company law.) It is stated that the users of financial statements will be better able to analyse the capacity of a firm, in terms of the timing and certainty of the cash flows it may generate, if they are provided with information focusing on its financial position, the results of its operations and changes in its financial position.

The essential quality of financial statement information is understandability by users. Its usefulness depends on three characteristics: relevance, reliability and comparability. The definitions of these three characteristics in the POC are derived from those in the US FASB's SFAC No. 2, published in 1980. The POC states that these characteristics, together with the concepts, principles and accounting rules, make it possible for general-purpose financial statements to give a true and fair view of the firm's financial position and the results of operations.

4.3 Accounting principles

Generally speaking, in Portugal accounting principles require legal expression or backing in order to be valid. There is no tradition of accounting principles gaining general acceptance through recognition by the accounting profession. The POC refers to the seven accounting principles listed in Table 5.6, where they are compared with the principles in the Fourth Directive.

The principles of continuity, consistency, accruals, and prudence are similar to those stated in the EC Fourth Directive. The directive also refers to the use of the cost (or entry price) basis of accounting for assets, but specifically allows the use of current cost as a member state option. The wording of the POC, however, is somewhat different: it requires the use of 'costs of acquisition or production, either in nominal or in constant escudos'. This suggests that current purchasing power accounting would be legally acceptable, but the acceptability of current cost accounting is more doubtful.

The principle of substance over form requires operations to be accounted for with regard to their substance and financial reality and not merely their legal form, i.e. in the spirit, not just the letter. With regard to the treatment of finance leases, the current accounting requirements are based on the legal form, but a change to treatment based on substance, i.e. finance lease capitalization, is planned.

Table 5.6 Accounting principles

POC	Principle	Fourth Directive
Section 4 (a)	Continuity	Article 31 (1) (a)
Section 4 (b)	Consistency	Articles 3 and 31 (1) (a)
Section 4 (c)	Accruals	Article 31 (1) (d)
Section 4 (d)	Historical cost	Articles 32 and 33
Section 4 (e)	Prudence	Articles 31 (1) (c) and 42 (1)
Section 4 (f)	Substance over form	} Various articles
Section 4 (g)	Materiality	

The principle of materiality requires financial statements to show all the items which are relevant and may affect the evaluation or decisions of interested users.

Financial accounting in Portugal remains essentially tax-orientated, so that an important influence on accounting practice in the sphere of valuation and income measurement is the body of decree laws and decrees dealing with the calculation of taxable profit and with tax treatments which are mandatory if certain tax allowances are to be obtained. Notwithstanding the fundamental principles enunciated in the POC, if the accounting treatment required to obtain a tax benefit differs from that which is consistent with the POC, it is the former which will prevail (although the POC requires the difference to be disclosed in the notes on the financial statements). On the other hand, Portuguese tax law does not set out to provide anything approaching a comprehensive set of accounting guidelines.

4.4 The overall Chart of Accounts

An important function of the POC has been to encourage the standardization of accounting terminology and classification. In part this has been achieved through the overall Chart of Accounts (section 10 of the POC), which includes the general ledger accounts (two digits). Table 5.7 reproduces the chart in both Portuguese and English versions.

Groups 1–5 include the balance sheet accounts (assets, groups 1–4; liabilities, group 2; net equity, group 5). Groups 6–8 include the income statement accounts. Code No. 88 is for the net result for the year and appears simultaneously in both statements. Groups 9 and 0 are free. Some companies use one or both of them for cost accounting.

The names and code numbers for the accounts are compulsory. Companies may not use the missing code numbers (e.g. 16 and 17) but may use classes 9 and 0. On the other hand, in the subdivisions of the accounts mentioned (which are listed in section 11 of the POC), companies are allowed to use names and code numbers for the accounts other than those in the detailed list of accounts.

Table 5.7 Overall Chart of Accounts in the POC (a) Portuguese original (*quadro de contas*)

1 Disponibilidades	2 Terceiros	3 Existências	4 Imobilizações	5 Capital, reservas e resultados transitados
11 Caixa	21 Clientes	31 Compras	41 Investimentos financeiros	51 Capital
12 Depósitos à ordem	22 Fornecedores	32 Mercadorias	42 Imobilizações corpóreas	52 Acções (quotas) próprias
13 Depósitos a prazo	23 Empréstimos obtidos	33 Produtos acabados e intermédios	43 Imobilizações incorpóreas	53 Prestações suplementares
14 Outros depósitos bancários	24 Estado e outros entes públicos	34 Subprodutos, desperdícios, resíduos e refugos	44 Imobilizações em curso	54 Prémios de emissão de acções (quotas)
15 Títulos negociáveis	25 Accionistas (sócios)	35 Produtos e trabalhos em curso		55 Reservas de reavaliação
	26 Outros devedores e credores	36 Matérias-primas, subsidiárias e de consumo		56 Reservas obrigatórias
	27 Acréscimos e diferimentos	37 Adiantamentos por conta de compras		57 Reservas especiais
18 Outras aplicações de tesouraria	28 Provisões para cobranças duvidosas	38 Regularização de existências	48 Amortizações acumuladas	58 Reservas livres
19 Provisões para aplicações de tesouraria	29 Provisões para riscos e encargos	39 Provisões para depreciação de existências	49 Provisões para investimentos finannanceiros	59 Resultados transitados

Table 5.7 Overall Chart of Accounts in the POC (b) English translation

1 Cash and banks	2 Third parties	3 Inventories	4 Fixed assets	5 Capital, reserves and past year's results
11 Cash	21 Trade accounts receivable	31 Inventory purchases	41 Investments	51 Capital
12 Sight deposits	22 Trade accounts payable	32 Goods	42 Tangible fixed assets	52 Own shares (quotas)
13 Term deposits	23 Loans from credit institutions	33 Finished and intermediate products	43 Intangible fixed assets	53 Supplementary capital
14 Other bank deposits	24 Public sector	34 Spoilage, waste defective units and scrap	44 Work in progress	54 Stock (quota) issue premium
15 Negotiable securities	25 Shareholders (partners)	35 Work in progress		55 Revaluation reserves
	26 Other debtors and creditors	36 Raw materials and consumables		56 Legal reserves
	27 Accruals and deferrals	37 Advances against purchases		57 Special reserves
18 Other short-term investments	28 Provisions for doubtful debts	38 Inventory adjustment	48 Accumulated depreciation	58 Free reserves
19 Provisions for short-term investments	29 Provisions for risks and charges	39 Provisions for inventory depreciation	49 Provisions for investments	59 Past year's results

6 Custos e perdas	7 Proveitos e ganhos	8 Resultados	9 Contabilidade de custos	0 –
61 Custo das mercadorias vendidas e das matérias consumidas	71 Vendas	81 Resultados operacionais		
62 Fornecimentos externos	72 Prestações de serviços	82 Resultados financeiros		
63 Impostos	73 Proveitos suplementares	83 (Resultados correntes)		
64 Custos com o pessoal	74 Subsídios à exploração	84 Resultados extraordinários		
65 Outros custos operacionais	75 Trabalhos para a própria empresa	85 (Resultados antes de impostos)		
66 Amortizações do exercício	76 Outros proveitos operacionais	86 Imposto sobre o rendimento do exercício		
67 Provisões do exercício				
68 Custos e perdas financeiros	78 Proveitos e ganhos financeiros	88 Resultado líquido do exercício		
69 Custos e perdas extraordinários	79 Proveitos e ganhos extraordinários	89 Dividendos antecipados		

6 Costs and losses	7 Revenues and gains	8 Results	9 Cost accounting	0 –
61 Cost of goods sold and materials consumed	71 Sales	81 Operating results		
62 External supplies and services	72 Services rendered	82 Financial results		
63 Taxes	73 Supplementary revenues	83 Current results		
64 Personnel expenses	74 Subventions received	84 Extraordinary results		
65 Other operating costs	75 Own work	85 Result before tax		
66 Depreciation of the year	76 Other operating revenues	86 Income tax of the year		
67 Provisions of the year				
68 Financial costs and losses	78 Financial income and gains	88 Net result of the year		
69 Extraordinary costs and losses	79 Extraordinary income and gains	89 Anticipated dividends		

5. PUBLICATION OF FINANCIAL STATEMENTS AND OTHER REPORTS

5.1 Publication of financial statements

The disclosure requirements for all corporations (*sociedades anónimas* and *sociedades em comandita por acções*) and limited liability companies (*sociedades por quotas*) above a certain size are the same. The following must be made public:

1   The balance sheet, profit and loss account and the notes on the financial statements.
2   The report of the board of directors.
3   The report of the statutory auditors.
4   The report of the audit board, where one is required.
5   Minutes of the general meeting approving the accounts and the distribution of profits.

Between 1986 and 1990 these documents were published in the official journal (*Diário da República*), deposited in the Commercial Registry and published, in a newspaper of the district in which the headquarters of the company were situated. Since 1990 the requirement of publication in a newspaper has ceased to apply.

For listed companies, special publication requirements in the official stock exchange gazette (Boletim das Coíções) apply; among other obligations, mid-year financial statements also have to be published in the gazette, though in less detail.

The above-mentioned and other detailed information must be made available to the shareholders at the company's headquarters one month before the date of the annual general meeting of shareholders.

5.2 Financial statements

The POC includes specific provision as to the format and content of financial statements. Under its terms companies must prepare:

1   A balance sheet.
2   A profit and loss account.
3   Notes to the financial statements.

Some small companies need only prepare simplified statements (balance sheet, profit and loss account and notes to the accounts).

Appendix A consists of a set of actual financial statements, in Portuguese and English, to illustrate what can be considered a representative example of Portuguese practice.

5.3 Report of the board of directors

The annual report must include at least a fair review of the development of the company's business and of its position. It should also mention any important events that have occurred since the end of the financial year, the likely course of the company's future development, activities in the field of research and development, and information concerning acquisitions of own shares.

5.4 Report of the statutory auditor

It is a requirement that companies should be audited by a qualified statutory auditor (*revisor oficial de contas*), who is a member of the company's audit board. When a company has such a body, the statutory audit complements the supervisory role of the audit board. His mandate is based on two criteria:

1 *The corporate form* adopted by the company. All SAs (*sociedades anónimas*) must be audited.

Example 5.1 **Legal certification of accounts by the statutory auditor (a) Portuguese original**

IP FINANCEIRA – Sociedade de Investimentos, Estudos e Participações Financeiras SA

Certificação legal de contas

Examinámos o balanço de IP Financeira – Sociedade de Investimentos, Estudos e Participações Financeiras, S.A. (uma sociedada anónima de direito português) em 31 de Dezembro de 1989 e as correspondentes demonstrações de resultados, de origem e aplicação de fundos e de variação nos recursos próprios para o exercício findo naquela data, documentos estes que foram preparados a partir dos livros, registos contabilísticos e documentos de suporte, mantidos em conformidade com os preceitos legais. O nosso exame foi efectuado de acordo com as Normas Técnicas de Revisão Oficial de Contas aprovadas pela Câmara dos Revisores Oficiais de Contas e com a profundidade que considerámos necessária nas circunstâncias.

Em nossa opinião as demonstrações financeiras acima referidas reflectem adequadamente a situação financeira da IP Financeira – Sociedade de Investimentos, Estudos e Participações Financeiras, S.A. em 31 de Dezembro de 1989, bem como os resultados das suas operações e a origem e a aplicação dos seus fundos para o exercício findo naquela data, de acordo com princípios de contabilidade geralmente aceites (Nota 2), aplicados numa base consistente com a do exercício anterior.

Lisboa, 23 de Fevereiro de 1990

Example 5.1 **Legal certification of accounts by the statutory auditor (b) English translation**

We have examined the balance sheet of IP Financeira – Sociedade de Investimentos, Estudos e Participações Financeiras SA (a Portuguese corporation) as of 31 December 1989 and the related statements of income, changes in financial position and changes in shareholders' investment in the company for the year then ended. All these statements have been prepared from the company's accounting records and supporting documentation, duly kept in accordance with legal requirements. Our examination was made in accordance with Normas Técnicas de Revisão Oficial de Contas (Portuguese auditing standards) approved by the Câmara dos Revisores Oficiais de Contas (the Portuguese Institute of Certified Auditors) and with the extent and scope we considered necessary in the circumstances.

In our opinion, the financial statements referred to above present fairly the financial position of IP Financeira – Sociedade de Investimentos, Estudos e Participações Financeiras SA as of 31 December 1989, and the results of its operations and changes in its financial position for the year then ended, in conformity with generally accepted accounting principles (Note 2) applied on a basis consistent with that of the preceding year.

Lisbon, 23 February 1990

2   *The size of the company. Sociedades por quotas* must be audited when, for two successive years, two of the following three limits have been exceeded:
   (a) Total assets: PTE 180 million.
   (b) Turnover: PTE 370 million.
   (c) Average number of employees: Fifty.

The statutory auditor must present an auditors' report, in a standard format. This is published as described below.

The audit is carried out in accordance with auditing standards issued by the auditors' institute, the Câmara dos Revisores Oficiais de Contas. The auditors' report is presented to the general meeting of shareholders. The statutory auditor must also monitor the company's activity and management on a continuous basis and issue a report on the results of this work.

Audits carried out by international audit firms in parallel with the statutory audit are becoming increasingly common. The standards set by the international firms have done much to raise auditing standards generally.

Example 5.2 **Audit board report (a) Portuguese original**

IP FINANCEIRA – Sociedade de Investimentos, Estudos e Participações Financeiras SA

Relatório e parecer do conselho fiscal

Ao Conselho de Administração e Accionistas da
IP Financeira – Sociedade de Investimentos,
Estudos e Participações Financeiras, S.A.

Examinámos o balanço da IP Financeira – Sociedade de Investimentos, Estudos e Participações Financeiras, S.A. em 31 de Dezembro de 1989, as demonstrações de resultados, de origem e aplicação de fundos e de variação nos recursos próprios, e respectivas notas anexas, e ainda o Relatório do Conselho de Administração para o exercício findo naquela data.
   O nosso exame foi efectuado de acordo com as disposições estatutárias e legais aplicáveis, sendo suportado, do ponto de vista técnico, pela Certificação Legal de Contas, com a qual expressamente concordamos, elaborada pelo Revisor Oficial de Contas deste Conselho, de acordo com as Normas Técnicas de Revisão Legal de Contas e com a profundidade por este considerada necessária nas circunstâncias.
   É nossa convicção que as demonstrações financeiras acima referidas reflectem adequadamente a situação financeira da Sociedade em 31 de Dezembro de 1989, bem como os resultados das suas operações e a origem e a aplicação de seus fundos para o exercício findo naquela data, de acordo com princípios contabilísticos geralmente aceites aplicados de forma consistente com o exercício anterior e que o Relatório do Conselho de Administração, na medida em que esclarece os elementos contabilísticos e as propostas nele expressas, está em conformidade com os requisitos legais e estatutários aplicáveis.
   O Conselho de Administração prestou-nos todos os esclarecimentos e provas que solicitámos.
   Assim, somos de parecer que a Assembleia Geral poderá aprovar o balanço em 31 de Dezembro de 1989, as demonstrações de resultados, de origem e aplicação de fundos e de variação nos recursos próprios para o exercício findo naquela data e o correspondente Relatório do Conselho de Administração, bem como as propostas nele expressas.
   Desejamos ainda manifestar ao Conselho de Administração o nosso apreço pela colaboração que nos prestou.

Lisboa, 23 de Fevereiro de 1990

Example 5.2 **Audit board report (b) English translation**

Report of the audit board

To the board of directors and the shareholders of IP Financeira – Sociedade de Investimentos, Estudos e Participações Financeiras SA

We have examined the balance sheet of IP Financeira – Sociedade de Investimentos, Estudos e Participações Financeiras SA as of 31 December 1989 and the related statements of income, changes in financial position and changes in shareholders' investment, and the respective notes on the accounts, as well as the board of directors' report for the year then ended.

Our examination was undertaken in accordance with prevailing legal and statutory requirements, supported from a technical point of view by the legal certification of accounts, with which we are in agreement, prepared by the statutory auditor of the board, in accordance with Normas Técnicas de Revisão Legal de Contas (Portuguese auditing standards) as we considered necessary in the circumstances.

In our opinion, the financial statements referred to above present fairly the company's financial position as of 31 December 1989 and the results of its operations and the changes in its financial position for the year then ended, in conformity with generally accepted accounting principles applied on a basis consistent with that of the preceding year, and the board of directors' report, to the extent that it clarifies the accounting data and the proposals it expresses, is in accordance with prevailing legal and statutory requirements.

The board of directors has at all times complied with our requests for clarification and supporting data.

We are of the opinion, therefore, that the shareholders' meeting may approve the balance sheet as of 31 December 1989 and the related statements of income, changes in financial position and changes in the shareholders equity for the year then ended, and the corresponding board of directors' report, as well as the proposals contained therein.

We also wish to express our appreciation to the board of directors for their collaboration.

Lisbon, 23 February 1990

5.5 Report of the audit board

For larger SAs the audit of the company is the responsibility of its audit board, one of whose members must be an ROC or a representative of a firm of ROCs. This body attends and presents to the annual general meeting a report separate from the statutory auditors' report. SAs with an issued capital of less than PTE 20 million may opt to have a single-member audit board, the single member then being the statutory auditor. *Lda* companies which exceed the above-mentioned size limits must have an audit board, which may consist of only one member (an ROC). The members of the audit board must meet the board of directors quarterly in order to review the actions of the board. Example 5.2 reproduces an audit board's report, in Portuguese and English, illustrating what may be considered a representative example of Portuguese practice.

6

Financial reporting (I) Valuation of assets, liabilities and shareholders' equity

3.8 Interim dividends
4   Assets and liabilities denominated in foreign currencies

In view of the recent publication of the new Official Accounting Plan (in 1989 and 1991), financial reporting by Portuguese companies has undergone some changes since 1990 with regard to the adoption of the new financial statement formats and the provision of more information in the notes to the accounts. Additionally, most groups of companies were obliged to prepare consolidated financial statements for the first time in the financial year beginning in 1991, and this led to the re-emergence of accounting practices forgotten in Portugal since 1974 – when private economic groups were broken up after the political revolution.

This chapter reviews the main groups of balance sheet accounts, and their valuation in accordance with Portuguese regulations and with regard to generally accepted accounting practice in Portugal, outlined in Chapter 5. Chapter 8 gives more detailed information on the individual classification of each item.

Information on valuation practices is typically included in the notes to the financial statements, for which a standardized numbering system exists. References to note numbers below are to those standardized numbers.

1 ASSETS
1.1 General valuation rules

The general principle of asset valuation applied by Portuguese companies is historical cost, adjusted to take into account value adjustments arising from the application of the principle of prudence.

Depreciation and decreases (considered as permanent) in the market value of assets are shown separately under the appropriate headings in the balance sheet, except for capitalized interest on loans used to finance tangible fixed asset acquisitions and some deferrals. The general rule may be set aside in the case of investments in group and associated companies, where the equity method is optional. Table 6.1 summarizes the general formula for calculating the book value of assets.

An asset is first valued at acquisition cost, or at production cost if it has been manufactured by the company. The value adjustments which give rise to a decrease in the original value may be due to wear and tear (in which case they are recorded as depreciation) or due to a decrease in the market value of the asset. If the decrease in market value is reversible or recoverable, a provision account is created. If, however, the decrease is permanent, the charge to income gives rise to a direct reduction in the asset account.

Companies may restate the carrying value of asset items when authorized by law, in which case there will be a legal restatement; in general, this will involve only tangible fixed assets.

Table 6.1 General rules of asset valuation

= Original cost	Acquisition cost
	Production cost
− Value adjustments:	
For wear and tear (depreciation)	Accumulated depreciated account
For decrease in the market value (reversible or permanent)	Asset provision account or reduction of asset account
+ Legal restatements	Occasionally permissible for fixed asset items

1.2 Intangible fixed assets

The individual balance sheet shows the following types of intangible assets, among others:

1   Formation expenses.
2   Research and development expenses.
3   Goodwill.

Formation expenses (*despesas de instalação*) are shown in the balance sheet as the first item under fixed assets and comprise legal or tax expenses incurred as a result of incorporation or an increase in capital, and expenses incurred in the pre-operating phase (for example, technical studies and projects, etc.) or for a subsequent increase in production capacity.

Formation expenses and research and development expenses may be capitalized but must normally be written off over a maximum of five years. Departures from this rule must be disclosed in the notes on the accounts. For tax purposes to be a deductible

Example 6.1 **Formation expenses (note 8)**

SOPORCEL – Sociededa Portuguesa de Celulose SA
Annual report, 1990 (author's translation)

	1990			1989		
Item	*Increases*	*Disposals*	*Depreciation*	*Increases*	*Disposals*	*Depreciation*
Account 431 – Formation expenses:						
Incorporation of the company		1568362			–	
Capital stock increases	59225		19740		–	7574
Studies and investment projects	26413	23930	201260	554930	–	184958
Total	85638	1592292	221000	554930	–	192532

Example 6.2 **Depreciation of goodwill (note 9)**

FETAL – Moda Internacional SA
Annual report, 1990 (author's translation)

Goodwill was not amortized because the board of directors of the company believes that the gross amounts included in the balance sheet are below the market value, owing to the location of the shops and their areas.

expense, the write-off period varies between three and six years from the date of inclusion in the balance sheet. An example is given in Example 6.1, which shows the relevant note in the annual report of a Portuguese company. However, very few Portuguese companies capitalize research and development expenses (*despesas de investigação e de desenvolvimento*).

In line with the Second EC Directive on companies, it is a legal requirement that, to ensure an appropriate asset amortization and write-down policy, no dividends can be distributed until the total of capitalized formation and research and development expenses have been fully amortized or until unrestricted reserves have been set up to an amount equal to the said total.

Example 6.3 **Details of the balance sheet values of intangible fixed assets (note 10)**

FISIPE – Fibras Sintécticas de Portugal SA
Annual report, 1990

10 Changes in fixed assets

Items	Opening balance	Revaluation	Increases	Sales	Transfers and reductions	Closing balance
Intangible fixed assets						
Research expenses	42 195 538$10		48 216 284$00		(6 753 868$10)	83 657 954$00
Industrial property and other rights	38 105 518$00		52 867 783$00			90 973 301$00
Fixed assets in progress	241 166 634$00		164 970 010$70		(20 800 106$00)	200 336 538$70
	321 467 690$10		266 054 077$70		(212 553 974$10)	374 967 793$70

Amortizations and provisions

Items	Opening balance	Increase	Adjustments	Closing balance
Intangible fixed assets				
Research expenses	31 580 490$00	15 796 402$00	(6 753 868$10)	40 623 023$90
Industrial property and other rights	12 681 773$00	10 600 356$00		23 282 129$00
	44 262 263$00	26 396 758$00	(6 753 868$10)	63 905 152$90

Goodwill (*trespasse*) should be amortized over a maximum of five years, but this period may be extended so long as it does not exceed the asset's useful life. In that case the notes to the accounts must justify the fact. An illustration is shown in Example 6.2. Although the POC requires amortization of goodwill, it is not a tax-deductible expense. Hence only a few companies do it, but the auditors' report commonly omits mention of the fact.

As for formation expenses and R&D expenses, supplementary schedules are required showing gross values and accumulated written-off goodwill (see Example 6.3).

1.3 Tangible fixed assets

Fixed assets are valued at the cost of acquisition or production. Such cost is to be determined using the same principles as those for inventories, explained below (section 2.5). Example 6.4 shows an actual instance. Supplementary information is disclosed in the notes as a breakdown by activities and categories of assets (Example 6.5).

Example 6.4 **Valuation principles for tangible fixed assets (note 5)**

SOPORCEL – Sociedade Portuguesa de Celulose SA
Annual report, 1990 (extract, author's translation)

3.2 Tangible fixed assets

Tangible fixed assets are valued at acquisition cost. This cost includes the amount invoiced by the supplier and additional purchase and assembling expenses. Financial costs incurred between the date of acquisition and the date of entry into use as well as exchange rate differences related to borrowing obtained for their acquisition which correspond to the period to 31 December 1985 are also included in the acquisition cost of tangible fixed assets.

Tangible fixed assets have been revalued, according to the laws mentioned under note 12 to the accounts. Until the year 1986, depreciation has been calculated from the year of entry into use according to the straight-line method and using minimum percentage rates for legal–fiscal purposes. Since 1987, inclusive, the company has decided to use percentages that match the estimated life of the assets, which correspond to percentages between the maximum and the minimum rates allowed for fiscal purposes (deductible costs) and the straight-line method continued to be used. This corresponds to the following average rates of annual depreciation for each of the years since 1987:

Item	Useful life (years)
Buildings and other constructions	50
Equipment	17
Vehicles	7
Tools	5
Furniture	8
Other tangible assets	10

All the assets which have been in use before 31 December 1988 were amortized according to the rates published in the annex to *Portaria* 737/81, 29 August, including corrections of *Portarias* 990/84, 29 December, and 85/88, 9 February. Other assets (those which came into use during 1989 or after) have been amortized according to the rates included in the annexes to Decree law 2/90, 12 January.

Expenses related to maintenance are included in the income statement for the year in which they were incurred.

The acquisition cost includes expenses incurred in making the asset operational; thereafter, costs may no longer be capitalized. Usually these capitalizable costs do not include indirect purchase taxes (for example, VAT), in so far as they are recoverable through sales and services rendered to customers. (Among the exceptions are cars, pleasure boats and aircraft.)

However, they may include financial costs associated with the financing of fixed assets, in so far as these are incurred during the period when the fixed asset was in the course of purchase or production. In the case where parts of an asset in the course of construction come into service at different dates, financial costs should cease to be imputed to each part as soon as it comes into service.

In the case of exchange differences on financing for fixed assets, it is permissible to impute the exchange differences to the cost of the fixed assets only during the period in which the fixed assets are acquired or in the course of construction.

The notes provide some information on the expenses capitalized during the financial year (see Example 6.6) as well as on the total capitalized costs at the balance sheet date.

Fixed assets having a limited useful life must be written off systematically over that life. In the case of tangible (or intangible) fixed assets, whether or not they have a limited useful life, if at the balance sheet date their value is less than the corresponding book value, and the reduction in value is expected to be permanent, an amount equal to the loss of value should be written off.

If the fixed asset has been manufactured by the company, it is valued on the basis of certain costs which must be capitalized and others which are optional. The compulsory ones are:

1 Raw materials.
2 Directly allowable personnel costs.
3 A reasonable proportion of the indirect costs incurred during the manufacturing period

and the optional ones:

1 Interest on loans used to finance the construction of own assets during the in-progress period.
2 Exchange differences on such loans during the in-progress period.

Although the fundamental accounting principles described in section 4 of the POC envisage the use of cost in terms of 'constant escudos', nothing further is said about this in the rules on fixed assets. However, tax law permits the revaluation of tangible fixed assets, using coefficients based on the consumer price index, so it may be supposed that the reference to the use of constant escudos is intended to bring this within the ambit of accounting principles.

Portugal has often suffered high inflation during the present century, especially in the 1970s and 1980s. This situation has been approached for accounting purposes by way of the tax laws, which sometimes authorized revaluation, but only of tangible fixed assets that had not been totally depreciated. In such cases, equity has been affected by the creation of a revaluation reserve which reflects the increase in the net book value of the

Example 6.5 Details of the balance sheet values of tangible fixed assets (notes 10 and 14)

FISIPE – Fibras Sintécticas de Portugal SA
Annual report, 1990

10 Changes in fixed assets

Items	Opening balance	Revaluation	Increases	Sales	Transfers and reductions	Closing balance
Tangible fixed assets						
Buildings and other constructions	2 425 312 647$70		38 249 401$00		(1 796 135$00)	2 461 765 940$70
Basic equipment	7 563 787 360$20	623 508 105$00	695 613 184$00		(75 185 931$00)	8 807 722 718$20
Transport equipment	87 428 595$00	13 741 885$00		5 422 572$00		95 747 908$00
Tools and utensils	96 400 972$80	28 288 096$00	24 565 344$00	434 745$00	(2 949 527$00)	145 870 140$80
Administrative equipment	162 851 677$00		621 301$00		(2 711 437$00)	160 761 541$00
Containers	18 272 283$10				(982 222$00)	17 290 061$10
Other tangible assets	2 794 503$00					2 794 503$00
Fixed assets in progress	1 642 095 498$00		365 451 131$00		(759 049 230$00)	1 248 497 399$00
Advances to fixed assets account	169 179 334$40		114 935 436$60		(265 471 623$50)	18 643 147$50
	12 168 122 898$20	665 538 086$00	1 239 435 797$60	5 857 317$00	(1 108 146 105$50)	12 959 093 359$30

Amortizations and provisions

Items	Opening balance	Increase	Adjustments	Closing balance
Tangible fixed assets				
Buildings and other constructions	812 735 785$00	100 354 515$00	(733 656$00)	912 356 644$00
Basic equipment	6 525 829 712$00	424 052 337$00	350 848 480$00	7 300 730 529$00
Transport equipment	58 238 294$00	7 674 679$00	3 786 505$00	69 699 478$00
Tools and utensils	55 514 404$00	34 564 555$00	14 258 333$00	104 337 292$00
Administrative equipment	127 096 120$00	5 550 476$00	(2 466 553$00)	130 180 043$00
Containers	18 139 763$00	66 260$00	(982 222$00)	17 223 801$00
Other tangible assets	2 293 193$00	87 095$00		2 380 288$00
	7 599 847 271$00	572 349 917$00	364 710 887$00	8 536 908 075$00

14 Tangible fixed assets involved in company activity and installed on property not belonging to the company

Buildings and other constructions	2 461 765 940$70
Basic equipment	8 807 722 718$20
Tools and utensils	145 870 140$80
Administrative equipment	160 761 541$00
Containers	17 290 061$10
Other tangible assets	2 794 503$00
Work in progress	1 248 497 399$00

Example 6.6 **Capitalized expenses (notes 11 and 14)**

FISIPE – Fibras Sintécticas de Portugal SA
Annual report, 1990

11 In the course of the year, financial costs relating to loans obtained for the financing of the company's investment in revamping, and which amounted to 66,317,569$60, were added to the assets.

---

revalued assets. Authorization to revalue has been given by the following decree laws:

Regulation No. 20258, 28 December 1963
Decree law No. 126/77, 2 April 1977
    353-B/77, 29 August 1977
    280/78, 8 September 1978
    430/78, 27 December 1978
    202/79, 2 July 1979
    24/82, 30 January 1982
    219/82, 30 June 1982
    195/83, 18 May 1983
    143/84, 9 May 1984
    399-G/84, 28 December 1984
    278/85, 19 July 1985
    118-B/86, 27 May 1986
    111/88, 2 April 1988
    49/91, 25 January 1991

Example 6.7 shows the disclosure of information about revaluation in the notes on the accounts.

1.4 Investments

This item includes participations in group companies, associated companies and others, as well as bonds and other securities held for more than a year. It also includes land and property (real estate) held as a financial investment. It is important to note that this item does not include own shares (which are recorded as a deduction on the liabilities side of the balance sheet, in the equity). Example 6.8 illustrates the information that has to be disclosed, in the notes to the accounts, about the participations (note 16).

Investments are generally valued at acquisition cost, adjusted according to the prudence principle. If at the balance sheet date the market value of such an asset is less than its book value, the latter may be correspondingly reduced, using the appropriate account. This provision should be reversed as soon as the loss of value ceases to be confirmed. See Example 6.9. The equity method is also a valid option for the valuation of shares in group and associated companies, according to the most recent version of the POC, dated July 1991.

An increase in the nominal capital of the investee company through the incorporation

Example 6.7 **Revaluation of tangible fixed assets (notes 12, 13 and 39)**

Teixeira Duarte Engenharia e Construções SA
Annual report, 1990

12 *Tangible fixed assets revaluation – Legal texts*:

The tangible fixed assets were revalued under the following decree laws:
– No. 49/91, of 25th January
– No. 111/88, of 2nd April
– No. 118-B/86, of 27th May
– No. 399-G/84, of 28th December
– No. 219/82, of 2nd June
– No. 430/78, of 27th December

13 *Table of revaluations*:

Item	Historical costs	Revaluations	Revalued amounts
Tangible fixed assets:			
Build. and other constructions	26.229	4.787	31.016
Basic equipment	649.518	121.462	770.980
Transp. equipment	130.716	24.523	155.239
Tools and fixtures	39.559	4.747	44.306
Office equipment	87.342	16.603	103.945
	933.364	172.122	1.105.486

39 *Changes in revaluation reserves*:

Item	Initial balance	Revaluations	Transfer	Final balance
Tangible fixed assets:				
– Decree Law No. 49/91		172.122		172.122
Financial investments:				
Adjusted res. of fin. invest.		1.089.550		1.089.550

of reserves is sometimes recorded in the assets of the investor company, up to the nominal value of the percentage of capital held.

Information about pension funds also must be disclosed, under note 18 to the accounts.

1.5 **Inventories (stocks)**

According to chapter 5 of the POC, the valuation basis for inventories is the cost of acquisition or production, unless it exceeds the market price, in which case the latter is to be used (the principle of the lower of cost and market value). The notes on the accounts must disclose the valuation basis used (see Example 6.10). In the case of assets that are not valued individually the comparison is by category of inventory against market price.

The cost of acquisition includes the purchase price and any expenditure incurred directly or indirectly in getting the item to its present state and location.

The cost of production includes the cost of raw materials, direct labour, variable

Example 6.8 **Statement of group companies, associated companies and other undertakings (note 16)**

VIDAGO, MELGAÇO E PEDRAS SALGADAS SA
Financial statements, 1990 (author's translation)

Company	% held	Share capital	Equity	Most recent year's result	Book value (000 escudos)
Companhia Portugesa de Águas Salus (Vidago) SA *Address* Vidago	99.75	200000000$00	308560420$94	(83288391$80)	199507
Insulana – Água de Mesa SA *Address* Auto-estrada Lisboa– Sintra, Km 2 Alfragide – 2700 Amadora	98.80	750000$00	1488686$00	(14457$00)	494
Meyrelles & Co. SA *Address* Rua das Laranjeiras 31 Ponta Delgado	60.00	7200000$00	3778782$00	(2032337$00)	7646
Sovipe – Soc. Desenv. Turístico de Vidago e Pedras Salgados SA *Address* Pedras Salgadas	75.00	1600000000$00	1602206933$00	1593764$00	900000
Empresa dos Casinos do Monte Estoril Lda *Address* Auto-estrada Lisboa– Sintra, Km 2 Alfragide – 2700 Amadora	65.30	235000$00	10271463$00	(7200$00)	7998
Sociedade Imobiliaria Ribamar Estoril Lda *Address* Auto-estrada Lisboa– Sintra, Km 2 Alfragide – 2700 Amadora	69.07	750000$00	1183543$00	(800$00)	518
Sociedade Propriet. do Hotel Universal Lda *Address* Pedras Salgadas	66.45	30000000$00	19443442$06	(5321144$60)	21370
Águas do Caramulo – Sociedade de Captação e Exploração de Águas Minerais Lda *Address* Varzielas – Oliveira de Frades	40.00	400000000$00	475896688$00	4372507$00	160000
Campos & Lameiro Lda *Address* Rua das Ameixoeiras, Francelos – 4405 Valadares	40.00	37000000$00	2021665$00	(15361007$00)	100000

Note: Equity and most recent year's result figures refer to 31 December 1989. Book value refers to 31 December 1990.

Example 6.9 **Valuation rules for investments (note 3)**

FISIPE – Fibras Sintécticas de Portugal SA
Annual report, 1990

FIXED ASSETS

Financial assets

These are valued at their purchase cost. During the year, the provision was adjusted to reflect the market value, based on the Lisbon Stock Exchange prices at 31 December 1990.

Example 6.10 **Inventory valuation rules (note 3)**

CELULOSE BEIRA INDUSTRIAL (CELBI) SA
Annual report, 1990

(e) *Stocks*

Are valued in accordance with the following criteria:

Raw materials (wood at mill) are valued at the average purchase price for the year, to mill site.

Other raw materials and consumables are valued at the average acquisition cost to mill site.

Products and work in progress:

– Timber in store is valued at an average purchase price, plus operating costs of storage.

– Felling in progress (own timber) is valued at the historical cost of thinning of own plantations plus felling costs or felling and forwarding costs according to the stage of processing.

– Felling in progress (standing timber) is valued at the average purchase price of standing timber plus felling costs or felling cost and forwarding costs according to the stage of processing.

– Plantations are stated at accumulated historical costs less costs of felled timber. This criterion includes, start-up expenses and all direct and indirect costs of forestry maintenance. Excludes the cost of land.

Finished products and work in progress are valued at average production cost, which includes raw materials, consumables, labour, maintenance costs and manufacturing overheads. The depreciation incorporated results from the maximum rates allowed for tax purposes on the nominal amounts of fixed assets. Fixed overheads are absorbed into stock on the basis of normal production capacity.

Merchandise is valued at the average cost of acquisition.

manufacturing costs plus fixed manufacturing costs necessarily incurred in producing the item and arriving at its present state and location. Fixed manufacturing costs may be imputed to cost of production, taking account of the normal capacity of the means of production. The costs of distribution or of general administration, and financial costs, are not to be incorporated in the cost of production.

Obsolescence, physical deterioration, a fall in price or analogous factors are to be dealt with according to the principle of the lower of cost and market value.

By-products, scrap, etc., are valued, in the absence of better criteria, at their net realizable value.

Example 6.11 **Difference between book value and market value (note 19)**

EPAL – Empresa Pública das Aguas Livres EP
Annual report, 1990 (author's translation)

The valuation rules adopted for inventories (average cost) and the nature of those items (chemical products for the treatment of water and pipelines for the distribution network) gave rise to differences between the accounting values and the market values at a given date, but the differences are not material.

Market price is to be understood as replacement cost for goods acquired for production, and as net realizable value for goods acquired for sale.

The following cost-flow conventions are permissible: specific cost, weighted average, FIFO, LIFO, standard cost. Standard cost may be used if it is checked and adjusted as necessary in accordance with accepted accounting principles. Adjustments should be made to take account of confirmed variances. Almost all the Portuguese companies use weighted average cost or standard cost.

In the case of agricultural, livestock and forestry operations, if the determination of production cost would be too burdensome, the following criterion may be used in valuing inventory: net realizable value less the normal profit margin. The same criterion may also be used in the extractive and fishing industries.

Merchandise inventories in retail sales establishments, where the variety of such items is great, may also be valued at net selling price less the profit margin included in such prices. Cash-and-carry outlets which sell predominantly small quantities of each type of merchandise to small retailers may also be considered as retail sales establishments for the present purpose.

In the case of work in progress under long-term contracts (for example, bridges, roads, etc.) either the percentage of completion method or the completed contract method may be used.

Raw materials and consumables may be accounted for using the base stock method at a fixed quantity and value, provided the following conditions are satisfied:

1 They turn over frequently.
2 They represent an overall value of relatively little importance to the business.
3 There are no significant variations in quantity, value or composition.

Example 6.12 **Inventories outside the company (note 22)**

FISIPE – Fibras Sintéctica de Portugal SA
Annual report, 1990

22 *Stocks held outside the company*

Materials in transit	3 962 804$60
Products being processed	63 093 255$50

In practice the application of these requirements is by no means as straightforward as it would appear.

It is a requirement that the notes to the accounts should disclose the total difference, by category of asset, between book value and market value, if it is material (note 19), and, in the case of items stated at a book value below the lower of cost and market value, the reasons for it (note 20). The former is illustrated in Example 6.11.

Disclosure is required of the global value of inventories located outside the company (note 22; Example 6.12).

1.6 Amounts due from third parties

Accounts receivable arising from operating transactions must be valued at their face value – that is, at the amount that the debtor has undertaken to pay by the due date, in accordance with the related invoice or bill of exchange.

With long-term receivables the asset is valued in the same way, but any interest included in the face value must also be recorded in a Deferred Receivable liability account, the amount of which is progressively taken to income.

In the case of amounts in foreign currencies, unrealized exchange gains or losses are generally to be dealt with in the same way as those on liquid assets. However, there are exceptions. In the case of medium and long-term loans, unrealized exchange gains should be deferred if there is a reasonable possibility that the gain may be reversed.

Value adjustments are possible in order to respect the prudence principle, e.g. in the case of doubtful debtors.

The VAT balance may appear as VAT recoverable on the assets side of the balance sheet, e.g. in the case of exporting companies.

As a minimum the notes to the accounts must disclose the following information about debtors:

1 The global value of doubtful debts for each category of assets (note 23).
2 Details of advances or loans to members of the board of administration, the board of directors or audit board of the company, including interest rates, rates, collateral, amount paid back, principal outstanding.
3 Global value of loans to employees (note 25).
4 Global value of debtors with bills of exchange not shown in the balance sheet (discounted) (note 26).

Example 6.13 illustrates information on these items to be disclosed in the notes on the accounts.

1.7 Liquid assets

Liquid assets in foreign currencies should be accounted for at closing rates, and unrealized exchange rate gains and losses are taken to the profit and loss account and reported under 'financial expenses and income'. The exchange rates used in the currency conversion must be disclosed in the notes to the accounts (see Example 6.14). Negotiable

Example 6.13 **Debts from third parties (notes 23, 25 and 26)**

SOCIEDADE FIGUEIRA PRAIA SA
Annual report, 1990 (author's translation)

Note 23 – Doubtful debts

Doubtful debts amount to a total of PTE 210235000; provision has been made according to the rules described under Note 3(e).

Note 25 – Debts from and to employees

Debts from employees amount to PTE 4330000 and credits from employees amount to PTE 43003000, including PTE 42200000 relating to holiday subsidies and salaries of the holiday month to be paid during 1991.

Note 26 – Secured debts not shown in the balance sheet

Customers with bills receivable (discounted) amount to PTE 88803000.

Example 6.14 **Exchange rates used for the translation of credits and debits in foreign currency (note 4)**

FISIPE – Fibras Sintécticas de Portugal, SA
Annual report, 1990

4 Exchange rates used for the conversion of credits and debits in foreign currency at 31 December 1990

	Credits	Debits
USD	133.333	133.867
DEM	89.321	89.679
FRF	26.188	26.292
ESP	1.395	1.4006
ITL	0.11819	0.11867
GBP	257.584	258.616
BEF	4.3213	4.3387
CHF	104.790	105.210
JPY	0.98702	0.99098
SEK	23.703	23.798
GRD	0.85329	0.85671

securities are treated according to the criteria set out for inventories, as far as they are applicable.

Generally securities include shares (usually listed shares) but not quotas held in other companies' capital, the latter are always recorded as investments (fixed financial assets).

Value adjustments are possible in deference to the prudence principle, e.g. creating provisions for negotiable securities (shares) when the market price at the balance sheet date is lower than the book value.

Losses and gains from the transfer of negotiable securities are reported as 'financial expenses and income' in the profit and loss account.

Companies are required to disclose, in the notes to the accounts (under note 17),

Example 6.15 **Negotiable securities (note 17)**

LISNAVE – Estaleiros Navais de Lisboa SA
Annual report, 1990 (author's translation)

The item 'Negotiable securities' includes temporary short-term investments in Treasury bills, amounting to a total of PTE 859 630 000.

---

information about shares recorded as negotiable securities whenever their book value in the holding company corresponds to more than 5 per cent of the gross *working* capital of that company. This requirement includes the name of the investee company, the number of shares held, their nominal value and their book value. It is fairly uncommon to find companies fulfilling the above-mentioned 5 per cent condition.

Example 6.15 illustrates such a disclosure practice.

1.8 Accruals and deferrals

The new POC uses the deferred accounts to record revenues and expenses which arise in one accounting period but which will be allocated to the profit and loss account in a future period. They are specific kinds of assets and liabilities (pre-payments, deferrals and accruals) and are not the same as ordinary creditors or debtors. On the assets side, the deferred item is subdivided into pre-paid expenses and deferred charges. The POC requires deferred charges to appear after liquid assets, at the foot of the balance sheet.

Examples already referred to in this chapter include, among others:

1 Interest to be received on long-term receivables.
2 Discounts arising on bond issues.
3 Redemption premiums on bond issues.

In these examples, the difference between the two amounts is considered as a financial expense to be allocated to the accounting years to which the transaction relates and is recorded as 'deferred charges' (*custos diferidos*) on the assets side of the balance sheet and must be disclosed in the notes (see Example 6.16).

Example 6.16 **Accruals and deferrals (note 33)**

SOPORCEL – Sociedade Portuguesa de Celulose SA
Annual report, 1990 (author's translation)

In the balance sheet, on 31 December 1990 and 31 December 1989, deferred charges accounts current balances include PTE 416 202 000 and PTE 15 461 000, respectively; they are unrealized exchange losses which occurred on medium and long-term debts denominated in foreign currency obtained to finance the investment in paper mill equipment in progress.

1.9 Leased assets

Under the 1976 version of the POC the lessor (which must be a *sociedade de locação financeira*, see Chapter 3, section 3.2.1) does not treat the leasing as a sale, whatever the terms of the contract, and the assets remain in its balance sheet as a tangible fixed asset. It is worth mentioning that the lessor's accounting does not follow the POC, but conforms to a special accounting plan approved by the Bank of Portugal, to which companies of this type periodically have to submit their accounts for scrutiny. This can justify the lessee in viewing the leasing arrangement as a rental agreement and the lease rentals as expenses of the period to which they refer, as an operating cost, and not subdividing them into repayment of principal and interest.

The new 1989 version of the POC refers to the capitalization of finance leases in the detailed comments on class 4 of the Chart of Accounts. It is envisaged that finance leases will be capitalized, using the approach of FAS 13/IAS 17, but implementation is hanging fire pending the revision of the accounting plan applicable to financial institutions.

However, the POC requires that the notes on the accounts should disclose, for each category of leased assets, information such as that revealed in Example 6.17.

Example 6.17 Leased assets (note 15)

CENTRAL DE CERVEJAS SA
Annual report, 1990 (author's translation)

Assets used under leasing contracts:

Telephone switchboard	955 090$	
Photocopying equipment	4 257 413$	5 212 503$

2 LIABILITIES
General valuation rules

Liabilities are classified in two groups, short-term and long-term, that is, debts to be repaid within one year and debts to be repaid over a longer period, respectively. Short-term liabilities are normally trade credits (for raw materials, purchases, employees' salaries, etc.). Long-term liabilities are very often bank loans, shareholders' loans (termed *suprimentos*) and bond loans; any portion of those liabilities falling due for repayment within one year is transferred to the short-term section of the balance sheet.

Short-term and long-term debts are valued on the basis of repayment value, and redemption premiums on debt securities are part of the value of related debt.

The basis for the valuation of a liability is the amount which will ultimately be repayable. The costs associated with issuing debt are normally expensed in the year the debt is issued, but it is also possible to amortize them over the life of the debt. If this is the option chosen, the amount is accounted for as a deferral expense on the asset side of the balance sheet, but the expense may not be deferred beyond the life of the debt to

Table 6.2 General valuation rules for liabilities

Trade debts	Repayable value
Non-trade debts	Repayable value
Foreign currency debts	Closing rate value
Provisions for liabilities and charges	Estimated value

which it relates. Table 6.2 summarizes the general valuation rules for liabilities.

The POC does not mention the case of debts in kind, but practice suggests that they should be valued at the market value and disclosed in the notes.

2.2 Trade liabilities

They are usually current and short-term debts, arising from purchases of raw materials and operating services, amounts due to employees, tax and social security, etc.

Debts in foreign currency are valued at the closing exchange rate, with exchange differences being recognized as financial costs and income even before they are effectively realized (see Example 6.18).

Example 6.18 **Debts in foreign currency (note 25)**

LISNAVE – Estaleiros Navais de Lisboa SA
Annual report, 1990 (author's translation)

Note 25
Debts from and to present and retired employees at the end of the financial year (PTE 000):

Debts to employees	61 459
Debts from employees	68 998

2.3 Non-trade liabilities

When a company arranges a line of credit with its bank, and draws against it as and when required, only the amount effectively drawn down is disclosed on the liabilities side of the balance sheet, the unused amount remaining undisclosed.

Borrowing has to be reported at the amount at which it is to be repaid, regardless of the amount received at the time the debt was contracted.

When the amount of foreign currency long-term loans payable exceeds that of corresponding loans receivable, the net unrealized difference on exchange may be treated as a deferred charge.

In the case of amounts in foreign currencies, unrealized exchange gains or losses are generally dealt with in the same way as those on liquid assets. However, there are exceptions. In the case of medium and long-term loans, unrealized exchange gains should be deferred if there is a reasonable likelihood that the gain may be reversed. (See also section 4 below.)

Example 6.19 **Supplementary disclosure of long-term debt (note 29)**

LISNAVE – Estaleiros Navais de Lisboa SA
Annual report, 1990 (author's translation)

Note 29
Debts to be paid after more than five years are as follows (PTE 000):

Loans to financial institutions	23 273 598
Other loans	262 800
State debts	2 362 577

Example 6.20 **Supplementary disclosure of guarantees (note 30)**

IMOVALOR – SGII SA
Annual report, 1990 (author's translation)

30 Debts to third parties covered by real estate guarantees rendered by the company:

– Financing of CGD, with real estate mortgage PTE 196 031 000
– Financing of CGD, with real estate mortgage PTE 5 million
– Financing of CPP, with real estate mortgage PTE 72 million

The disclosure of the value of non-trade debt is supplemented in the notes to the financial statements with other details such as:

1 The currency in which the debts are contracted, indicating which exchange rates have been used to calculate the conversion and also whether exchange differences have been provided for (note 4).
2 Maturity date, giving a breakdown by its nature of long-term debt in the case of maturities of more than five years, showing separately debts to group companies, to associated companies and to other companies (note 29).
3 Effective guarantees of debts (note 30).

As an illustration of supplementary disclosure of non-trade liabilities, Examples 6.14 and 6.19–20 show the information provided by Portuguese companies.

2.4 Special financial liabilities

Financial instruments have been created which obscure the distinction between equity and liabilities. Also an increasing number of commitments entered into by a company will not appear among the liabilities in the balance sheet, but may be disclosed in the notes to the accounts. Hence the need to disclose them on the liabilities side of the balance sheet and the valuation rules for them raise some questions concerning their hybrid nature, e.g.:

Example 6.21 **Special financial liabilities: convertible securities (note 27)**

TERTIR – Terminais de Portugal SA
Annual report, 1990

27 The loan in convertible debentures to PTE 1 498 750 000, represented by 272 500 debentures with a nominal value of PTE 5 500 each, earns the debenture holders the right to convert to shares on the basis of one for one (initial basis of conversion), where each convertible debenture may be converted into one share with a nominal value of PTE 1 000.

1 Debt which can be redeemed in shares.
2 Perpetual loans.
3 Convertible bonds.
4 Warrants.
5 Bonds with warrants.
6 Zero coupon bonds.
7 *Títulos de participação* (participating certificates).

In the case of convertible bonds and *títulos de participação* the main features of each issue – interest rate, maturity, guarantees, redemption or conversion conditions, etc. (see Example 6.21) – should be disclosed.

Títulos de participação are a kind of undated loan which appeared in 1985 and are similar to the French *titres de participation*. Only state-owned companies and very large undertakings may issue them, depending upon legal authorization, on a case-by-case basis.

The issuing company will show them in the balance sheet as liabilities, although they are non-refundable loans except at the option of the issuer and only after ten years from their issue. In some cases they are exchanged against nominal capital; in others, they give the owner prior rights in the nominal capital increases of the issuing company.

Usually they are listed on the stock exchange. A company holding investments in *títulos de participação* will show them either as fixed financial assets or as negotiable securities, according to the length of time they are expected to be held. They earn interest which consists of a fixed element and a variable element indexed to net turnover, cash flow, gross profit, etc. (see Chapter 3).

2.5 Provisions for liabilities and charges

Provisions for liabilities and charges include items such as pension arrangements, litigation, duty rights. They are considered as liabilities in the balance sheet (where debt is divided into three groups: short-term debt, medium to long-term debt, and provisions for liabilities and charges). In the income statement the charges in respect of this group of provisions are included with the provisions for asset depreciation.

According to the current version of the POC, events against which provision is to be made should involve an element of risk (that is, uncertainty having a probability of occurrence less than unity).

Under the old POC the concept of provision was broader than in the new, 1989 one. It included some debts which were certain to have to be repaid in the future and the only thing that was uncertain was the actual amount that would fall due on the date of the report. Such debts were accounted for by estimated amounts, which would not necessarily correspond to the amount eventually paid. Income tax is an example: it was accounted as a provision under the old POC (based on the fact that the exact amount of the tax to be paid – part of it in the year following the one to which the accounts relate – does not always coincide with the amount calculated (estimated) and presented in the annual report). According to the new POC, income tax not pre-paid is included under the short-term debt group in the balance sheet.

2.6 Accruals and deferrals

On the liabilities side, the deferred item is subdivided into revenues received in advance and accrued expenses of the current year that will be paid in the future. The POC requires accrued expenses to appear at the bottom of the liabilities side of the balance sheet. Among other things, this item includes:

1   Interest to be paid.
2   Insurance premiums received in advance.

2.7 Financial commitments not shown in the balance sheet

In Portugal as elsewhere the importance of financial commitments not shown in the balance sheet is tending to increase. This kind of information is given in the notes on the accounts and may differ a good deal from company to company. Example 6.22 shows a case involving guarantees.

Example 6.22 Disclosure of off-balance sheet guarantees (notes 31–2)

TEIXEIRA DUARTE, Engenharia e Construções SA
Annual report, 1990

31 *Financial commitments not included in the balance sheet*: Discounted clients' bills: Esc. 157.558.556$50

32 *Responsibilities for guarantees given*: Guarantees to clients: Esc. 8.467.611.000$00

---

3 SHAREHOLDERS' EQUITY

The Accounting Plan places great emphasis on shareholders' equity, the difference between a company's assets and its liabilities. Thus shareholders' equity comprises the following items, which together form the last separately totalled group of accounts in a Portuguese balance sheet:

1   Nominal capital.

2   Own shares or quotas.
3   Share or quota premiums.
4   Revenue reserves.
5   Revaluation reserves.
6   Retained earnings or accumulated deficit.
7   Result of the year (profit or loss).
8   Interim dividends.

3.1 Nominal capital

Nominal capital is the face value of the shares or quotas. This amount may be altered if a qualified majority of the shareholders or quotaholders approve the change. An extraordinary general meeting is sometimes called. The nominal value of the capital must be totally subscribed, but the value may be paid in several instalments (see Chapter 2 for details). Capital may not be issued at a discount from the nominal value, but among existing companies the issue at a premium is common, especially where new members are becoming quotaholders or shareholders. There is no requirement for shares or quotas to have exactly the same voting rights or entitlement to dividends, but usually the shares of a company are alike as far as the related rights of their owners are concerned.

Example 6.23 **Nominal capital value (notes 35–7)**

TERTIR – Terminais de Portugal SA
Annual report, 1990

35 The share capital is fully paid up. There was an increase in share capital of PTE 350 000 000$00 through the issue of 350 000 shares each with a nominal value of PTE 1 000$00 at an issue price of PTE 1 700$00.

36 Share capital is represented by 3 850 000 shares of PTE 1 000$00 each, being:
Nominative   1 041 784
Bearer   2 808 216.

37 Shareholding by any member greater than 20%:
TERNOR   27,37%
Rodoviária Nacional   25,11%.

Example 6.23 is an instance of disclosure in the notes on the accounts relating to the nominal capital that includes the minimal obligatory information. From Example 6.23 it can be concluded that the differences in rights do not appear in the financial statements. However, according to the POC, companies are required to disclose in the notes on the accounts the number of shares of each category into which the capital stock is divided, the nominal value, subscribed capital during the year, unpaid capital, the nature of capital stock increases during the year, etc.

3.2 Own shares or quotas

According to the POC, the value of own shares or quotas acquired should be shown under a suitable heading of its own in the equity (and not on the assets side of the balance sheet, as was normal before the recent accounting reforms and according to the 1977 version of the POC).

The acquisition of own shares is closely circumscribed and is considered a reimbursement of capital to the shareholders, not as the company investing in itself. In line with the rules of the Second EC Directive relating to the capital of companies whose capital is divided into shares, Portuguese legislation limits the ownership by a company of its own shares, stipulating that:

1   No company can hold more than 10 per cent of its own capital stock.
2   Own shares may be acquired from third parties but may not be subscribed direct nor subscribed by a nominee.
3   Before its own shares can be acquired the company must have available reserves equal to at least double the amount to be paid for the shares.
4   A company which holds its own shares must maintain as 'restricted' reserves an amount at least equal to the amount it paid for them throughout the period it holds the shares.

3.3 Premiums

Issue premiums arise as a result of issuing new shares at a price (or prices) higher than their nominal value. There are no regulations governing or limiting the price at which the shares may be sold, apart from the nominal value being the minimum. In some cases company law gives the existing shareholders a prior right to subscribe for new shares, and that right can be sold on the market in the case of public companies.

Although the nominal capital can be paid in several instalments, the issue premiums must be paid in total during the subscription period.

The issue premiums can be incorporated into the nominal capital when future increases occur, e.g. by means of bonus issues.

The share issue costs may be accounted for either as costs of the period when the shares were issued (not very common, unless they are not material expenses) or capitalized as formation costs and written off within a five-year period. Usually depreciation is over three or six years, this span representing the lower and upper useful lives for these costs to be accepted as tax-deductible. The POC suggests five years as the normal useful life.

3.4 Revenue reserves

Usually in Portuguese the term *reservas* is used to mean profits retained against future difficulties, i.e. to offset losses that may arise. But there are reserves which originate for other reasons, namely the revaluation reserve and certain donations received by the company.

Reserves are classified as one of the following:

1   Compulsory reserves.
2   Free reserves.
3   Revaluation reserves.

Compulsory reserves are those specified by law, by the statutes of the company or by any contractual clause (e.g. in the case of state authorization to render specific services or enter particular industries).

Companies formed under any of the legal forms prescribed in the Companies Act must constitute a legal reserve by setting aside 5 per cent of the profits of each year until the reserve is equal to 20 per cent of the nominal value of the shareholders' or quota-holders' capital. Sometimes the articles of association may call for the automatic transfer of a higher proportion of the profit of the year to reserves.

Free reserves are those decided by the annual general meeting, on the basis of the board of directors' (or managers') recommendation and voted by the members out of profits.

In general terms, a reserve is always created *after* payment of any tax due. Corrections of prior-year errors are not made directly to reserves. The normal practice is to show them as extraordinary items called *resultados transitados* (preceding year's income not appropriated and/or losses carried forward) in the profit and loss account for the year in which the correction takes place.

The POC requires the disclosure in the notes on the accounts of movements on reserves during the course of the year (note 40). Example 6.24 illustrates the fact.

Example 6.24 **Disclosure of movements in reserves (note 40)**

TERTIR – Terminais de Portugal SA
Annual report, 1990

40 Explanations of movements in other accounts in shareholders' funds

Account	Opening balance	Increase	Decrease	Closing balance
Share capital	3 500 000	350 000	–	3 850 000
Own shares				
Nominal value	(969)	(74 460)	(42 570)	(32 859)
Premiums and discounts	(1 183)	(120 874)	(20 160)	(101 897)
Share premiums	150 000	245 000	–	395 000
Legal reserves	86 137	67 277	–	153 414
Free reserves	709 589	862 540	–	1 572 129
Net profit for the period	1 345 542	2 317 948	(1 345 542)	2 317 948

Justification for the increases

Share premiums: Resulting from the increase in share capital.
Legal reserve: Resulting from the distribution of results.
Free reserves: Resulting from the distribution of results – 860 394 c. Resulting from the sale of own shares – 2 146 c.
Net profits: Decrease due to distribution of 1989 results. Increase due to 1990 results.

3.5 Revaluation reserves

The revaluation reserves result from the methodology applied to the revaluation of tangible fixed assets explained below (see also section 1.3 above).

Table 6.3 Indices used for revaluation

Year	Coefficient	Year	Coefficient
Up to 1900	2,051.01	1965	30.30
1901–3	2,093.29	1966	28.94
1904–10	1,948.60	1967–9	27.07
1911–14	1,868.93	1970	25.07
1915	1,662.77	1971	23.87
1916	1,360.99	1972	22.31
1917	1,086.48	1973	20.28
1918	775.17	1974	15.55
1919	594.09	1975	13.29
1920	392.54	1976	11.12
1921	256.12	1977	8.55
1922	189.68	1978	6.69
1923	116.09	1979	5.26
1924	97.72	1980	4.76
1925–36	84.22	1981	3.89
1937–9	81.79	1982	3.24
1940	68.82	1983	2.58
1941	61.12	1984	2.00
1942	52.77	1985	1.67
1943	44.95	1986	1.51
1944–50	38.16	1987	1.38
1951–7	34.99	1988	1.27
1958–63	32.91	1989	1.12
1964	31.44	1990	1

Source: Ministry of Finance, *Portaria* No. 332/91, dated 1 April 1991 (authors' translation).

Revaluation of the gross value of the tangible fixed assets is effected by multiplying the acquisition (or previously restated) values by indices which are published annually in the *Diário da República* for capital gains tax purposes. The indices to apply are those for the year of acquisition of the assets or for the year when the assets were last revalued.

Restatement of the accumulated depreciation is done using the same index for the whole amount, that is, the same index that was used to revalue the gross value of the asset. Although the accumulated depreciation was set up over a number of years, this procedure is used for the sake of simplicity. Table 6.3 shows some of the indices which were used in the last revaluation, to be included in the 1990 balance sheet.

The difference between the new net book value of the tangible fixed asset and the old is accounted for as 'Revaluation reserve' and represents a net increase in the assets and also in the equity of the company. The revaluation procedures as well as the movements of the revaluation reserve within the year must be disclosed in the notes to the accounts (notes 13 and 39 respectively).

The revaluation reserve may not be distributed as dividends, but it is possible to use it to increase the nominal value of the capital (though only if there are no accumulated losses to be offset against the reserve).

Example 6.25 **Disclosure of revaluation procedure (notes 12 and 13)**

IMOVALOR, SGII, SA
Annual report, 1990

12 Indication of legal documents on which the revaluation of tangible fixed assets or of financial investments was based. Decree law No. 237/81 of 12th June, Article 10.
13 Chart on Revaluations

Revaluations (item 13)

Description	Historic costs (a)	Revaluations (a) (b)	Revalued accounting values (a)
Tangible fixed assets:			
Land and natural resources	312.454.828	822.779.288	1.135.234.116
Buildings and other constr.	1.123.218.319	1.854.007.202	2.977.225.521
Basic equipment	1.417.369		1.417.369
Transport equipment	92.080		92.080
Administrative equipment	5.447.368		5.447.368
	1.442.629.964	2.676.786.490	4.119.416.454

(a) Net values.
(b) Includes successive revaluations.

Example 6.26 **Movements in the revaluation reserve (note 39)**

IMOVALOR, SGII, SA
Annual report, 1990

39 Variation of reserves for revaluation occurring during the year.
Reserve for revaluation decree law 237/87:
Revaluation of the year 2,327,901 thousand Esc.
Previous balance 505,567 thousand Esc.
Final balance 2,833,468 thousand Esc.

3.6 Retained earnings or accumulated losses

Where the profit (or the loss) for the year, or part of it, has not been taken to reserves or distributed as dividend this is shown in the balance sheet as 'retained earnings' or 'accumulated losses' until a decision has been reached as to the final treatment.

3.7 Result for the year

See Chapter 7, on profit and loss account valuation, as that is the bottom line of this statement. It is the linking item between the balance sheet and the income statement and is the only one that appears simultaneously in both statements. Example 6.27 shows a minute of a general meeting, dealing with profit appropriation. Such a minute must appear in the annual report.

3.8 Interim dividends

The result for the year may be transferred to reserves or distributed to the shareholders as dividends, subject to the following:

1   At least 5 per cent of the net income for the year must be transferred to the legal reserve until the reserve reaches at least 20 per cent of the subscribed capital. The legal reserve may be used to offset losses (articles 218, 295 and 296, CSC).
2   Non-voting shares take priority in the distribution of dividends, including outstanding year balances.

Dividends may be distributed against reserves even if there is a loss for the year or the income for the year is insufficient, but only if the remaining equity is no lower than the amount of capital stock plus restricted reserves, plus the non-depreciated formation expenses, research and development expenses and goodwill (articles 217 and 294 of the Companies Act). However, interim dividend distribution is more restricted under article 297 of the Companies Act. They may be distributed only as authorized by the statutes of the company and only during the second half of the financial year, and may never exceed half the expected income for the year, based on estimated statements for the year.

Example 6.27   **Disclosure of appropriation of profits**

IP FINANCEIRA – Sociedade de Investimento, Esudos e Participações Financeiras
Annual report, 1990

Aplicação de resultados

A conta de resultados apresenta um saldo positivo de ESC. 141 655 321$30.

Dando cumprimento aos preceitos legais e estatutários e com o objectivo de reforçar os Capitais Próprios da sociedade nesta fase de consolidação da sua presença no mercado, o Conselho de Administração da IP FINANCEIRA propõe que não se proceda este ano à distribuição de dividendos e que os resultados apurados tenham a seguinte aplicação:

Fundo de Reserva Legal	ESC. 14 165 532$10
Para Reserva Especial	ESC. 7 082 276$60
Para Reservas Livres	ESC. 120 407 512$60

dos quais ESC. 20 000 000$00 se consideram afectados ao pagamento da contrapartida das acções próprias que a sociedade eventualmente venha a adquirir.

Appropriation of profits

The net profit for the year was PTE 141 655 321,30.

The board of directors proposes that in order to comply with the law and its articles of association and to strengthen the company's own capital during this phase in which it is consolidating its position in the market, there should be no dividend this year and that the net profit be applied in the following way:

– to the Legal Reserve Fund	PTE	14 165 532,10
– to the Special Reserve	PTE	7 082 276,60
– to Free Reserves	PTE	120 407 512,60

of which 20 000 000 escudos are considered to be reserved for the eventual acquisition by the company of its own shares.

---

4 ASSETS AND LIABILITIES DENOMINATED IN FOREIGN CURRENCIES

Portuguese accounting law (the POC) requires disclosure only of the method used in the translation of foreign currency transactions, whether for individual accounts or for consolidated accounts. An explanation of the method must be included in the notes on the accounts. The POC does not deal with the translation of foreign currency financial statements.

Translation of foreign currency transactions. The POC also includes some specific pronouncements relating to foreign currency translation. Essentially, these require the following (see Chapter 5):

1   *Cash and bank balances.* These items are translated as at the balance sheet date (closing rate). Exchange rate variations should be considered as financial gains or losses to be included in the profit and loss account of the year.
2   *Short-term receivables and payables.* Initially these items are translated at the historical exchange rate (the date of the transaction), unless a different rate of exchange has been agreed for it. Subsequently, at the balance sheet date, the items which have so far been recorded at the historical exchange rate must be revalued at the balance sheet date according to the closing rate. Exchange rate variations must be considered as financial gains or losses and are included in the income statement of the year.
3   *Long-term receivables and payables.* The same procedure referred to in (2) above, except that the unrealized gains are required to be deferred in the balance sheet if it seems possible that such gains will be reversible. The gains will be deferred to the period when they are definitely realized.
4   *Financing of fixed assets in progress.* Exchange rate fluctuations may be capitalized in the financed asset during the period of construction.
5   *Other assets (stocks and fixed assets).* The valuation is at purchase cost (as at the day of the transaction).

7

Financial reporting (II) The profit and loss account

1 INTRODUCTION

This chapter deals with expenses, revenues, losses and gains which in turn determine the net income for the year.

The income statement of a Portuguese company is a single document which records all expenses, revenues, losses and gains, grouped by category. This statement may be abridged (depending on the size of the company) but in any case must be in horizontal rather than in vertical form. The latter has not been used in Portugal.

Expenses are classified in the income statement as follows:

1   Operating expenses.
2   Financial expenses and losses.

3   Extraordinary expenses and losses.
4   Tax on the company's income for the year.

The revenue side of the income statement is subdivided as follows:

1   Operating revenues.
2   Financial revenues and gains.
3   Extraordinary revenues and gains.

The stringency of corporate income tax regulations is such that only amounts recorded in the financial statements (and not all of those, in some instances) may be considered as deductible expenses for tax purposes.

The basic principles of income reporting are:

Expenses   Accruals and prudence
Revenues   Recognition basis

Accounting methods may vary from those described in chapter 5 of the POC (see Chapter 5 above for details) as between reporting periods only in exceptional circumstances and in order to ensure a 'true and fair view' (*imagem verdadeira e apropriada*). In such a case the notes on the accounts must disclose the relevant information to permit comparison with prior-year figures (note 1). Example 7.1 shows disclosure of this sort. When there is a change in accounting principles or valuation rules, the comparative information must be modified accordingly or the impossibility of doing so must be stated in the notes on the accounts (note 2).

Example 7.1 **Exceptional variation to achieve a true and fair view (note 1)**

FETAL-MODA INTERNACIONAL SA
Annual report, 1990 (author's translation)

Requirements of the Official Accounting Plan which have not been applied

In order to achieve a true and fair view, goodwill has not been depreciated. Justification for that procedure is given under note 9 on the accounts.

The notes on the accounts must disclose the differences arising from changes in accounting methods and require the figures of the previous year to be adjusted in order to permit comparisons in the balance sheet and the profit and loss account (note 2). This is what happened in financial figures disclosed for 1990, the first year of application of the 1989 version of the POC. In fact the introduction of the new POC as well as the tax reform of 1988 (given that accounting in Portugal is still heavily influenced by tax regulations) made some changes possible:

1   Own shares, formerly considered as investment assets, must now appear in the balance sheet as a capital deduction.

Example 7.2 **Comparative information modified (note 2)**

EMPRESA PÚBLICA DAS AGUAS LIVRES EP
Annual report, 1990 (author's translation)

During the current year, because of changes which have occurred in the Official Accounting Plan, the contents of the accounts mentioned below do not permit comparability between the figures of the year 1990 and those of the previous year (1989) and so adjustments were made as follows:

Account code			Balance sheet, 1989 (PTE 000)	
1990	1989	Account name	Debit	Credit
2624	233	Loans to third parties	223	
2721	47	Capitalized expenses	2 151 167	
2719	2682	Revenues receivable	730 998	
2732	2681	Deferred costs		22 877
2734	2683	Interest receivable on loans		221 312

Account code			Income statement, 1989 (PTE 000)	
1990	1989	Account name	Debit	Credit
69	82	Extraordinary losses	85 616	
69	83	Prior years' losses	1 030 916	
79	82	Extraordinary gains		306 097
79	83	Prior years' gains		471 483
79	79	Provisions (utilization)		177 997

2   In accounting for advances from customers and to suppliers the separation of monetary and non-monetary items is now a requirement. Only the former are classed as receivables.

3   Real property held as an investment is now treated as such. It was previously considered as a tangible fixed asset.

The following sections discuss these issues. The reader should also refer to Chapter 8, where the income statement layouts are presented and analysed in detail.

2 OPERATING EXPENSES

Of the two alternative methods of classifying operating expenses permitted by the Fourth EC Directive, Portugal opted for the classification by the nature of the expense. According to this classification, operating expenses include the following headings: purchases of materials and merchandise; purchases of external services; personnel expenses; provisions for depreciation and the amortization of fixed assets; provisions against reductions in the value of working capital items (receivables and inventories); and other operating expenses.

Purchases of materials and merchandise are referred to in the Portuguese classification as *Custos das mercadorias vendidas e das matérias consumidas*, that is, 'Costs of goods sold and materials consumed'. However, it should be understood that this heading refers to costs of *purchases* (inputs) for sale and production. Correspondingly, inventory increases or decreases in finished goods and work in progress during the financial period are included as additions or deductions on the revenue side of the profit and loss account under the heading 'Variação da produção' ('Variation in production').

2.1 Cost of materials consumed and goods sold

'Custo das mercadorias vendidas e das matérias consumidas' includes stock balances of raw materials, other consumables and merchandise. They are shown on the left-hand side of the income statement, under costs. Valuation is according to acquisition cost.

Under normal circumstances purchases of materials and merchandise are invoiced with VAT, which is not usually charged to the cost of sales, unless it is not recoverable.

Additional expenses or purchases necessary to bring the asset into use, such as transport costs, duties, insurance, warehouse costs, etc., may be included in the cost of goods sold. For more details on the valuation of cost of merchandise sold and materials consumed see Chapter 6, section 1.5. The breakdown of the cost of goods sold and materials consumed must be disclosed in the notes on the accounts (note 41). This information completes the income statement.

Example 7.3 **Breakdown of cost of goods sold and materials consumed (note 41)**

VIDAGO, MELGAÇO E PEDRAS SALGADAS SA
Annual report, 1990 (author's translation)

	Merchandise	Materials
Initial balances	66 668 000	37 563 000
Purchases	1 201 481 000	325 315 000
Inventory adjustments	0	0
Final balances	91 624 000	78 968 000
Cost of goods sold and materials consumed during the year	1 176 525 000	283 910 000

If the balance sheet valuation of raw materials and merchandise shows that the carrying values are too high, this will give rise to the creation of a provision. So the change in inventories that appears in the above-mentioned note on the accounts, shown in Example 7.3, is accounted for at gross values (that is, excluding provisions). The same thing happens with the change in inventories of finished goods.

2.2 Personnel expenses

Note that holiday payments are considered a cost not in the year when they are paid by the company but in the previous year, being also recorded on the liabilities side of the balance sheet as a provision.

Pension expenses are considered as operating expenses in two cases:

1   When payments are made by the company into an external pension fund which will pay retired employees the pensions in the future.
2   When payment is made by the company to employees already retired, as a supplement to their pensions.

The notes on the accounts complete the information on the personnel expenses, disclosing the amounts of the remuneration of the members of the board of directors and the audit board. Commitments regarding retirement pensions for them must also be disclosed (note 43).

The costs of employers' contributions to employee pension funds, the voluntary insurance of employees and similar expenses are tax-deductible up to a maximum of 15 per cent of salary costs.

Example 7.4 **Disclosure of remuneration (note 43)**

SABEL – Santos & Bento SA
Annual report, 1990 (author's translation)

Board of directors	11 333 258$
Audit board (ROC)	690 000$

2.3 Depreciation of fixed assets

Depreciation of tangible and intangible fixed assets is part of the operating expenses, but depreciation of real property held as an investment is treated as a financial expense, although the methods and percentages of depreciation applied are the same. The notes on the accounts include a reference to the method of adjusting the values of the assets (note 3), i.e. the method of depreciating fixed assets (see Example 7.5). Disclosure of the depreciation of the year as well as of the accumulated depreciation is required (note 10), including a breakdown by category of fixed assets (see Example 7.6). If the income of the year has been affected because the amount attributed to depreciation was higher than it would have been under the company's normal depreciation rules, the tax effect must be disclosed in the notes (note 6; see Example 7.14).

Goodwill must be written off, but if a period longer than five years is chosen to depreciate it, the reasons must be disclosed in the notes (note 9). Some companies do not depreciate goodwill and in this way they follow the tax rules, which do not authorize the depreciation of goodwill.

Example 7.5 **Value adjustment method (note 3)**

FITOR – Companhia Portuguesa de Têxteis SA
Annual report, 1990 (extract, author's translation)

(c) Depreciation for the year was calculated using the straight-line method and the highest percentages allowed for tax purposes, according to the estimated useful life.

The POC is silent upon the methods and percentages to be used for fixed asset depreciation. However, the tax rules on depreciation, which are very detailed, tend to be followed in most companies. Under tax law, depreciation may be based on either the straight line or the declining balance method, but not on the sum-of-years-digits method. For many categories of asset the maximum and minimum straight-line depreciation rates are specified by tax law, the minimum rates being 50 per cent of the maxima. Some representative rates are indicated in Table 7.1. If rates lower than the minima are used, the difference cannot be made up by additional depreciation in subsequent years.

If the declining balance method is used, the corresponding straight-line rates are increased by the following coefficients:

1   For useful lives of less than five years, 1.5.
2   For useful lives of five or six years, 2.0.
3   For useful lives longer than six years, 2.5.

Under some circumstances, companies may charge additional depreciation under the regime of 'intensive use of assets'. Intensive use is defined as using the assets for two or

Example 7.6 **Disclosure of the year's depreciation (note 10)**

TEIXEIRA DUARTE, Engenharia e Construções SA
Annual report, 1990 (extract)

Depreciation and provisions (PTE 000)

Item	Initial balance	Reinforc.	Revaluation	Regulariz.	Final balance
Intangible fixed assets:					
Operating expenses	24.336	11.193			35.529
	24.336	11.193			35.529
Tangible fixed assets:					
Build. and other constructions	75.569	18.776	7.898	− 764	101.479
Basic equipment	1.738.714	446.482	141.356	− 87.724	2.238.828
Transp. equipment	246.607	142.261	49.680	− 1.490	437.058
Tools and fixtures	437.669	202.590	9.494	− 107	649.646
Office equipment	141.301	66.996	14.630		222.927
	2.639.860	877.105	223.058	− 90.085	3.649.938

Table 7.1 Selected depreciation rates (%)

Buildings	
Commercial and administrative	2.0
Industrial	5.0
Hotels, restaurants, etc.	5.0
Fixtures	
Water, electrical, compressed air, refrigeration and telephones	10.0
Machinery	
Electronic machines	20.0
Typewriters and other office machinery	20.0
Machine tools	
Light	20.0
Heavy	12.5
Vehicles	
Light	25.0
Heavy	25.0

more shifts per day (each shift comprises eight hours of work). Article 9 of the decree 2/90, dated 12 January 1990 allows the normal maximum rates to be increased by 25 per cent in the case of two shifts, and by 50 per cent in the case of more than two. There are restrictions on allowable depreciation for light vehicles (cars), the maximum depreciable value being PTE 4 million.

For fixed assets of low value (under PTE 20,000), on the other hand, 100 per cent write-off in the year of acquisition is allowed.

The rates above are general for the assets indicated. In addition, there are a large number of rates for assets specific to particular industries.

Annual depreciation of the revalued items would be calculated using the revalued amount, but the extra depreciation relating to the revaluation is not wholly a tax-deductible cost: 40 per cent of such extra depreciation may not be deducted from the income for the year for tax purposes.

2.4 Provisions against working capital items

At the year end there are usually some situations where revenue or expense (and corresponding debtor and creditor amounts) are not recognized although the circumstances make it reasonably probable that the revenue or an expense will materialize. The prudence principle points to the incorporation in the accounts of the probable expenses, which are tax-deductible in legally defined circumstances, referred to below.

Provisions against receivables, and inventories are usually an operating expense, but write-downs of negotiable securities and investments are recorded as a financial expense.

The notes to the accounts include reference to the methods of value adjustment to take account of the prudence principle through provisions (note 3). Additional information about provisions is usually required in the notes, namely the accumulated adjustments and the adjustments of the year (note 34). The information disclosed in the notes, such as that in Example 7.7, is very often insufficient to enable the reader to

Example 7.7 **Value adjustment through provisions (note 3)**

LISNAVE – Estaleiros Navais de Lisboa SA
Annual report, 1990 (extract, author's translation)

3.4 Inventories are valued at acquisition or production cost, according to the following:
  – Materials: average cost of acquisition, including all expenses prior to their storage.
  – Work in progress and finished products: cost of production, including raw materials, salaries and overhead costs.
3.5 Accounts receivable and payable in currencies other than the Portuguese escudo are valued at the exchange rate(s) ruling at the balance sheet date. Positive and negative exchange rate differences are recognized as gains and losses for the year.

understand and assess the content of it. The Tax Tables are much more complete.

The tax orientation of Portuguese accounting means that tax rules for provisions will usually have been assimilated in the financial reports of Portuguese companies. The most important ones are outlined below.

Provisions for write-downs of negotiable securities are not tax-deductible, although the prudence principle suggests that they should be seriously considered in cases where the acquisition value (or, more precisely, the book value) is higher than the market price. By contrast, bad debt and inventory provisions may be tax-deductible costs.

Tax law lays down the maximum allowable for bad debts, based on the age of the debts, as shown in Table 7.2. However, to take full advantage of the tax deductions, the company must demonstrate that all reasonable efforts have been made to collect the items and the debt must be recorded in the 'Doubtful debtors' account.

If a debtor is declared bankrupt during the year, amounts owing by that debtor are treated as losses for tax purposes, and do not need to be provided for via the provisions account. They are considered an extraordinary item.

Example 7.8 **Disclosure of adjustments to provisions (note 34)**

CENTRAL DE CERVEJAS SA
Annual report, 1990 (author's translation)

	Initial balance	Increase	Decrease	Final balance
28 Provisions for bad debts				
281 Customers	458977388$80	366341183$72	341597780$22	483720792$30
288 Other debtors		18719700$00		18719700$00
29 Provisions for liabilities and charges				
298 Other liabilities and charges	499374494$70			499374494$70
39 Provisions for inventory write-offs				
396 Raw materials	32070193$00		32070193$00	
49 Provisions for investments				
495 Other investments	952700$00			952700$00

Table 7.2 Maximum allowable percentages for
bad debt provisions

Age (months)	Provision allowed (%)
6–12	25
13–18	50
19–24	75
Over 24	100

If a debtor holds 10 per cent or more of the creditor company's share capital, or is a company in which the creditor holds 10 per cent or more of the share capital, then no bad debt provision is tax-deductible. No bad debt provisions are tax-deductible on accounts of amounts owed by government agencies.

Deductible provisions for inventories are limited to the difference between the cost of acquisition, or production, and market value at the balance sheet date, if lower. Market value is replacement cost for raw materials and selling price for finished goods. A special case exists for publishers, who may write off old editions which have been in stock over two years.

2.5 Other operating expenses

Confidential expenses are expenses of an undivulged nature which have an appropriate heading in the POC Chart of Accounts. These expenses are subject to 10 per cent income tax in addition to normal taxation, and tax is payable even if the company is paying no normal income tax or is reporting losses.

Provisions for liabilities and charges are also operating expenses; these include pension provisions, and the amounts of holiday payments to be paid only in the next year.

3 OPERATING REVENUES

Operating revenues include net turnover, changes in finished goods and work-in-progress inventories, capitalized items and other operating revenues. 'Capitalized costs' are estimated by the company and offset against related expenses (for example, self-constructed assets).

A number of issues arising in the context of income recognition by Portuguese companies are discussed in the following paragraphs.

3.1 Sales and services

Sales of goods are recognized at the time of delivery. Services are recognized as time elapses, in the case of services rendered on a continuous basis, or after the service has been rendered, and in the case of services rendered on an occasional basis, respectively. These are the moments when it is possible to invoice. Sales and services revenues correspond to the amount of net sales, net of returns, rebates and trade discounts, but not

Example 7.9 **Analysis of sales of goods and services (note 44)**

SOPORCEL – Sociedade Portuguesa de Celulose SA
Annual report, 1990 (author's translation)

	1990				1989			
	Domestic market		Exports		Domestic market		Exports	
Account	Amount	%	Amount	%	Amount	%	Amount	%
71 Sales of goods	1620931	5.04	30492229	94.92	3586277	8.42	39009670	91.57
72 Services	8172	0.03	1449	0.01	4921	0.01	105	–
Total	1629103	5.07	30493678	94.93	3591198	8.43	39009775	91.57

cash discounts, which are financial expenses to be accounted for separately even when included in the invoice.

Under normal circumstances, sales and services rendered (an exception is the case of exports) are invoiced with IVA (value-added tax). This 'output' IVA is a percentage added to the price of goods and services invoiced to the customer, and is subsequently paid to the state after deduction of some of the 'input' IVA paid to suppliers of services, inventory and tangible fixed assets.

There is no difference between the information disclosed in the detailed profit and loss account and notes relating to sales and services and that disclosed in the abridged versions. In both cases, in the notes on the accounts, sales and services rendered must be revealed, analysed by activity and geographical area (note 44). In practice Portuguese companies generally disclose this information without very much detail. Maybe the idea that 'secrecy is the soul of the business' is still lying in the mind of managers and shareholders.

In Example 7.9 the disclosed values are net, except those of financial discounts, which are disclosed separately under the financial income statement (see below, section 4).

Construction contracts to be executed in Portugal are nowadays subject to the *Directriz Contabilística* 2/91, approved by the Accounting Standardization Committee on 28 August 1991. The following conditions are necessary if the *Directriz* is to apply:

1   The contract is for the construction of an asset or a combination of assets which together constitute a single project, such as a bridge, a dam, a ship, a building or a complex piece of equipment.
2   The date at which the contract activity is embarked upon and the date when the contract is completed fall in different accounting periods.

Construction contracts generally fall into two basic types: fixed-price contracts (in some cases subject to cost escalation clauses) and cost-plus contracts (the contractor is reimbursed to the extent of his costs, plus a percentage of those costs or a fixed fee).

Two methods of accounting for construction contracts may be used by contractors: the

Example 7.10 **Accounting for long-term contracts**

During year *n* a contract with a term of two and a half years is signed between companies ABC and DEF. This example is therefore concerned with ABC's accounting for the contract.

   The total contract price is 10 million PTE, and there is no price variation clause. Payment terms are: 30 per cent advance on signature, 20 per cent after eighteen months and 50 per cent on completion. At the end of the first year the situation is as follows:

	PTE
Costs incurred to date	270,000
Estimated costs to complete	660,000
Invoices issued	200,000
Received from customer (DEF)	
Advance of 30 per cent	300,000
Payment of invoices, less 30 per cent	
70 per cent of 200,000	140,000

Revenue recognized on percentage of completion basis:

$$\frac{\text{Costs incurred to date}}{\text{Total costs to complete}} \times \text{Total contract price} - \text{Amount invoiced to date}$$

$$= 270{,}000/270{,}000 + 660{,}000 \times (1{,}000{,}000 - 200{,}000)$$
$$= 90{,}323$$

Journal entries by ABC in year 1:

		Debit	Credit
Costs incurred	Work in progress	270,000	
	Operating income/expense		270,000
Invoices issued	Customers (DEF)	200,000	
	Sales		200,000
Accrued income	Accrued receivables	90,323	
	Sales		90,323
Transfers	Operating income/expense (cost of sales)	270,000	
	Work in progress		270,000
Cash receipts	Cash and banks	440,000	
	Advances from customers		300,000
	Customers (against invoices)		140,000
Transfers	Advances from customers	60,000	
	Customers		60,000

The gross profit would therefore be:

Sales (200,000 + 90,323)	290,323
Cost of sales	270,000
Gross profit	20,323

Source: Extracted from an example in the *Directriz contabilística* 2/91.

'percentage of completion' method or the 'completed contract' method. Under the former, revenue is recognized as the contract activity progresses and the costs incurred are matched with that revenue. Consequently a profit for the year can be calculated on the basis of the proportion of work completed. Under the latter method, revenue is recognized only when the contract is complete, or substantially complete, the costs incurred having accumulated during the course of the contract. The percentage of completion method should not be used if the cost estimates are suspected not to be reliable.

The criteria adopted in selecting the methods constitute an accounting policy which must be consistently applied. Once a contractor has used a method for a particular contract then all other contracts that meet similar criteria should be accounted for by the same method. However, the completed contract method can be used in the case of some projects of lesser importance.

Revenues and costs on construction contracts in progress which have already been included in the calculation of the results of the company should be disclosed in the notes to the accounts (note 48). Amounts received and receivable related to construction work in progress should also be disclosed under the same note to the accounts.

Example 7.10 illustrates the percentage of completion method.

Revenues in foreign currencies must be translated into escudos at the exchange rate ruling on the transaction date (if there is no agreement otherwise), or at an average exchange rate if the transactions were spread over a period of time, provided the rate chosen is a representative one.

3.2 Increase (decrease) in inventories

The notes to the accounts must disclose the change in inventories of finished goods and work in progress (note 42). Example 7.11 shows an example of this type of disclosure.

If the balance sheet valuation shows that the carrying value is too high, this will give rise to the creation of a provision and so, the inventory change that appears in the profit and loss account and in the calculation of cost of sales is accounted for at gross value (that is, excluding provisions).

Example 7.11 **Disclosure of changes in inventories (note 42)**

FIACO – Fiação de Algodões de Coimbra SA
Annual report, 1990 (author's translation)

Movements for the year	Finished and intermediate products	Scrap, residues, etc.	Work in progress
+ Final balances	126 508 372$	–	18 871 128$
– Initial balances	124 911 634$	–	12 541 365$
± Increases/decreases	1 596 738$	–	6 329 763$

'Variação de produções' includes stock balances of work in progress, intermediate goods and finished goods. It is shown on the revenue (right-hand) side of the income statement. Valuation is according to production cost. Production cost includes raw materials, labour costs, overheads, depreciation, etc.

3.3 Other operating revenues

Other operating revenues consist of sundry revenues from regular operations, operating subsidies and any over-provision for contingencies and expenses.

4 FINANCIAL INCOME

In addition to the interest on a company's short and long-term debts, financial expenses include losses on the sale of negotiable securities, (but not those arising from the disposal of financial investments, which are considered to be extraordinary losses), write-offs and provisions against financial investments and foreign currency exchange losses. Correspondingly, financial income includes interest and dividends from financial investments, gains on sales of negotiable securities (but not on financial investments, which are considered to be extraordinary gains), and foreign currency exchange gains.

The principle that is generally accepted by companies and prescribed in Portuguese accounting standards is that financial revenues should be recognized over time, using the accrual method.

The notes on the accounts must include a statement that analyses the financial expenses and revenues (note 45), which appear in aggregate in the profit and loss account. Example 7.12 illustrates this disclosure.

Cash discounts on trade debts and credits are recognized when payment occurs.

Provisions against negotiable securities and investments are not tax-deductible, even though they may be required in order to give a true and fair view. For financial sector enterprises such as banks and insurance companies there are special tax rules, and in any case the accounting rules are not those in the POC.

It is worth mentioning that in the case of dividends from group companies (and also associated companies in which the holding is at least 25 per cent) only 5 per cent of the gross dividend received is counted for tax purposes (see Chapter 4).

5 EXTRAORDINARY INCOME

Extraordinary income consists primarily of gains and losses that are atypical or infrequent, including capital grants transferred to income, donations, prior-year items and gains and losses on disposals of fixed assets or own shares and quotas, extraordinary assets adjustments, penalties, fines, etc.

There are specific headings in the profit and loss account for the extraordinary income and extraordinary losses, and there is a special line for disclosing the net extraordinary result before tax. More information has to be disclosed in the notes on the accounts, which include a statement in which the extraordinary items are analysed. Example 7.13 illustrates such disclosure. As can be seen, the POC does not make it obligatory to disclose the portion of corporate income tax relating to the extraordinary result separately from the income tax on the ordinary result.

Although extraordinary items include a wide variety of profit and loss items, the list of accounts in the POC includes a number of examples, such as those arising from accidents, indemnity payments, penalties, fines, the recovery of bad debts, fire, flood,

Example 7.12 Financial income statement (note 45)

TRANSINSULAR – Transportes Marítimos Insulares SA
Annual report, 1990

45 Statement of financial results (PTE 000)

Costs and losses	Financial year	
	1990	*1989*
Interest paid	268 646 485$90	47 798 934$90
Provisions against investments	8 684 593$90	
Foreign exchange losses	67 815 086 30	69 684 139$80
Discounts granted for prompt payment	56 562 533$20	13 502 854$40
Other costs and financial losses	25 814 529$10	29 340 701$10
Financial results	(283 752 488$80)	78 818 340$20
	143 770 739$60	239 144 970$40

Income and profits	Financial year	
	1990	*1989*
Interest received	90 567 306$60	152 082 322$60
Income from participation certificates	5 515 606$50	10 965 894$20
Income from capital holdings	266 917$00	933 309$20
Foreign exchange profits	42 809 985$40	60 756 747$30
Discounts obtained for prompt payment	4 569 297$60	8 047 225$00
Other financial income and profits	41 626$50	6 359 472$10
	143 770 739$60	239 144 970$40

Example 7.13 **Breakdown of extraordinary items (note 46)**

TERTIR – Terminais de Portugal SA
Annual report, 1990

46 Extraordinary items

Expenditure	1990	1989	Income	1990	1989
Donations	12030	–	Gains and disposals	1217244	365910
Loss on fixed asset disposals	4654	2419	Prior year adjustment	139	294061
Fines and penalties	43	50	Other	12547	11836
Prior year adjustments	1380	352346			
Other	62670	1460			
Extraordinary Items (net)	1149153	315532			
	1229930	671807		1229930	671807

prior-year items, gains and losses on the sale of tangible fixed assets or securities, etc. We only mention in detail the following extraordinary items here: donations for cultural purposes, capital subsidies and prior years' items.

Tax deductions in respect of such donations are limited to 0.2 per cent of turnover for the financial year, unless the recipient is the government or one of its agencies or branches, in which case the limit does not apply.

Capital subsidies must be capitalized: they are shown on the liabilities side of the balance under the heading 'Accruals and deferrals'. The rate of allocation of these subsidies to income must be the same as the depreciation rate of the subsidized asset, unless the asset is not depreciable, in which case the company recognizes the income only when the asset is sold.

A special word needs to be said about items from prior years. These are included in the extraordinary gains or losses, and so do not appear separately in the profit and loss account, but are shown among the extraordinary items in the notes on the accounts. When prior years' items are not material they can be included alongside expenses and revenues of a similar nature in the income statement for the year. In some cases, when they are very important, they are not allowed to affect the income statement for the year but are shown in the balance sheet as equity under the heading 'Accumulated losses or unattributed profits'.

In the 1977 version of the POC, prior-year items were distinguished from extra-ordinary items. In practice, it sometimes happened that prior-year items included losses for which the incumbent management disclaimed responsibility. The 1989 version of the POC includes prior-year items with extraordinary items.

6 THE IMPACT OF TAX RULES ON FINANCIAL ACCOUNTING AND THE INFLUENCE IN FUTURE YEARS' TAXATION OF ACCOUNTING PRINCIPLES

Portuguese companies have traditionally prepared their accounts on the basis of tax rules, particularly with regard to the calculation of income tax. In fact the Companies' Income

Example 7.14 **Accounting principles and taxation (note 6)**

TERTIR – Terminais de Portugal SA
Annual report, 1990 (author's translation)

Owing to investments undertaken, the following amounts are available for set-off against taxable income in the following years:

1990 Deduction of reinvestment of profits – PTE 326 414 476
1991 Deduction of reinvestment of profits – PTE 274 214 239

Tax Code of 1988 provides a set of rules for the valuation and recording of items in order to determine the taxable income. However, the income tax return which companies must complete in order to calculate their corporate income tax includes a table ('Table 17') that is used to calculate the adjustments of the accounting result for the year in order to calculate the company's taxable income. The differences shown between the taxable profit and the accounting profit (which is also detailed in its constituent parts in another table in the return where the accounting figures of the profit and loss account are listed by type in the same way as they were presented to the annual general meeting) are nevertheless important.

The tax rules affect financial accounting in the following areas:

1 Inventory valuation.
2 Revaluation of fixed assets.
3 Depreciation of fixed assets.
4 Provisions for reductions in the value of assets.
5 Confidential expenses.
6 Costs of social provisions in the workplace.
7 Donations for cultural purposes.
8 Capital gains and losses.
9 Tax charges and liabilities.
10 Dividends from group companies and other undertakings.

The timing of the recognition of expenses for tax purposes may differ from the timing for accounting purposes, as mentioned in Chapter 4.

This chapter has referred at various points to some of the tax influences on financial reporting and accounting valuation. In some cases the tax rules do not differ from the accounting rules, only adding more detail. As an example, the tax treatment of inventories is the same in all material respects as that laid down in the POC, except for the matter of provisions for obsolescence, where the tax rules are much more detailed (see under provisions, section 2.4 above).

In other cases the tax rules conflict with accounting law. This is the case with the depreciation of goodwill. The POC requires it to be written off, normally over five years, but over up to twenty years if there is an explanation in the notes. However, amortization or other write-downs of goodwill are not tax-deductible. Only 60 per cent of the additional annual depreciation on revalued assets is deductible for tax purposes, although all the additional depreciation must be shown in the accounts. Tax losses can be carried forward against the profits of the following five years, and so this can be the subject of tax planning devices.

Changes in accounting principles during the financial year in order to obtain fiscal advantages must be disclosed in the notes (note 5). Also, the notes on the accounts must not omit to disclose (under note 6) the influence of accounting principles in future years' tax. Example 7.14 illustrates this disclosure.

8

Presentation of annual accounts and other financial reports

1 INTRODUCTION

The accounting practices directly related to the presentation of financial statements in line with the accounting principles and standards prevailing in Portugal have been described in Chapter 5. It should be noted that all such financial statements must be expressed in Portuguese currency and in the Portuguese language.

The requirements of the POC are based on those of the Fourth Directive, and thus encompass the balance sheet, the profit and loss statement and an annex comprising the notes to the financial statements. There is no requirement for a statement of the sources and applications of funds or of cash flows.

Up to 1990 companies were not required to publish group accounts, although they have been able to submit tax returns on a group basis since 1988. This situation has recently changed as a result of an extension of the POC in July 1991 to require consolidated accounts as set out in the Seventh Directive. It will apply to financial statements for financial years beginning on or after 1 January, 1991. Some companies present supplementary information relating to value added, ratios, forecasts, social responsibility, etc.

2 BALANCE SHEET LAYOUT AND CONTENT

The POC opted for the horizontal format provided in the Fourth Directive. As is usual

Table 8.1 Detailed balance sheet (a) Portuguese original (*balanço analítico*)

Códigos das contas		Activo	Exercícios			
			N			N − 1
CE[1]	POC		AB	AP	AL	AL
C		Imobilizado:				
I		Imobilizações incorpóreas:				
1	431	Despesas de instalação	●	●	●	●
1	432	Despesas de investigação e de desenvolvimento	●	●	●	●
2	433	Propriedade industrial e outros direitos	●	●	●	●
3	434	Trespasses	●	●	●	●
4	441/6	Imobilizações em curso	●		●	●
4	449	Adiantamentos por conta de imobilizações incorpóreas	●		●	●
			●	●	●	●
			—	—	—	—
II		Imobilizações corpóreas:				
1	421	Terrenos e recursos naturais	●	●	●	●
1	422	Edifícios e outras construções	●	●	●	●
2	423	Equipamento básico	●	●	●	●
2	424	Equipamento de transporte	●	●	●	●
3	425	Ferramentas e utensílios	●	●	●	●
3	426	Equipamento administrativo	●	●	●	●
3	427	Taras e vasilhame	●	●	●	●
3	429	Outras imobilizações corpóreas	●	●	●	●
4	441/6	Imobilizações em curso	●		●	●
4	448	Adiantamentos por conta de imobilizações corpóreas	●		●	●
			●	●	●	●
			—	—	—	—
III		Investimentos financeiros:				
1	4111	Partes de capital em empresas do grupo	●	●	●	●
2	4121 + 4131	Empréstimos a empresas do grupo	●	●	●	●
3	4112	Partes de capital em empresas associadas	●	●	●	●
4	4122 + 4132	Empréstimos a empresas associadas	●	●	●	●
5	4113 + 414 + 415	Títulos e outras aplicações financeiras	●	●	●	●
6	4123 + 4133	Outros empréstimos concedidos	●	●	●	●
6	441/6	Imobilizações em curso	●		●	●
6	447	Adiantamentos por conta de investimentos financeiros	●		●	●
			●	●	●	●
			—	—	—	—
D		Circulante:				
I		Existências:				
1	36	Matérias-primas, subsidiárias e de consumo	●	●	●	●
2	35	Produtos e trabalhos em curso	●	●	●	●
3	34	Subprodutos, desperdícios, resíduos e refugos	●	●	●	●
3	33	Produtos acabados e intermédios	●	●	●	●
3	32	Mercadorias	●	●	●	●
4	37	Adiantamentos por conta de compras	●		●	●
			●	●	●	●
			—	—	—	—

Table 8.1 Detailed balance sheet (b) English translation

EC[1] codes	Assets	GA	DP	NA	NA
		Year		n	n − 1

EC[1] codes	Assets	GA	DP	NA	NA
C	Fixed assets				
I	Intangible fixed assets				
1	Formation expenses	•	•	•	•
1	Research and development expenses	•	•	•	•
2	Industrial property and other rights	•	•	•	•
3	Goodwill	•	•		•
4	Expenses in progress	•		•	•
4	Advances to suppliers	•		•	•
		•	•	•	•
		—	•	—	•
II	Tangible fixed assets				
1	Land and natural resources	•	•	•	•
1	Buildings and other constructions	•	•	•	•
2	Machinery and equipment	•	•	•	•
2	Transport equipment	•	•	•	•
3	Tools and utensils	•	•	•	•
3	Containers	•	•	•	•
3	Furniture and office equipment	•	•	•	•
3	Other fixed assets	•	•	•	•
4	Construction in progress	•		•	•
4	Advances to suppliers of fixed assets	•		•	•
		•	•	•	•
		—	—	—	—
III	Investments				
1	Investments in group companies	•	•	•	•
2	Loans to group companies	•	•	•	•
3	Investments in associated companies	•	•	•	•
4	Loans to associated companies	•	•	•	•
5	Securities and other investments	•	•	•	•
6	Other loans	•	•	•	•
6	Investments in progress	•		•	•
6	Advances	•		•	•
		•	•	•	•
		—	—	—	—
D	Current assets				
I	Inventories				
1	Raw materials and consumables	•	•	•	•
2	Work in progress	•	•	•	•
3	Spoilage, waste and scrap	•	•	•	•
3	Finished and semi-finished products	•	•	•	•
3	Merchandise	•	•	•	•
4	Advances to suppliers	•		•	•
		•	•	•	•
		—	—	—	—

Table 8.1 (a) Portuguese original (*continued*)

Códigos das contas			Exercícios			
			N			N − 1
CE[1]	POC	Activo	AB	AP	AL	AL
II		Dívidas de terceiros – Médio e longo prazo[2]	•	•	•	•
II		Dívidas de terceiros – Curto prazo:				
1	211	Clientes, c/c	•	•	•	•
1	212	Clientes – Títulos a receber	•	•	•	•
1	218	Clientes de cobrança duvidosa	•	•	•	•
2	252	Empresas do grupo	•	•	•	•
3	253 + 254	Empresas participadas e participantes	•	•	•	•
4	251 + 255	Outros accionistas (sócios)	•	•	•	•
4	229	Adiantamentos a fornecedores	•		•	•
4	2619	Adiantamentos a fornecedores de imobilizado	•		•	•
4	24	Estado e outros entes públicos	•	•	•	•
4	262 + 266 + 267 + 268 + 221	Outros devedores	•	•	•	•
5	264	Subscritores de capital	•	•	•	•
III		Títulos negociáveis:				
1	1511	Acções em empresas do grupo	•	•	•	•
3	1521	Obrigações e títulos de participação em empresas do grupo	•	•	•	•
3	1512	Acções em empresas associadas	•	•	•	•
3	1522	Obrigações e títulos de participação em empresas associadas	•	•	•	•
3	1513 + 1523 + 153/9	Outros títulos negociáveis	•	•	•	•
3	18	Outras aplicações de tesouraria	•	•	•	•
IV		Depósitos bancários e caixa:				
	12 + 13 + 14	Depósitos bancários	•		•	•
	11	Caixa	•		•	•
E		Acréscimos e diferimentos:				
	271	Acréscimos de proveitos	•		•	•
	272	Custos diferidos	•		•	•
		Total de amortizações		•		
		Total de provisões		•		
		Total do activo	•	•	•	•

[1] Em conformidade com o artigo 9.º da 4.ª Directiva da CE.
[2] A desenvolver, segundo as rubricas existentes no «curto prazo», atendendo às previsões de cobrança ou exigibilidade da dívida ou de parte dela, a mais de um ano.
Abreviaturas: AB activo bruto, AP amortizações e provisões acumuladas, AL activo líquido.

Table 8.1 (b) English translation (*continued*)

EC[1] codes	Assets	Year n GA	Year n DP	Year n NA	Year n−1 NA
II	Medium and long-term receivables[2]	•	•	•	•
II	Short-term receivables				
1	Trade accounts receivable – current account	•	•	•	•
1	Trade accounts receivable – bills receivable	•	•	•	•
1	Doubtful debtors	•	•	•	•
2	Group companies	•	•	•	•
3	Other participations	•	•	•	•
4	Other shareholders and partners	•	•	•	•
4	Advances to suppliers	•		•	•
4	Advances to suppliers of fixed assets	•		•	•
4	State and other public entities	•	•	•	•
4	Other debtors	•	•	•	•
5	Share and quota subscribers	•	•	•	•
III	Negotiable securities				
1	Shares in group companies	•	•	•	•
3	Bonds in group companies	•	•	•	•
3	Shares in associated companies	•	•	•	•
3	Bonds in associated companies	•	•	•	•
3	Other negotiable securities	•	•	•	•
3	Other short-term investments	•	•	•	•
IV	Cash and bank balances				
	Bank deposits	•		•	•
	Cash	•		•	•
E	Accruals and deferrals				
	Accrued income	•		•	•
	Deferred expenses	•		•	•
	Total accumulated depreciation		•		
	Total provisions		•		
	Total assets	•	•	•	•

Notes:
[1] EC Fourth Directive, article 9.
[2] Broken down like the short-term receivables.
GA gross assets, *DP* depreciation and provisions, *NA* net assets.

Table 8.1 (a) Portuguese original (*continued*)

Códigos das contas		Capital próprio e passivo	Exercícios	
CE[1]	POC		N	N − 1
A		Capital próprio:		
I	51	Capital	+ ●	+ ●
	521	Acções (quotas) próprias – Valor nominal	− ●	− ●
	522	Acções (quotas) próprias – Descontos e prémios	± ●	± ●
	53	Prestações suplementares	+ ●	+ ●
II	54	Prémios de emissão de acções (quotas)	+ ●	+ ●
III	55	Ajustamentos de partes de capital em filiais e associadas	± ●	± ●
	56	Reservas de reavaliação	+ ●	+ ●
IV		Reservas:		
1/2	571	Reservas legais	+ ●	+ ●
3	572	Reservas estatutárias	+ ●	+ ●
4	573	Reservas contratuais	+ ●	+ ●
4	574 a 579	Outras reservas	+ ●	+ ●
V	59	Resultados transitados	± ●	± ●
		Subtotal	± ●	± ●
VI	88	Resultado líquido do exercício	± ●	± ●
	89	Dividendos antecipados	− ●	− ●
		Total do capital próprio	± ●	± ●
		Passivo:		
B		Provisões para riscos e encargos:		
1	291	Provisões para pensões	●	●
2	292	Provisões para impostos	●	●
3	293/8	Outras provisões para riscos e encargos	●	●
			●	●
C		Dívidas a terceiros – Médio e longo prazo[2]	●	●
C		Dívidas a terceiros – Curto prazo:		
1		Empréstimos por obrigações:		
	2321	Convertíveis	●	●
	2322	Não convertíveis	●	●
1	233	Empréstimos por títulos de participação	●	●
2	231 + 12	Dívidas a instituições de crédito	●	●
3	269	Adiantamentos por conta de vendas	●	●
4	221	Fornecedores, c/c	●	●
4	228	Fornecedores – Facturas em recepção e conferência	●	●
5	222	Fornecedores – Títulos a pagar	●	●
5	2612	Fornecedores de imobilizado – Títulos a pagar	●	●
6	252	Empresas do grupo	●	●
7	253 + 254	Empresas participadas e participantes	●	●
8	251 + 255	Outros accionistas (sócios)	●	●
8	219	Adiantamentos de clientes	●	●
8	239	Outros empréstimos obtidos	●	●
8	2611	Fornecedores de imobilizado, c/c	●	●
8	24	Estado e outros entes públicos	●	●

Table 8.1 (b) English translation (*continued*)

EC[1] codes	Net equity and liabilities		Year	
			n	n − 1
A	Net equity			
I	Capital		+ ●	+ ●
	Own shares (quotas) − nominal value		− ●	− ●
	Own shares (quotas) − premiums and discounts		± ●	± ●
	Supplementary capital		+ ●	+ ●
II	Share issue premiums (quotas)		+ ●	+ ●
III	Net equity adjustments in group and associated companies		± ●	± ●
	Revaluation reserves		+ ●	+ ●
IV	Reserves			
1/2	Legal reserves		+ ●	+ ●
3	Statutory reserves		+ ●	+ ●
4	Contractual reserves		+ ●	+ ●
4	Other reserves		+ ●	+ ●
V	Past years' results		± ●	± ●
		Subtotal	± ●	± ●
VI	After tax result of the year		± ●	± ●
	Anticipated dividends		− ●	− ●
		Total net equity	± ●	± ●
	Liabilities			
B	Provisions for risks and charges			
1	Provisions for pensions		●	●
2	Provisions for taxes		●	●
3	Provisions for other risks and charges		●	●
			●	●
C	Medium and long-term liabilities[2]		●	●
C	Short-term liabilities			
1	Bond borrowing			
	Convertible bonds		●	●
	Non-convertible bonds		●	●
1	Participating bond borrowing		●	●
2	Debits to credit institutions		●	●
3	Advances to customers		●	●
4	Suppliers − current accounts		●	●
4	Suppliers − invoices outstanding		●	●
5	Suppliers − bills payable		●	●
5	Accounts payable to fixed asset suppliers − bills		●	●
6	Group companies		●	●
7	Other participations and participating companies		●	●
8	Other shareholders and quotaholders		●	●
8	Advances from customers		●	●
8	Other borrowing		●	●
8	Suppliers of fixed assets − current accounts		●	●
8	State and other public entities		●	●

Table 8.1 (a) Portuguese original (*continued*)

| Códigos das contas | | | Exercícios | | | |
| | | | N | | | N − 1 |
CE¹	POC	Capital próprio e passivo	AB	AP	AL	AL
	$8 \left\{ \begin{array}{c} 262 + 263 + 264 + \\ + 265 + 267 + 268 + 211 \end{array} \right\}$	Outros credores		•		•
				•		•
D		Acréscimos e diferimentos:				
	273	Acréscimos de custos		•		•
	274	Proveitos diferidos		•		•
				•		•
		Total do passivo		•		•
		Total do capital próprio e do passivo		•		•

Table 8.1 (b) English translation (*continued*)

	Net equity and liabilities	Year	
		n	*n − 1*
	8 Other creditors	●	●
D	Accruals and deferrals		
	Cost accruals	●	●
	Deferred income	●	●
		●	●
	Total liabilities	●	●
	Total net equity and liabilities	●	●

Table 8.2 Abridged balance sheet (a) Portuguese original (*balanço sintético*)

Códigos das contas		Activo	Exercícios			
			N			N − 1
CE	POC		AB	AP	AL	AL
C		Imobilizado:				
I	43 + 441/6 + 449	Imobilizações incorpóreas	•	•	•	•
II	42 + 441/6 + 448	Imobilizações corpóreas	•	•	•	•
III	41 + 441/6 + 447	Investimentos financeiros	•	•	•	•
			−	−	−	−
D		Circulante:				
I	32 a 37	Existências	•		•	•
II	21 + 22 + 24 + 25 + 26	Dívidas de terceiros:				
		Médio e longo prazo	•		•	•
		Curto prazo	•		•	•
III	15 + 18	Títulos negociáveis	•	•	•	•
IV	11 a 14	Depósitos bancários e caixa	•		•	•
			−	−	−	−
E	27	Acréscimos e diferimentos	•		•	•
			−	−	−	
		Total do activo	•	•	•	•

Capital próprio e passivo	Códigos das contas		Exercícios	
	CE	POC	N	N − 1
Capital próprio:	A			
Capital	I	51	•	•
Prémios de emissão de acções (quotas)	II	54	•	•
Reservas de reavaliação	III	56	•	•
Reservas legais	IV	571	±	±
Restantes reservas e outros capitais próprios		52 + 53 + 55 + 572/9	±	±
Resultados transitados	V	59	±	±
Subtotal				
Resultado líquido do exercício	VI	88	±	±
Dividendos antecipados		89	−	−
Total do capital próprio			±	±
Passivo:				
Provisões para riscos e encargos	B	29	•	•
Dívidas a terceiros:	C	21 + 22 + 23 + 24		
Médio e longo prazo		+ 25 + 26	•	•
Curto prazo			•	•
Acréscimos e diferimentos	D	27	•	•
			−	−
Total do passivo			•	•
			−	−
Total do capital próprio e do passivo			•	•

Note: *AB* activo bruto, *AP* amortizações e provisões, *AL* activo líquido.

Table 8.2 Abridged balance sheet (b) English translation

Assets

EC codes	Assets	Year n GA	DP	NA	Year n−1 NA
C	Fixed assets:				
I	Intangible fixed assets	•	−	•	•
II	Tangible fixed assets	•	−	•	•
III	Investments	•	−	•	•
D	Current assets:				
I	Inventories	•		•	•
II	Receivables:				
	Medium and long-term	••		••	••
	Short-term	•••	−	•••	•••
III	Negotiable securities	•	−	•	•
IV	Cash and bank balances	•	−	•	•
E	Accruals and deferrals	•		•	•
	Total assets	•	•	•	•

Net equity and liabilities

EC codes	Net equity and liabilities	Year n	Year n−1
A	Net equity:		
I	Capital	•	•
II	Shares (quotas) issued premiums	•	•
III	Revaluation reserves	•	•
IV	Legal reserves	•	•
	Other reserves	•	•
V	Past year's results	•	•
		(±)	(±)
VI	After-tax result of the year	(−)	(−)
	Anticipated dividends	(±)	(±)
	Total net equity		
B	Liabilities:		
	Provisions for risks and charges	••	••
		−	−
C	Liabilities:		
	Medium and long-term	••	••
	Short-term	•	•
D	Accruals and deferrals	•	•
		−	−
	Total liabilities	•	•
	Total net equity and liabilities	•	•

Note. GA gross assets, DP depreciation and provisions, NA net assets.

Table 8.3 Detailed profit and loss account (a) Portuguese original (*demonstração dos resultados*)

Códigos das contas			Exercícios			
CE	POC		N		N − 1	
A		**Custos e perdas**				
2(a)	61	Custo das mercadorias vendidas e das matérias consumidas:				
		Meradorias	•		•	
		Matérias	•	•	•	•
2(b)	62	Fornecimentos e serviços externos		•		•
3		Custos com o pessoal:				
3(a)	641 + 642	Remunerações	•		•	
3(b)		Encargos sociais:				
	643 + 644	Pensões	•		•	
	645/8	Outros	•	•	•	•
4(a)	66	Amortizações do imobilizado corpóreo e incorpóreo	•		•	
4(b)	67	Provisões	•	•	•	•
5	63	Impostos	•		•	
5	65	Outros custos e perdas operacionais	•	•	•	•
		(*A*)		•		•
6	682	Perdas em empresas do grupo e associadas		•		•
6	683 + 684	Amortizações e provisões de aplicações e investimentos financeiros	•		•	
7		Juros e custos similares:				
		Relativos a empresas do grupo	•		•	
		Outros	•	•	•	•
		(*C*)		•		•
10	69	Custos e perdas extraordinários		•		•
		(*E*)		•		•
8 + 11	86	Imposto sobre o rendimento do exercício		•		•
		(*G*)		•		•
13	88	Resultado líquido do exercício		± •		± •
				•		•
B		**Proveitos e ganhos**				
1	71	Vendas:				
		Mercadorias	•		•	
		Produtos	•		•	
1	72	Prestações de serviços	•	•	•	•
2		Variação da produção		± •		± •
3	75	Trabalhos para a própria empresa		•		•
4	73	Proveitos suplementares	•		•	
4	74	Subsídios à exploração	•		•	
4	76	Outros proveitos e ganhos operacionais	•	•	•	•

Table 8.3 Detailed profit and loss account (b) English translation

EC accounts code		Year n		Year n − 1	
A	**Expenses and losses**				
2(a)	Costs of goods sold and materials consumed:				
	Goods	•		•	
	Materials	•	•	•	•
2(b)	External supplies and services		•		•
3	Personnel expenses:				
3(a)	Wages and salaries	•		•	
3(b)	Social security costs:				
	Pension costs	•		•	
	Other	•	•	•	•
4(a)	Depreciation of intangible and tangible fixed assets	•		•	
4(b)	Provisions	•	•	•	•
5	Taxes	•		•	
5	Other operating costs	•	•	•	•
	(A)		•		•
6	Losses in group and associated companies		•		•
6	Depreciation and provisions for investments	•		•	
7	Interest expenses and similar costs:				
	Group and associated companies	•		•	
	Other	•	•	•	•
	(C)		•		•
10	Extraordinary costs and losses		•		•
	(E)		•		•
8 + 11	Income tax of the year		•		•
	(G)		•		•
13	Net result for the year		± •		± •
			•		•
B	**Revenues and gains**				
1	Sales:				
	Goods	•		•	
	Products	•		•	
1	Services	•	•	•	•
2	Increase or decrease in stocks of finished products and work in progress		± •		± •
3	Work performed by the undertaking for its own purposes		•		•
4	Supplementary revenues	•		•	
4	Subventions received	•		•	
4	Other operating revenues	•	•	•	•

Table 8.3 (a) Portuguese original (*continued*)

Códigos das contas			Exercícios			
CE	POC		N		N − 1	
		(B)		•		•
5	782	Ganhos em empresas do grupo e associadas	•		•	
5	784	Rendimentos de participações de capital	•		•	
6		Rendimentos de títulos negociáveis e de outras aplicações financeiras:				
		Relativos a empresas do grupo	•		•	
		Outros	•		•	
7		Outros juros e proveitos similares:				
		Relativos a empresas do grupo	•		•	
		Outros	•	•	•	•
		(D)		•		•
9	79	Proveitos e ganhos extradinários		•		•
		(F)		•		•

Resumo:

Resultados operacionais: $(B) - (A) =$			•	•
Resultados financeiros: $(D - B) - (C - A) =$			•	•
Resultados correntes: $(D) - (C) =$			•	•
Resultados antes de impostos: $(F) - (E) =$			•	•
Resultado líquido do exercício: $(F) - (G) =$			•	•

throughout Europe, the balance sheet items are ordered from lower to higher liquidity on the assets side and from lower to higher claimability on the liabilities side. Accordingly, the assets side begins with tangible and intangible fixed assets and ends up with cash, whereas the liabilities side begins with shareholders' equity and ends with current liabilities.

The balance sheet and the income statement prescribed in the Official Accounting Plan largely conform to Portuguese accounting tradition. Only the horizontal layout is permissible for the balance sheet. Although the vertical layout, by function, may be used for the income statement, the option is merely additional to, and does not supersede, the horizontal layout organized according to the nature of the expenses.

The notes to the accounts (in the annex, or appendix) constitute an extensive document in themselves, with almost fifty notes. They include not only explanations of the accounting rules and valuation methods used but also supplementary accounting statements (regarding financial costs and income, extraordinary items, statements of movements on fixed assets or and on the equity, etc.) and detailed analyses of particular account headings.

With regard to the content of the balance sheet, the POC gives a highly detailed exemplar, in which most lines of the balance sheet correspond to a single two or three-digit account code within the national Chart of Accounts. There is also a summary

Table 8.3 (b) English translation (*continued*)

EC accounts code		Year	
		n	*n − 1*
	(B)	●	●
5	Gains in group and associated companies	●	●
5	Dividends on shares and profits from undertakings	●	●
6	Income from negotiable securities and other short-term investments:		
	From group and associated companies	●	●
	Other	●	●
7	Other financial revenues:		
	From group and associated companies	●	●
	Other	● ● ●	● ●
	(D)	●	●
9	Extraordinary revenues and gains	●	●
	(F)	●	●
	Summary:		
	Operating result: $(B) - (A) =$	●	●
	Financial result: $(D - B) - (C - A) =$	●	●
	Current result: $(D) - (C) =$	●	●
	Result before tax: $(F) - (E) =$	●	●
	After-tax result for the year: $(F) - (G) =$	●	●

version, in which most lines correspond to a combination of account codes and which may be used by smaller enterprises, i.e. those which during the last two successive years have not exceeded two out of the following three size criteria (from the Companies Act):

50 employees
PTE 370,000,000 turnover
PTE 180,000,000 total assets

Table 8.1 illustrates the detailed format, with the description of line items in Portuguese and English. It will be noticed that three columns are provided for the current year's balance sheet figures: these are for the gross values of assets, provisions for depreciation of amortization, and net values, respectively.

Comparative figures must be presented for the preceding year and must be restated to conform with the current year presentation, which may require adjustment to the preceding year's financial statements. Such may be the case when, for example, there has been a change in the accounting method or in the name of the account or if the grouping of the accounts has been changed during the year.

Accounts receivable and payable between the same parties must not be offset in the balance sheet. Also, if a given account has both short-term and long-term maturities, these must be separated in the balance sheet for presentation purposes, although the

Table 8.4 Abridged profit and loss account (a) Portuguese original (*demonstração dos resultados*)

Códigos das contas			Exercícios			
CE	POC		N		N − 1	
A		**Custos e perdas**				
2(a)	61	Custo das mercadorias vendidas e das matérias consumidas	•		•	
2(b)	62	Fornecimentos e serviços externos	•	•	•	•
3		Custos com o pessoal:				
3(a)	641 + 642	Remunerações	•		•	
3(b)	643 a 648	Encargos sociais[1]	•	•	•	•
4(a)	66	Amortizações do imobilizado corpóreo e incorpóreo	•		•	
4(b)	67	Provisões	•	•	•	•
5	63	Impostos	•		•	
5	65	Outros custos e perdas operacionais	•	•	•	•
		(*A*)		•		•
6	683 + 684	Amortizações e provisões de aplicações e investimentos financeiros	•		•	
7		Juros e custos similares	•	•	•	•
		(*C*)		•		•
10	69	Custos e perdas extraordinários		•		•
		(*E*)		•		•
8 + 11	86	Imposto sobre o rendimento do exercício		•		•
		(*G*)		•		•
13	88	Resultado líquido do exercício		± •		± •
				•		•
B		**Proveitos e ganhos**				
1	71 + 72	Vendas e prestações de serviços		•		•
2		Variação da produção		± •		± •
3	75	Trabalhos para a própria empresa		•		•
4	74	Subsídios à exploração	•		•	
4	73 + 76	Outros proveitos e ganhos operacionais	•	•	•	•
		(*B*)		•		•
5	784	Rendimentos de participações de capital	•		•	
6		Rendimentos de títulos negociáveis e de outras aplicações financeiras	•		•	
7		Outros juros e proveitos similares	•	•	•	•
		(*D*)		•		•
9	79	Proveitos e ganhos extradinários		•		•
		(*F*)		•		•

Resumo:

Resultados operacionais: (*B*) − (*A*) =   • •
Resultados financeiros: (*D* − *B*) − (*C* − *A*) =   • •
Resultados correntes: (*D*) − (*C*) =   • •
Resultados antes de impostos: (*F*) − (*E*) =   • •
Resultado líquido do exercício: (*F*) − (*G*) =   • •

[1] Evidenciar os custos de 'Pensões', quando for caso disso.

Table 8.4 Abridged profit and loss account (b) English translation

		Year	
EC codes		*n*	*n − 1*
A	**Expenses and losses**		
2(a)	Costs of goods sold and materials consumed	•	•
2(b)	External supplies and services	• • •	• •
3	Personnel expenses:		
3(a)	Wages and salaries	•	•
3(b)	Social security and pension costs[1]	• • •	• •
4(a)	Depreciation of intangible and tangible fixed assets	•	•
4(b)	Provisions	• • •	• •
5	Taxes	•	•
5	Other operating costs	• • • •	• • • •
	(A)	•	•
6	Depreciation and provisions for investments	•	•
7	Interest expenses and similar costs	• • • •	• • • •
	(C)	•	•
10	Extraordinary costs and losses	•	•
	(E)	•	•
8 + 11	Income tax of the period	•	•
	(G)	•	•
13	Net result for the period	± •	± •
		•	•
B	**Revenues and gains**		
1	Sales and services	•	•
2	Increase or decrease in stocks of finished products and work in progress	± •	± •
3	Work performed by the undertaking for its own purposes	•	•
4	Subventions received	• •	•
4	Other operating revenues	• • • •	• • • •
	(B)	•	•
5	Dividends on shares and profits from undertakings	•	•
6	Income from negotiable securities and other short-term investments	•	
7	Other financial revenues	• • • •	• • • •
	(D)	•	•
9	Extraordinary revenues and gains	•	•
	(F)	•	•

Summary:

	n	*n − 1*
Operating result: $(B) − (A) =$	•	•
Financial result: $(D − B) − (C − A) =$	•	•
Current result: $(D) − (C) =$	•	•
Result before tax: $(F) − (E) =$	•	•
Net result for the period: $(F) − (G) =$	•	•

[1] Pension costs to be broken down as necessary.

Table 8.5 Income balances

	Operating income (loss)
+	Financial income (loss)
=	Ordinary income (loss)
±	Extraordinary income (loss)
=	Income (loss) before taxes
+	Corporate income tax
=	Income (loss) of the year

Table 8.6 Vertical layout of profit and loss account, by function (a) Portuguese original (*demonstração dos resultados por funções*)

		Exercícios	
		N	*N − 1*
1	Vendas e prestações de serviços	●	●
2	Custo das vendas e prestações de serviços	− ●	− ●
3	Resultados brutos	●	●
4	Custos de distribuição	− ●	− ●
5	Custos administrativos	− ●	− ●
6	Outros proveitos operacionais	●	●
	Resultados operacionais	●	●
7	Rendimentos de participações de capital:		
	Relativos a empresas interligadas	●	●
	Relativos a outras empresas	●	●
8	Rendimentos de títulos negociáveis e de outras aplicações financeiras:		
	Relativos a empresas interligadas	●	●
	Outros	●	●
9	Outros juros e proveitos similares:		
	Relativos a empresas interligadas	●	●
	Outros	●	●
10	Amortizações e provisões de aplicações e investimentos financeiros	− ●	− ●
11	Juros e custos similares:		
	Relativos a empresas interligadas	− ●	− ●
	Outros	− ●	− ●
	Resultados correntes	●	●
14	Proveitos e ganhos extraordinários	●	●
15	Custos e perdas extraordinários	− ●	− ●
	Resultados antes de impostos	●	●
	Imposto sobre o rendimento do exercício	− ●	− ●
19	Resultado liquido do exercício	●	●

notes on the accounts may provide further information on those items which have been subdivided between short-term and long-term.

The abridged format of the balance sheet is shown in Table 8.2.

3 PROFIT AND LOSS STATEMENT LAYOUT AND CONTENT

Of the four formats offered by the Fourth Directive, the POC opts for the horizontal format classified by the nature of the items (according to article 24), with expenses and losses on the left-hand side and revenues and income for the year on the right, as shown in Table 8.3. As with the balance sheet, so far as content is concerned the full version is relatively detailed, and smaller enterprises may produce an abridged version, presented

Table 8.6 Vertical layout of profit and loss account, by function (b) English translation

		Year	
		n	*n − 1*
1	Sales and services rendered	•	•
2	Costs of sales and services rendered	− •	− •
3	Gross result	•	•
4	Distribution costs	− •	− •
5	Administrative costs	− •	− •
6	Other operating revenues	•	•
	Operating result	•	•
7	Income from undertakings:		
	From group and associated companies	•	•
	From other participations	•	•
8	Income from short-term investments:		
	From group and associated companies	•	•
	Other	•	•
9	Other interest received and similar revenues		
	From group and associated companies	•	•
	Other	•	•
10	Depreciation and provisions for investments	− •	− •
11	Interest and similar expenses:		
	From group and associated companies	− •	− •
	Other	− •	− •
	Current result	•	•
14	Extraordinary revenues and gains	•	•
15	Extraordinary costs and losses	− •	− •
	Result before income tax	•	•
	Income tax of the year	− •	− •
19	Net result of the year	•	•

in Table 8.4. However, there is much less difference between the amount of detail in the two versions than in the case of the balance sheet.

As shown in Tables 8.3 and 8.4, the profit and loss account format requires intermediate income balances to be calculated and presented. These balances are calculated in accordance with the step-by-step approach to income calculation, summarized in Table 8.5. It should be noted that certain items in the standard profit and loss account may be negative, namely variation of inventories and income for the year (if a loss).

'Cost of goods sold and materials consumed' includes stock balances of raw materials, other consumables and merchandise. They are shown on the left-hand side, under costs. Valuation is according to acquisition cost.

'Increase/decrease in stocks of finished products and work in progress' includes the balances of stocks and work in progress, intermediate goods and finished goods. It is shown on the revenue (right-hand) side. Valuation is according to production cost. Production cost includes raw materials, labour costs, overheads, depreciation, etc.

The POC also provides a vertical format arranged by function, based on that given in the Fourth Directive (article 25). This alternative may be adopted in addition to the required horizontal format but cannot replace it. Table 8.6 shows the vertically organized profit and loss format.

4 THE ANNEX (NOTES TO THE ACCOUNTS)

The annex required by the POC is designed to meet the requirements of the Fourth Directive. It includes a set of information intended to amplify and explain items in the financial statements. The POC stresses that the quality of the financial information given by companies is heavily dependent on the content of the notes.

Containing nearly fifty items as they do, the notes on the accounts are too numerous to list here in detail, but the most significant are those requiring disclosure of:

1 Any departure from the requirement of the POC on exceptional grounds in order to show a true and fair view, and the reasons for such departure.
2 Any items in the balance sheet or profit and loss statement that are not comparable with those of the previous year, with an explanation.
3 The valuation principles and methods of calculating depreciation and provisions.
4 Exchange rates used to translate amounts originally expressed in foreign currency for inclusion in the balance sheet and profit and loss statement.
5 Accounting methods used in order to obtain tax benefits:

   (a) The use of asset valuation principles different from those referred to above.
   (b) Depreciation in excess of that which is economically justified.
   (c) Extraordinary provisions (write-downs) against assets.

6 Situations having an impact on future taxation.
7 Comments on organization costs and research and development costs, and on goodwill and other intangibles if amortized over more than five years.
8 Supplementary schedules of fixed assets, including intangibles, property, plant and equipment, and financial fixed assets.

9 Further information on fixed assets, such as interest capitalized during the year, revaluations, a breakdown by sector of economic activity and other analyses relevant for tax or EC purposes.

10 Assets held under financial leases. (As noted above, assets held under finance leases are not at present capitalized, but will be in the future.)

11 A list of subsidiaries, associated companies and participations in which the parent company holds at least 10 per cent of the capital. (Associated companies and concerns in which a participation is held which are not required to publish their financial statements may be omitted.)

12 Information on investments in other companies included under negotiable securities if these have a carrying value amounting to more than 5 per cent of the working capital of the reporting entity.

13 Analysis of assets held on account of restricted funds, e.g. pension funds.

14 For items of working capital:

   (a) The total difference by category of asset between book value and market value, if it is material.
   (b) In the case of items stated at a book value below the lower of cost and market value, the reasons for this.
   (c) An indication of and the reasons for any extraordinary provisions for decline in value.

15 The global value of inventories belonging to the entity but not in its possession.

16 The global value of doubtful debts for each category of receivables.

17 Details of advances or loans to members of the board of administration, the executive board or the audit board of the company.

5 THE STATEMENT OF THE SOURCES AND APPLICATION OF FUNDS

Under the Official Accounting Plan the statement of the sources and applications of funds, the *mapa de origens e aplicações de fundos*, is not compulsory. Table 8.7 shows in summary form the structure of this statement.

The concept of funds underlying the statement is not equivalent to cash or financial assets and liabilities. It corresponds to the notion of working capital (*fundos circulantes*).

The statement starts with the funds obtained from operations (net profit after tax, plus depreciation and other adjustments for non-funds items), to which are added the other funds obtained (increases in long-term financing and fixed asset sales), and ends with the total funds obtained.

Applications include any loss from operations, dividends, investments in fixed assets or loan repayments. The total application of funds is the sum of all these items.

The net movement in working capital appears as a balancing item, either as a source if it is a decrease or as an application if it is an increase. This movement is analysed by component of working capital in a separate table attached to the statement, as shown in Table 8.8.

The statement does not separately identify sources or applications of funds pertaining to extraordinary operations.

Table 8.7 Statement of the sources and application of funds (a) Portuguese original (*demonstração da origem e da aplicação de fundos*)

Origem dos fundos			Aplicação dos fundos		
Internas:			Distribuições:		
Resultado líquido do exercício	± •		Por aplicação de resultados	•	
Amortizações	•		Por aplicação de reservas[1]	•	•
Variação de provisões	± •	± •		—	
	⎯⎯		Diminuições dos capitais próprios:		
Externas:			Diminuições de capital e de		
Aumentos dos capitais próprios:			prestações suplementares		•
Aumentos de capital e de			Movimentos financeiros a médio e		
prestações suplementares	•		longo prazo:		
Aumentos de prémios de			Aumentos de investimentos		
emissão e de reservas			financeiros[1]	•	
especiais	•		Diminuições das dívidas a terceiros		
Cobertura de prejuízos	•	•	a médio e longo prazo[1]	•	
	⎯⎯		Aumentos das dívidas de terceiros a		
Movimentos financeiros a médio e			médio e longo prazo[1]	•	•
longo prazo:				—	
Diminuições de investimentos					
financeiros[1]	•		Aumentos de imobilizações:		
Diminuições das dívidas de terceiros			Trabalhos da empresa para ela		
a médio e longo prazo[1]	•		própria[1]	•	
Aumentos das dívidas a terceiros a			Aquisição de imobilizações[1]	•	•
médio e longo prazo[1]	•	•		—	
	⎯⎯				
Diminuições de imobilizações:					
Cessão de imobilizações (pelo valor					
contabilístico líquido)[1]	•				
Diminuição dos fundos circulantes	•	Aumento dos fundos circulantes		•
	⎯⎯			⎯⎯	
	•			•	

[1] A desenvolver segundo as rubricas do balanço.

Table 8.8 Statement of movements in working capital

Increase in inventories	•	Decrease in inventories		•
Increase in short-term receivables	•	Decrease in short-term receivables		•
Decrease in short-term liabilities	•	Increase in short-term liabilities		•
Increase in cash and bank balances	•	Decrease in cash and bank balances		•
Decrease in working capital	•	Increase in working capital		•
	⎯			⎯
	•			•

6 OTHER FINANCIAL REPORTS

The accounting practices of Portuguese companies generally conform with the requirements of the Official Accounting Plan, and, accordingly, they only rarely prepare

Table 8.7 Statement of the sources and application of funds (b) English translation

Source of funds				Application of funds		
Internal sources:				Profit distributions and dividends:		
Net profit for the year	± •			Profit allocations	•	
Depreciation	•			Reserve allocations	•	•
Variation of provisions	± •	± •			—	
	—			Decrease in equity capital:		
External sources:				Decrease in issued capital	•	
Increase in equity capital				Medium and long-term movements:		
Increase in issued capital	•			Increase in investments[1]	•	
Increase in share premium				Increase in medium and long-term		
account special reserves	•			debt[1]	•	
Loss offset	•	•		Decrease in medium and long-term		
	—			loans[1]	•	•
					—	
Medium and long-term movements:						
Decrease in investments[1]	•			Increases in tangible fixed assets:		
Decrease in medium and long-term				Self-made[1]	•	
debt[1]	•			Acquisitions[1]	•	•
Increase in medium and long-term					—	
loans[1]	•	•				
	—					
Decrease in tangible fixed assets:						
Fixed assets disposals (net book						
value)[1]	•					
Decrease in working capital	•			Increase in working capital	•	
	—				—	
Total sources of funds	•			*Total applications of funds*	•	

[1] Breakdown according to balance sheet items.

financial statements other than those mentioned above as compulsory. However, certain companies do prepare and disclose other types of financial information, either because of particular requirements or simply because they have decided to do so. Such information often includes interim financial statements. A brief summary follows of some of the main types of information of this sort.

Only listed companies are required to lodge interim statements with the stock exchange twice a year, and most of them comply with the requirement. The statements are usually published.

Apart from those relating to listed companies, no rules about interim statements have been issued for companies in general. Banks and other financial institutions, however, as well as insurance companies, must prepare confidential monthly balance sheets for the Bank of Portugal and the Insurance Institute of Portugal respectively.

Annual reports do not usually include a forecast, although the management report sometimes does. The board of directors is solely responsible for the preparation and disclosure of the forecast. Like the Fourth and Seventh EC Directives, the POC requires sales to be broken down only by type of activity and geographical market area (in note 44). There are no regulations about the identification of market or industry segments or about the treatment of common costs and inter-segment transactions. In some cases companies do in fact reveal such information.

Some public companies include information in their annual report about variations in the share price, the effect of capital increases or bond conversions, and the return on shareholders' investment during the year.

Many companies disclose a series of ratios together with their financial statements and generally also provide comparative three or even five-year data. Since this accounting practice has not been standardized, the companies select widely varying ratios, depending on the industry in which they operate, the information they want or do not want to disclose, etc. The most commonly used ratios include the following:

1   Current ratio.
2   Debt ratio.
3   Margins on sales.
4   Inventory turnover.
5   Receivables collection period.
6   Asset turnover.
7   Return on equity.
8   Return on investment.

These ratios are sometimes compared with those of the industry or sector in which the company operates.

There is a requirement, similar to the French *bilan social*, which applies to companies with more than 100 employees (law 141/85). This report must include information on employment conditions, such as salaries, absenteeism, the age structure of the workforce, their qualifications, the percentage of men and of women employed, fringe benefits, the resources devoted to training, industrial accidents, and general welfare facilities.

Although there is no obligation to disclose value added statements, some companies include a statement in their annual report, expressed either in monetary terms or as a percentage of the turnover of the year. Usually value added is presented gross (including depreciation).

9

Consolidated accounts

1 INTRODUCTION

Until 1991 there was no legal requirement to present consolidated accounts. The law concerned itself only with individual company accounts, although undertakings could include consolidated accounts as supplementary information. The usual practice was to present unconsolidated accounts and to reflect investments at cost.

Preparations were made in 1991 to implement the EC Seventh Directive in Portuguese law, and to this end a set of draft requirements for consolidated financial statements was prepared by a working group of the Accounting Standardization Committee (CNC). These requirements were approved by the general council of the CNC and published in the *Official Journal* on 2 July 1991 (decree law 238/91). This law also includes the requirements of the Seventh Directive regarding the audit and publication of consolidated accounts and those regarding the annual report on group activities. Under it, consolidated accounts are mandatory for financial years beginning on or after 1 January 1991.

It is too early as yet to evaluate the impact of the Seventh Directive. However, it is not unreasonable to see the adoption of the Seventh Directive as a significant achievement for the CNC, considering the difficulties of reconciling in one document the wide variety of opinions and practice regarding consolidated accounts. It is also of great relevance to the business community because of the changes that will be required in corporate reporting practices.

An important contribution of the new law is the requirement that consolidated accounts should give a true and fair view of the group's results and financial position. This perhaps marks a distinct departure from established practice in Portugal, where financial reporting has been heavily influenced by tax considerations and more weight is attached to form than to substance.

Banks and other financial institutions, together with insurance companies are still not yet obliged to prepare consolidated accounts as the relevant EC Directives have yet to be implemented. The law is silent on the subject of consolidated accounts for banks, except as regards Portuguese-based credit institutions with a participation in the credit institutions of other EC countries. The Bank of Portugal and the Insurance Institute of Portugal are in the process of preparing draft legislation covering the group accounts of banks, insurance companies and other financial institutions. The new regime was expected to come into force by the end of 1992.

2 WHO MUST PREPARE CONSOLIDATED ACCOUNTS?

2.1 Scope of application

The scope of application is as laid down in the Seventh Directive. The following types of legal entity must prepare consolidated accounts, subject to criteria stated below:

1 *Sociedades anónimas* (SAs, approximately equivalent to the British PLC).
2 *Sociedades por quotas de responsabilidade limitada* (*Lda*s, private limited companies like a British 'Ltd').
3 *Sociedades em comandita por acções* (SCAs) (Limited partnerships).

State-owned companies and co-operatives are not obliged to present consolidated accounts.

Companies to be consolidated are defined in terms of ability to control or exert a dominant influence at the ordinary annual general meeting, through a majority of votes or through contracts or agreements.

2.2 Exemptions

The size criteria for exemption from the requirement of preparing consolidated accounts are as shown below. A company can be exempted only when it has not exceeded two out of three limits during two successive financial years:

Total assets: PTE 1,500 million.
Total turnover: PTE 3,000 million.
Number of employees: 250.

However, these size exemptions do not apply to groups if one or more of their member companies is listed on any EC stock exchange.

The Seventh Directive's exemption of sub-groups (cf. article 7 of the directive), when it is the ultimate 'parent' company that prepares consolidated accounts, also applies, subject to the same condition as to their not being listed on an EC stock exchange.

2.3 Exclusions

As required by the Seventh Directive, subsidiaries *must* be excluded from consolidation if their activities are of such a different nature from those of the rest of the group that their inclusion would militate against a true and fair view.

Following the directive, subsidiaries *may* be excluded on grounds of immateriality. A further optional exclusion exists in the case of subsidiaries in foreign countries over which the group's control is restricted by the policies of the governments of those countries. A subsidiary may also be excluded from consolidation if it is impossible to obtain any accounts from it without disproportionate expense or undue delay. Subsidiaries may also be excluded if the interest in them is held on a short-term basis only (temporary control).

2.4 Changes in the scope of the consolidation

If the composition of the undertakings included in the consolidation has changed significantly in the course of a financial year, additional information must be given (either in the balance sheet or in the notes on the accounts) in order to provide the necessary comparability.

3 HOW SHOULD CONSOLIDATED ACCOUNTS BE PREPARED?
3.1 Object of consolidated accounts

The object of group accounts is to give a true and fair view (*imagem verdadeira e apropriada*) of the assets, liabilities, financial position and profit or loss of the undertakings included in the consolidation, taken as a whole. In order to achieve this object, the methods and procedures of consolidation must be applied consistently from one financial year to the next.

When the effects of failure to comply are not material to the presentation of a true and fair view, it is not necessary to:

1   Consolidate the accounts of a subsidiary which is not of material importance to the undertaking. (However, if two or more immaterial subsidiaries become material in aggregate, they must be consolidated.)
2   Eliminate immaterial inter-company accounts, transactions or profits.
3   Apply uniform accounting valuation principles if the difference in results is immaterial.
4   Apply the equity method to account for an investment in an associated undertaking which is not of material importance.

The notes on the accounts should be used to disclose information related to this object.

3.2 Date of consolidated accounts

The group accounts should be drawn up at the same date as the annual accounts of the parent undertaking, except when another date may be preferable in order to take account of the largest number or the most important of the undertakings included in the consolidation. Where use is made of this derogation, the fact must be disclosed in the notes on the consolidated accounts together with the reasons.

Where an undertaking's balance sheet date precedes the consolidated balance sheet date by more than three months, that undertaking must be consolidated on the basis of interim accounts drawn up as of the consolidated balance sheet date.

3.3 Consolidation methods

The full or global method is the rule in the case of subsidiaries (*afiliadas*). This is the line-by-line method, with assets, liabilities, income and expense being included in full and with minority interests shown where appropriate. No option allowing the use of the 'merger' or 'pooling of interests' method was included in the law. Associated companies (*associadas*), as well as some excluded subsidiary companies, should be consolidated using the equity method.

Joint ventures (those jointly controlled) may be brought in by the equity method or by proportional consolidation. The latter method involves consolidating the appropriate proportion of the joint venture on a line-by-line basis.

4 SUBSIDIARY COMPANIES

4.1 Valuation criteria

These should conform to the criteria laid down by the POC and must be the same as those used in the annual accounts of the parent undertaking. If necessary, consolidating adjustments should be made to the figures of companies being consolidated in order to meet these criteria.

The assets and liabilities, the income and the expenditure of undertakings included in a consolidation must be incorporated in full in the consolidated balance sheet and the consolidated profit and loss account, respectively.

4.2 Eliminations

The POC, following article 26 of the Seventh Directive, requires elimination of:

1   Debts and claims between undertakings included in the consolidation.
2   Income and expenses relating to transactions between those undertakings.
3   Profits and losses from such transactions included in the book values of assets.

The prudence principle applies whenever a transaction has been concluded under normal market conditions. Also, derogation from the need to eliminate may be accepted if elimination would involve undue expense or if the transaction giving rise to the profit or loss originated outside the group.

4.3 Presentation of minority interests

The amount attributable to shares in subsidiary undertakings included in the consolidation held by persons other than undertakings included in the consolidation must be shown in the consolidated balance sheet as a separate item under the heading 'Interesses minoritários', to appear between liabilities and equity capital. The amount of any profit or loss attributable to them has to be shown in the consolidated profit and loss account as a separate item under the heading 'Interesses minoritários'.

The POC does not mention the presentation of minority interests in cases where accumulated losses become so large that the total of the capital and reserves of the subsidiary undertaking becomes a deficit amount.

4.4 Goodwill

Accounting for goodwill is based on the acquisition value, as described below. Goodwill is calculated in a two-stage process. The investment in the subsidiary is set off against the group's share of the book value of its net assets at the date of acquisition, then any difference is allocated to individual assets and liabilities up to their fair values. Any remaining difference is goodwill. This can be capitalized and then depreciated over up to five years (or over its useful life if longer). Negative goodwill is treated as a reserve or as a provision for future losses.

When consolidated accounts are first prepared for a group which has already been in existence for some time the amount of 'pre-acquisition' capital and reserves of subsidiary undertakings may be taken as the amount at the date of the first consolidation rather than as at the date of the original acquisition. However, this needs to be explained in a note.

Where goodwill corresponds to a positive consolidation difference which arose before the date of the first consolidated accounts, the goodwill must be written off systematically over a limited period of no more than five years as from the date of the first consolidated accounts drawn up in accordance with the law.

Where goodwill corresponds to a negative consolidation difference it will not be imputed to the profit and loss account unless the 'prudence principle' so requires.

4.5 Tax differences

The POC requires adjustments in the consolidated accounts for valuations or charges in individual companies' accounts that result purely from the use of tax rules.

Account must be taken in the consolidated financial statements of any difference arising on consolidation between the tax chargeable for the financial year and for the preceding financial years, and the amount of tax paid or payable in respect of those years.

5 ASSOCIATED COMPANIES

Associated companies are defined as those over which the group has significant influence, which is presumed to be the case where the power exists to exercise 20 per cent or more of the votes at the annual general meeting. Such participating interests should be shown in the consolidated balance sheet as a separate item with an appropriate heading.

Participating interests should be shown in the consolidated balance sheet valued by the equity method. When the equity method is being used for the first time the participating interest should be shown in the consolidated balance sheet either:

1   At its book value, calculated in accordance with the valuation rules laid down in the Fourth Directive. The difference between that value and the amount corresponding to the proportion of capital and reserves represented by that participating interest must be disclosed separately in the notes on the accounts, or
2   At an amount corresponding to the proportion of the associated undertaking's capital and reserves represented by that participating interest. The difference between that amount and the book value calculated in accordance with the valuation rules laid down in the Fourth Directive should be disclosed separately in the consolidated balance sheet.

The difference should be calculated as at:

a) *Participations which were acquired before the first year of consolidation*: calculation as at the beginning of the first year of group accounts (date at which the equity method is first used). The difference is always presented in the equity on the balance sheet, under the heading *Ajustamentos de transição*. Some argue that the positive part of the difference may not be depreciated. Separation between positive and negative differences is only shown in the notes to the accounts.
b) *Participations which were acquired during or after the first year of consolidation*: calculation as at the date of acquisition. Positive differences are presented on the assets side of the balance sheet (as an intangible fixed asset) under the heading *Diferenças de consolidação*, and may be depreciated on a five yearly basis. For depreciation over a longer period, explanation must be given in the notes to the group accounts. The depreciation for the year is a cost to be included in the group

income statement. Negative differences are presented in the consolidated balance sheet under the heading *Diferenças de consolidação*. Past years' depreciation of positive differences are deducted from the section *Diferenças de consolidação*.

Where an associated undertaking's assets or liabilities have been valued by methods other than those used for consolidation, they may, for the purpose of calculating the difference mentioned, be revalued by the methods used for consolidation. Such a revaluation must be carried out unless there is good reason otherwise. Where no such revaluation has been carried out, the fact must be disclosed in the notes on the accounts.

The book value referred to in (1) above, or the amount corresponding to the proportion of the associated undertaking's capital and reserves referred to in paragraph (2) above, should be increased or reduced by the amount of any variation which has taken place during the financial year in the proportion of the associated undertaking's capital and reserves represented by that participating interest; it should be reduced by the amount of the dividends relating to that participating interest.

In so far as the positive difference referred to above cannot be related to any category of assets or liabilities it should be dealt with in the same way as goodwill (see section 4.4 above).

The proportion of the profit or loss of the associated undertaking attributable to such a participating interest should be shown in the consolidated profit and loss account as a separate item under an appropriate heading.

The eliminations referred to in section 4.2 above must be effected in so far as the facts are known or can be ascertained.

Where an associated undertaking draws up consolidated accounts, the foregoing provisions apply to the capital and reserves shown in such consolidated accounts.

6 PROPORTIONAL CONSOLIDATION

According to the POC, the method of proportional consolidation may be used if an undertaking included in the consolidated accounts manages another undertaking in conjunction with one or more undertakings that are not represented in the consolidated accounts. In that case the inclusion of the jointly managed undertaking in the consolidated accounts may be in proportion to the rights in its capital held by the undertaking that is included in the consolidated accounts.

Points 4.1–5 apply, *mutatis mutandis*, to the proportional consolidation but the equity method does not apply if the undertaking proportionally consolidated is an associated undertaking, as defined in section 5 above.

7 FOREIGN UNDERTAKINGS

The POC only requires disclosure of the method used in the translation of foreign currency transactions, both for individual accounts and for consolidated accounts. Of course, the method should be followed consistently from year to year.

The notes on the accounts must set out information about the valuation methods applied to the various items in the annual accounts as well as the methods employed in

Table 9.1 Consolidated balance sheet (a) Portuguese original (*balanço consolidado*)

			Exercícios	
		N		N − 1
Activo	AB	AP	AL	AL
Immobilizado:				
Imobilizações incorpóreas:				
Despesas de instalação	●	●	●	●
Despesas de investigação e desenvolvimento	●	●	●	●
Propriedade industrial e outros direitos	●	●	●	●
Trespasses	●	●	●	●
Imobilizações em curso	●		●	●
Adiantamentos por conta de imobilizações incorpóreas	●		●	●
Diferenças de consolidação	●	●	●	●
	—	—	—	—
Imobilizacões corpóreas:				
Terrenos e recursos naturais	●	●	●	●
Edifícios e outras construções	●	●	●	●
Equipamento básico	●	●	●	●
Equipamento de transporte	●	●	●	●
Ferramentas e utensílios	●	●	●	●
Equipamento administrativo	●	●	●	●
Taras e vasilhame	●	●	●	●
Outras imobilizações corpóreas	●	●	●	●
Imobilizações em curso	●		●	●
Adiantamentos por conta de imobilizações corpóreas	●	●	●	●
	—	—	—	—
Investimentos financeiros:				
Partes de capital em empresas associadas	●	●	●	●
Empréstimos a empresas associadas	●	●	●	●
Partes de capital em outras empresas participadas	●	●	●	●
Empréstimos a outras empresas participadas	●	●	●	●
Títulos e outras aplicações financeiras	●	●	●	●
Outros empréstimos concedidos	●		●	●
Imobilizações em curso	●		●	●
Adiantamentos por conta de investimentos financeiros	●	●	●	●
	—	—	—	—
Circulante:				
Existências:				
Matérias-primas, subsidiárias e de consumo	●	●	●	●
Produtos e trabalhos em curso	●	●	●	●
Subprodutos, desperdícios, resíduos e refugos	●	●	●	●
Produtos acabados e intermédios	●	●	●	●
Mercadorias	●		●	●
Adiantamentos por conta de compras	●	●	●	●
	—	—	—	—
Dívidas de terceiros – Médio e longo prazo	●	●	●	●
	—	—	—	—
Dívidas de terceiros – Curto prazo:				
Clientes, c/c	●	●	●	●
Clientes – Títulos a receber	●	●	●	●
Clientes de cobrança duvidosa	●	●	●	●
Empresas associadas	●	●	●	●
Empresas participadas e participantes	●	●	●	●

Table 9.1 Consolidated balance sheet (b) English translation

	Year			
	n			*n − 1*
Assets	GA	DP	NA	NA
Fixed assets:				
Intangible fixed assets:				
Formation expenses	•	•	•	•
Research and development expenses	•	•	•	•
Industrial property and other rights	•	•	•	•
Goodwill (excluding goodwill on consolidation)	•	•	•	•
Expenses in progress	•		•	•
Advances to suppliers	•		•	•
Goodwill on consolidation	•	•	•	•
	—	—	—	—
Tangible fixed assets:				
Land and natural resources	•	•	•	•
Buildings and other constructions	•	•	•	•
Machinery and equipment	•	•	•	•
Transport equipment	•	•	•	•
Tools and utensils	•	•	•	•
Furniture and office equipment	•	•	•	•
Containers	•	•	•	•
Other fixed assets	•	•	•	•
Construction in progress	•		•	•
Advances to suppliers of fixed assets	•		•	•
	—	—	—	—
Investments:				
Investments in associated companies	•	•	•	•
Loans to associated companies	•	•	•	•
Investments in other related companies	•	•	•	•
Loans to other related companies	•	•	•	•
Securities and other investments	•	•	•	•
Other loans	•	•	•	•
Investments in progress	•		•	•
Advances	•		•	•
	—	—	—	—
Current assets:				
Inventories:				
Raw materials and consumables	•	•	•	•
Work in progress	•	•	•	•
Spoilage, waste and scrap	•	•	•	•
Finished and semi-finished products	•	•	•	•
Merchandise	•	•	•	•
Advances to suppliers	•		•	•
	—	—	—	—
Medium and long-term receivables	•	•	•	•
	—	—	—	—
Short-term receivables:	—	—	—	—
Trade accounts receivable – current account	•	•	•	•
Trade accounts receivable – bills receivable	•	•	•	•
Doubtful debtors	•	•	•	•
Group companies	•	•	•	•
Other related companies	•	•	•	•

Table 9.1 (a) Portuguese original (*continued*)

Activo	Exercícios			
	N			N − 1
	AB	AP	AL	AL
Outros accionistas (sócios)	●	●	●	●
Adiantamentos a fornecedores	●		●	●
Adiantamentos a fornecedores de imobilizado	●		●	●
Estado e outros entes públicos	●	●	●	●
Outros devedores	●	●	●	●
Subscritores de capital	●	●	●	●
	—	—	—	—
Títulos negociáveis:				
Acções em empresas associadas	●	●	●	●
Obrigações em empresas associadas	●	●	●	●
Outros títulos negociáveis	●	●	●	●
Outras aplicações de tesouraria	●	●	●	●
	—	—	—	—
Depósitos bancários e caixa:				
Depósitos bancários	●		●	●
Caixa	●		●	●
	—		—	—
Acréscimos e diferimentos:				
Acréscimos de proveitos	●		●	●
Custos diferidos	●		●	●
	—		—	—
Total de amortizações		●		
		—		
Total de provisões		●		
		—		
Total do activo	●	●	●	●

Notas: *AB* activo bruto, *AP* amortizações e provisões, *AL* activo líquido.

calculating the value adjustments. For items included in the consolidated accounts which are or were originally expressed in foreign currency, the basis of conversion used to express them in local currency must be disclosed.

8 DISCLOSURE REQUIREMENT FOR CONSOLIDATED ACCOUNTS
8.1 Consolidated financial statements

These must comprise a balance sheet, a profit and loss statement and notes on the accounts (annex). The documents should comprise a composite whole. The legally prescribed formats are similar to those required of the individual companies and are outlined below. The preparation of a statement of the sources and application of funds is also recommended, but not required by law. No particular format is mandatory.

Table 9.1 (b) English translation (*continued*)

Assets	Year n GA	Year n DP	Year n NA	Year n−1 NA
Other shareholders and partners	•	•	•	•
Advances to suppliers	•		•	•
Advances to suppliers of fixed assets	•		•	•
State and other public entities	•	•	•	•
Other debtors	•	•	•	•
Shareholders or quotaholders	•	•	•	•
Negotiable securities:				
Shares in associated companies	•	•	•	•
Bonds in associated companies	•	•	•	•
Other negotiable securities	•	•	•	•
Other short-term investments	•	•	•	•
Cash and bank balances:				
Bank deposits	•		•	•
Cash	•		•	•
Accruals and deferrals:				
Accrued income	•		•	•
Deferred expenses	•		•	•
Total accumulated depreciation		•		
Total provisions		•		
Total assets	•	•	•	•

Note: *GA* gross assets, *DP* depreciation and provisions, *NA* net assets.

The layouts required for the three main statements are set out in the POC (Tables 9.1–2). They are essentially the same as those to be used for the parent company's accounts in line with articles 9 (balance sheet), 24 and 25 of the Fourth Directive (profit and loss accounts). One exception relates to minority interests that may appear in the group accounts and another to shares in or loans to affiliated undertakings, which can be omitted.

The notes to the consolidated accounts constitute an extensive document in themselves, running to nearly fifty points or more. Some of the points may be inapplicable in particular cases, but, if so, the fact needs to be stated.

The requirements for group accounts are intended to be flexible, so that a number of 'derogations' from the POC are permitted. However, any such derogations must be mentioned in the notes, with reasons and implications being stated. In addition the notes

Table 9.1 (a) Portuguese original (*continued*)

Capital próprio e passivo	Exercícios	
	N	N − 1
Capital próprio:		
Capital	●	●
Acções (quotas) próprias − Valor nominal	− ●	− ●
Acções (quotas) próprias − Descontos e prémios	± ●	± ●
Prestações suplementares	●	●
Prémios de emissão de acções (quotas)	●	●
Diferenças de consolidação	± ●	± ●
Ajustamentos de partes de capital em filiais e associadas	± ●	± ●
Reservas de reavaliação	●	●
Reservas:		
Reservas legais	●	●
Reservas estatutárias	●	●
Reservas contratuais	●	●
Outras reservas	●	●
Resultados transitados	± ●	± ●
Resultado líquido do exercício	± ●	± ●
Dividendos antecipados	± ●	± ●
Total do capital próprio	± ●	± ●
Interesses minoritários	± ●	± ●
Passivo:		
Provisões para riscos e encargos:		
Provisões para pensões	●	●
Provisões para impostos	●	●
Outras provisões para riscos e encargos	●	●
	●	●
Dívidas a terceiros − Médio e longo prazo	●	●
Dívidas a terceiros − Curto prazo:		
Empréstimos por obrigações:		
Convertíveis	●	●
Não convertíveis	●	●
Empréstimos por títulos de participação	●	●
Dívidas a instituições de crédito	●	●
Adiantamentos por conta de vendas	●	●
Fornecedores, c/c	●	●
Fornecedores − Facturas em recepção e conferência	●	●
Fornecedores − Títulos a pagar	●	●
Fornecedores de imobilizado − Títulos a pagar	●	●
Empresas associadas	●	●
Empresas participadas e participantes	●	●
Outros accionistas (sócios)	●	●
Adiantamentos de clientes	●	●
Outros empréstimos obtidos	●	●
Fornecedores de imobilizado, c/c	●	●
Estado e outros entes públicos	●	●
Outros credores	●	●

Table 9.1 (b) English translation (*continued*)

Net equity and liabilities	Year	
	n	*n − 1*
Net equity:		
Capital	●	●
Own shares (quotas) − nominal value	− ●	− ●
Own shares (quotas) − premiums and discounts	± ●	± ●
Supplementary capital	●	●
Share issue premiums (quotas)	●	●
Capital reserve on consolidation	± ●	± ●
Net equity adjustments in group and associated companies	± ●	± ●
Revaluation reserves	●	●
Reserves:		
Legal reserves	●	●
Statutory reserves	●	●
Contractual reserves	●	●
Other reserves	●	●
Past years' results	± ●	± ●
Subtotal	± ●	± ●
After-tax result of the year	± ●	± ●
Proposed dividends	± ●	± ●
Total net equity	± ●	± ●
Minority interests	± ●	± ●
Liabilities:		
Provisions for risks and charges:		
Provisions for pensions	●	●
Provisions for taxes	●	●
Provisions for other risks and charges	●	●
	●	●
Medium and long-term liabilities	●	●
Short-term liabilities:		
Bond borrowing:		
Convertible bonds	●	●
Non-convertible bonds	●	●
Participating bond borrowing	●	●
Debits to credit institutions	●	●
Advances from customers	●	●
Suppliers − current accounts	●	●
Suppliers − invoices outstanding	●	●
Suppliers − bills payable	●	●
Accounts payable to fixed asset suppliers − bills	●	●
Group companies	●	●
Other participations and participating companies	●	●
Other shareholders and quotaholders	●	●
Advances from customers	●	●
Other borrowing	●	●
Suppliers of fixed assets − current accounts	●	●
State and other public entities	●	●
Other creditors	●	●
	●	●

Table 9.1 (a) Portuguese original (*continued*)

	Exercícios	
Capital próprio e passivo	N	N − 1
Acréscimos e diferimentos: Acréscimos de custos Proveitos diferidos	• • •	• • •
Total do passivo	•	•
Total do capital próprio, dos interesses minoritários e do passivo	•	•

on the accounts must set out information in respect of *at least* the following matters:

1 Group and other undertakings.
2 The presentation of a true and fair view.
3 Consolidation procedures.
4 Commitments.
5 Accounting policies.
6 Specific items in consolidated accounts.
7 The classification of the accounts.

Table 9.1 (b) English translation (*continued*)

	Year	
Net equity and liabilities	*n*	*n − 1*
Accruals and deferrals:		
Cost accruals	●	●
Deferred income	●	●
	●	●
Total liabilities	●	●
Total net equity and liabilities	●	●

8.2 Consolidated annual report

The consolidated annual report must accompany the consolidated accounts. It must include a fair review of the development of the business and the position of the consolidated undertakings taken as a whole, and brief statements concerning the consolidated undertakings, namely:

1 Any important events that have occurred subsequent to the end of the financial year.
2 The likely future development of the undertakings consolidated.
3 Their research and development activities.
4 The number and nominal or accounting par value of parent undertaking shares held by the parent undertaking, other group undertakings or their nominees.

Table 9.2 Consolidated profit and loss account (a) Portuguese original (*demonstração consolidada dos resultados*)

	Exercícios			
	N		N − 1	
Custo e perdas				
Custo das mercadorias vendidas e das matérias consumidas:				
Mercadorias	•		•	
Matérias	•	•	•	•
Fornecimentos e serviços externos		•		•
Custos com o pessoal:				
Remunerações	•		•	
Encargos sociais:				
Pensões	•		•	
Outros	•		•	•
Amortizações do imobilizado corpóreo e incorpóreo	•		•	
Provisões	•	•	•	•
Impostos	•		•	
Outros custos e perdas operacionais	•	•	•	•
(A)		•		•
Amortizações e provisões de aplicações e investimentos financeiros		•		•
Juros e custos similares:				
Relativos a empresas associadas	•		•	
Outros	•	•	•	•
(C)		•		•
Perdas relativas a empresas associadas		•		•
Custos e perdas extraordinários		•		•
(E)		•		•
Imposto sobre o rendimento do exercício		•		•
(G)		•		•
Interesses minoritários		± •		± •
Resultado consolidado líquido do exercício		± •		± •
Proveitos e ganhos				
Vendas:				
Mercadorias	•		•	
Produtos	•		•	
Prestações de serviços	•	•	•	•
Variação da produção		± •		± •
Trabalhos para a própria empresa		•		•
Proveitos suplementares	•		•	
Subsídios à exploração	•		•	
Outros proveitos e ganhos operacionais	•	•	•	•
(B)		•		•
Ganhos de participações de capital:				
Relativos e empresas associadas	•		•	
Relativos a outros empresas	•		•	
Rendimentos de títulos negociáveis e de outras aplicações financeiras:				
Relativos a empresas associadas	•		•	

Table 9.2 Consolidated profit and loss account (b) English translation

	Year			
	n		*n − 1*	
Expenses and losses				
Costs of goods sold and materials consumed:				
Goods	•		•	
Materials	•	•	•	•
External supplies and services		•		•
Personnel expenses:				
Wages and salaries	•		•	
Social security costs:				
Pension costs	•		•	
Others	•	•	•	•
Depreciation of intangible and tangible fixed assets	•		•	
Provisions	•	•	•	•
Taxes	•		•	
Other operating costs	•	•	•	•
(A)		•		•
Losses in associated companies		•		•
Depreciation and provisions for investments	•		•	
Interest expenses and similar costs:				
Associated companies	•		•	
Others	•	•	•	•
(C)		•		•
Losses in associated companies		•		•
Extraordinary costs and losses		•		•
(E)		•		•
Income tax of the year		•		•
(G)		•		•
Minority interests (result for the year)		± •		± •
Group net result for the year		± •		± •
Revenues and gains				
Sales:				
Goods	•		•	
Products	•		•	
Services	•	•	•	•
Increase or decrease in stocks of finished products and work in progress		± •		± •
Work performed by the undertaking for its own purposes		•		•
Supplementary revenues	•		•	
Subventions received	•		•	
Other operating revenues	•	•	•	•
(B)		•		•
Dividends on shares and profits from undertakings:				
Gains in associated companies	•		•	
Gains in other related companies	•		•	
Income from negotiable securities and other short-term investments:				
From associated companies	•		•	

Table 9.2 (a) Portuguese original (*continued*)

	Exercícios			
	N		N − 1	
Outros	●		●	
Outros juros e proveitos similares:				
Relativos a empresas associadas	●		●	
Outros	●	●	●	●
(D)		●		●
Proveitos e ganhos extraordinários		●		●
(F)		●		●

Resumo:
Resultados operacionais: $(B) - (A) =$ ● ●
Resultados financeiros: $(D - B) - (C - A) =$ ● ●
Resultados correntes: $(D) - (C) =$ ● ●
Resultados antes de impostos: $(F) - (E) =$ ● ●
Resultado consolidado com os interesses minoritários do exercício:
$(F) - (G) =$ ● ●

8.3 Consolidated auditors' report

An auditor (or auditors) authorized to audit accounts under Portuguese law must audit the consolidated accounts. He or she must verify that the consolidated annual report is consistent with the related consolidated accounts. In practical terms, it may be prudent to regard the consolidated accounts as taking precedence and to bring any conflicting information in the consolidated annual report into line with it.

8.4 Publication and filing

The duly approved consolidated accounts, the consolidated annual report and the auditors' report must be lodged with the established registry office. In addition, the consolidated accounts and the auditors' report must be published in the official journal designated for the purpose in the parent undertaking's articles. The consolidated annual report must also be published. However, under the Portuguese law the publication of these documents is not required if the parent undertaking which prepared the consolidated accounts is not one of the legal forms of organization listed in section 2.1 above. In that case the consolidated annual report must be available for inspection by the public at its registered office and copies of part or the whole of the documents must be supplied on request at no more than cost.

Table 9.2 (b) English translation (*continued*)

	Year	
	n	*n − 1*
Other	●	●
Other financial revenues:		
From associated companies	●	●
Other	●	● ● ●
(D)	●	●
Extraordinary revenues and gains	●	●
(F)	●	●
Summary:		
Operating result: $(B) − (A) =$	●	●
Financial result: $(D − B) − (C − A) =$	●	●
Current result: $(D) − (C) =$	●	●
Result before tax: $(F) − (E) =$	●	●
Group result including minority rights for the year: $(F) − (G) =$	●	●

9 TRANSITIONAL PROVISIONS UPON FIRST CONSOLIDATION

Under the terms of the POC, when a participating interest in an undertaking is included in a consolidation for the first time, the amount to be included in the consolidated balance sheet should equal the capital and reserves of the undertaking. The difference between that amount and the book value of the participating interest in the parent's accounts (i.e. goodwill) should be disclosed separately within the intangible fixed assets in the consolidated balance sheet at the relevant date. The treatment of goodwill in the terms of the POC is outlined in section 4.4 above.

Participations in subsidiaries and associated companies acquired in the year to which the accounts refer must be valued according to one of the following rules:

1   Valuation at purchase price without any changes. It must be disclosed in the Notes on the Accounts.
2   Valuation by the equity method, the items having been previously recorded at the acquisition value, which has to be increased or reduced in line with the effect on the profits or losses of the subsidiary or associated company (reckoned as financial gains or costs) and other changes in the equity of the subsidiary or associated company (included in the balance sheet, within the equity capital, under the item 'Undertakings adjustments').
3   The deduction of the dividends paid and the addition of the losses covered must also be taken into account.

In the case of participations in subsidiary and associated companies acquired in previous years the book value or the amount which corresponds to the proportion of capital and reserves has to be increased or reduced by the amount of the variation which has taken

Table 9.3 Consolidated profit and loss account, vertical layout by function (a) Portuguese original (*demonstração consolidada dos resultados por funções*)

		Exercícios	
		N	N − 1
1	Vendas e prestações de serviços	●	●
2	Custo das vendas e prestação de serviços	− ●	− ●
3	Resultados brutos	●	●
4	Custos de distribuição	− ●	− ●
5	Custos administrativos	− ●	− ●
6	Outros proveitos e ganhos operacionais	●	●
	Resultados operacionais	●	●
7	Rendimento de participações de capital:		
	Relativos a empresas associadas	●	●
	Relativos a outras empresas	●	●
8	Rendimentos de títulos negociáveis e de outras aplicações financeiras:		
	Relativos a empresas associadas	●	●
	Outros	●	●
9	Outros juros e proveitos similares:		
	Relativos a empresas associadas	●	●
	Outros	●	●
10	Amortizações e provisões de aplicações e investimentos financeiros	− ●	− ●
11	Juros e custos similares:		
	Relativos a empresas associadas	− ●	− ●
	Outros	− ●	− ●
	Resultados correntes	●	●
14	Proveitos e ganhos extraordinários	●	●
15	Custos e perdas extraordinários	− ●	− ●
	Resultados antes de impostos	●	●
16	Imposto sobre o rendimento do exercício	− ●	− ●
		●	●
17	Interesses minoritários	± ●	± ●
18	Resultado consolidado do exercício	± ●	± ●

place during the financial year in the proportion of capital and reserves represented by that participating interest. It must be reduced by the amount of dividends relating to the participating interest.

Participations of less than 20 per cent must be valued at the acquisition price. Valuation according to the equity method is not allowed in such cases.

Shares in subsidiaries and associated companies must be written down in the parent company's accounts whenever the market price is lower than the acquisition value.

10 TRANSLATION OF FOREIGN SUBSIDIARIES' FINANCIAL STATEMENTS

The POC requires disclosure of the method used in the translation of foreign currency

Table 9.3 Consolidated profit and loss account, vertical layout by function (b) English translation

		Year	
		n	$n-1$
1	Sales and services rendered	•	•
2	Costs of sales and services rendered	– •	– •
3	Gross result	•	•
4	Distribution costs	– •	– •
5	Administrative costs	– •	– •
6	Other operating revenues	•	•
	Operating result	•	•
7	Income from undertakings:		
	From associated companies	•	•
	From other related companies	•	•
8	Income from short-term investments:		
	From associated companies	•	•
	Other	•	•
9	Other interest received and similar revenues:		
	From and associated companies	•	•
	Other	•	•
10	Depreciation and provisions for investments	– •	– •
11	Interest and similar expenses:		
	From associated companies	– •	– •
	Other	– •	– •
	Current result	•	•
14	Extraordinary revenues and gains	•	•
15	Extraordinary costs and losses	– •	– •
	Result before income tax	•	•
16	Income tax of the year	– •	– •
		•	•
17	Minority interests	± •	± •
18	Consolidated net result of the year	± •	± •

transactions, both for individual accounts and for consolidated accounts. An explanation must be included in the notes on the accounts. The POC does not deal with the translation of foreign currency financial statements.

The POC specifies only that the notes on the accounts should set out information about the valuation methods applied to the various items in the annual accounts as well as the methods employed in calculating the value adjustments. For items included in the consolidated accounts which are or were originally expressed in foreign currency, the basis of conversion used to express them in local currency must be disclosed. In fact this is no more than is required by the Seventh Directive on consolidated accounts.

Example 9.1 **Merger accounting**

On 30 April 19XX company ABC combined with company XYZ. It is assumed that both the companies apply the same accounting principles and valuation rules. Company ABC exchanged 150,000 of its shares (with a nominal value PTE 1,000 and a market value of PTE 2,500). Company ABC received all the shares of company XYZ, that is 100,000 shares, with a nominal value of PTE 1,000. Company ABC also incurred the following expenses: auditing costs (PTE 4,000), notarial expenses (PTE 2,500 – deed and PTE 1,000 – register), intermediation (PTE 9,000), printing of shares (PTE 2,000) and other expenses (PTE 1,500).

XYZ balance sheet at 30 April 19XX (PTE 000)

Current assets	100,000
Fixed assets	300,000
Other assets	60,000
	460,000
Current liabilities	50,000
Non-current liabilities	100,000
Issued capital	100,000
Share premium	70,000
Reserves	140,000
	460,000

The board of directors of company ABC assumed the following fair values for XYZ's assets and liabilities:

Current assets	115,000
Fixed assets	340,000
Other assets	60,000
Current liabilities	50,000
Non-current liabilities	95,000

11 MERGER ACCOUNTING

On 8 August 1991 the general council of the Accounting Standardization Committee published *Directiz Contabilística* No. 1/91, *Accounting for Business Combinations (Mergers and Acquisitions)*. The *directriz* includes two methods of accounting for business combinations: the purchase method and the pooling of interests method. It is the former that now governs the accounting in the case of a business combination; the latter is retained as an exception applicable only to joint ventures.

With the purchase method, the acquired assets and liabilities are accounted for at 'fair values'; assets and liabilities not included in the balance sheet should also be taken into account. Business combination costs can be capitalized and depreciated. The difference between fair values and book values may be either depreciated (when positive) or considered as deferred income (when negative) for a period no longer than five years. Goodwill is depreciated over a period of five years (which may, however, be extended up to twenty years).

To illustrate the use of the purchase method, take the case of a business combination

Example 9.2 **Accounting for business combinations by the purchase method (PTE 000)**

In company ABC			Debit	Credit
Acquisition of XYZ by	Investments	(1)	375,000	
issue of shares	Issued capital			150,000
	Issue premium	(2)		225,000
Additional expenses	Investments	(3)	11,500	
	Issued capital	(4)	8,500	
	Cash and bank			20,000
Inclusion of assets and	Current assets		115,000	
liabilities of XYZ in	Fixed assets		340,000	
group accounts	Other assets		60,000	
	Liabilities discount		5,000	
	Goodwill	(5)	16,500	
	Current liabilities	(7)		50,000
	Non-current liabilities	(7)		100,000
	Investments	(6)		386,500

(1) 150000 × 2.5 = 375,000.
(2) 150000 × 1.5 = 225,000.
(3) Deed expenses and intermediation = 11,500.
(4) Other issuing expenses not included in (3).
(5) = (6) − (7).
(6) = 375,000 + 11 500 = (1) + (3).
(7) = (115,000 + 340,000 + 60,000 + 5,000) − (50,000 + 100,000).

In company XYZ		Debit	Credit
Elimination of the	Current liabilities	50,000	
company	Non-current liabilities	100,000	
	Issued capital	100,000	
	Share premium	70,000	
	Reserves	140,000	
	Current assets		100,000
	Fixed assets		300,000
	Other assets		60,000

(regardless of the type of combination) such as that shown in Example 9.1. Example 9.2 shows the use of the purchasing method. The example is a translation of part of *Directriz* No. 1/91.

With the pooling of interests method, assets, liabilities, capital and reserves are recorded at book values and goodwill is not recognized. Business combination expenses are considered as a cost of the year in which the combination takes place. Example 9.3 illustrates the use of the pooling of interests method. For ease of comparison, it uses the same situation as Examples 9.1–2.

When one company ceases to exist, the transaction can take place through an exchange of shares, but there can be a cash payment in some cases.

The valuation of the items in the financial statements of the combining companies is included in the related balance sheets prior to the merger, which must be audited and submitted to the shareholders' meetings of the companies that will approve them. Also, according to Companies Law the exchange ratio of the shares of the combining companies must be specified in a report prepared by an independent appraiser and must have the opinion of a Statutory Auditor.

Example 9.3 **Accounting for business combinations using the pooling of interests method (PTE 000)**

In company ABC			Debit	Credit
Additional expenses	Combination expenses		20,000	
		Cash and bank		20,000
Inclusion of assets and	Current assets		100,000	
liabilities of XYZ in	Fixed assets		300,000	
group accounts	Other assets		60,000	
		Current liabilities		50,000
		Non-current liabilities		100,000
		Issued capital		150,000
		Share premium (1)		20,000
		Reserves		140,000

(1) Capital and share premium of XYZ less nominal value of shares issued by ABC = 170,000 − 150,000 = 20,000.

In company XYZ			Debit	Credit
Elimination of the	Current liabilities		50,000	
company	Non-current liabilities		100,000	
	Issued capital		100,000	
	Share premium		70,000	
	Reserves		140,000	
		Current assets		100,000
		Fixed assets		300,000
		Other assets		60,000

Part III
Appendices

Appendix A
Illustrative financial statements

1 INTRODUCTION

The financial statements of Somincor are reproduced from the company's bilingual 1992 Annual Report and Accounts (*Relatório e Contas*) for the year ended 31 December 1992. The financial statements are presented in accordance with generally accepted accounting principles in Portugal and with the disclosure requirements of the Official Chart of Accounts.

Somincor is engaged in the extraction and processing of copper ore and tin ore, and the sale of metal concentrates on the international market. Its results are influenced by the world copper price and the exchange rate between the US dollar and the Portuguese escudo, and its activities are financed by equity and long term debt denominated mainly in US dollars and ECU.

SOMINCOR
Sociedade Mineira de Neves Corvo SA
Report for the year ended 31 December 1992

Contents

BALANÇOS EM 31 DE DEZEMBRO DE 1992 E 1991
(Valores expressos em milhares de Escudos)

ACTIVO	Notas	Activo bruto (1992)	Amortização e provisões (1992)	Activo líquido (1992)	1991	CAPITAL PRÓPRIO E PASSIVO	Notas	1992	1991
IMOBILIZADO						**CAPITAL PRÓPRIO**			
Imobilizações Incorpóreas:									
Despesas de instalação	10	238,112	181,693	56,419	104,041	Capital	37	14,650,000	14,650,000
Despesas de invest. e de desenvolv.	10	394,381	73,630	320,751	312,926	*Reservas:*			
Trespasses	10	70,000	-	70,000	70,000	Reservas legais	40	1,868,015	1,399,978
Despesas de inst. arranque mina	10	1,116,140	644,075	472,065	663,004	Reservas especiais	40	874,000	824,000
Despesas de treino form. profissional	10	421,507	84,301	337,206	358,281	Reservas livres	40	17,214,947	13,866,024
						Resultado líquido do exercício	40	8,865,293	9,360,736
		2,240,140	983,699	1,256,441	1,508,252				
						Total do capital próprio		43,472,255	40,100,738
Imobilizações Corpóreas:									
Terrenos e recursos naturais	10	131,462	-	131,462	131,462	**PASSIVO**			
Edifícios e outras construções	10	9,149,907	1,236,777	7,913,130	7,671,611				
Equipamento básico	10	64,314,533	13,858,967	50,455,566	52,667,754	**PROVISÕES PARA RISCOS**			
Equipamento de transporte	10	546,556	368,291	178,265	242,421	**E ENCARGOS**			
Ferramentas e utensílios	10	1,708,465	979,383	729,082	773,962	Outras Prov. para riscos e encargos	34	50,935	444,343
Equipamento administrativo	10	997,962	659,458	338,504	379,481				
Taras e vasilhame	10	168,962	120,525	48,437	72,487	**DÍVIDAS A TERCEIROS - Médio e longo prazo**			
Outras imobilizações corpóreas	10	43,348	20,514	22,834	27,855	Dívidas a instituições de crédito	48	27,706,141	29,176,696
Imobilizações em curso	10	2,920,444	-	2,920,444	2,900,931	Accionistas	27	3,050,000	3,050,00
Adiantamentos por conta imob. corp.	10	47,374	-	47,374	17,420				
		80,029,013	17,243,915	62,785,098	64,885,384			30,756,141	32,226,696
						DÍVIDAS A TERCEIROS - Curto prazo			
CIRCULANTE						Dívidas a instituições de crédito	48	2,473,949	2,552,212
Existências:						Fornecedores c/c		1,198,827	1,804,303
Matérias-primas, subsid. e de consumo		2,053,916	-	2,053,916	2,386,241	Fornecedores fact. recep. conf.		299,183	427,197
Produtos acabados e intermédios		548,679	-	548,679	1,743,930	Accionistas	27	610,000	610,000
						Fornecedores de imob. c/c		-	33,726
		2,602,595	-	2,602,595	4,130,171	Estado e outros entes públicos	50	1,147,756	1,179,188
						Outros credores		8,140	13,162
Dívidas de Terceiros - curto prazo:									
Clientes, conta corrente		6,027,441	-	6,027,441	6,866,942			5,737,855	6,619,788
Adiantamentos a fornecedores		153,209	-	153,209	605,914				
Estado e outros entes públicos	50	630,528	-	630,528	1,278,602	**ACRÉSCIMOS E DIFERIMENTOS**			
Outros devedores		33,206	-	33,206	89,138	Acréscimos de custos	51	884,473	866,161
						Proveitos diferidos	51	929,312	2,616,846
		6,844,384	-	6,844,384	8,840,596				
								1,813,785	3,483,007
Títulos Negociáveis:									
Outras aplicações de tesouraria		5,366,776	-	5,366,776	2,070,760				
		5,366,776	-	5,366,776	2,070,760				
Depósitos Bancários e Caixa:									
Depósitos bancários		115,692	-	115,692	322,150				
Caixa		1,434	-	1,434	2,732				
		117,126	-	117,126	324,882				
ACRÉSCIMOS E DIFERIMENTOS									
Acréscimos de proveitos	51	33,934	-	33,934	24,804				
Custos diferidos	51	2,824,617	-	2,824,617	1,089,723				
		2,858,551	-	2,858,551	1,114,527				
Total de amortizações			18,227,614						
Total de provisões			-						
Total do activo		100,058,585	18,227,614	81,830,971	82,874,572	Total do capital próprio e do passivo		81,830,971	82,874,572

As notas anexas fazem parte integrante destes balanços

BALANCE SHEETS AS AT 31 DECEMBER 1992 AND 1991
(Amounts expressed in thousands of Portuguese Escudos)
(Translation of a reput originally issued in Portuguese Note 52)

ASSETS	Notes	Total assets	Depreciation and provisions	Net assets	1991
			1992		
MEDIUM AND LONG-TERM ASSETS					
Intangible assets:					
Installation costs	10	238,112	181,693	56,419	104,041
Research and development	10	394,381	73,630	320,751	312,926
Goodwill	10	70,000	-	70,000	70,000
Expenses related with the start-up of mining operations	10	1,116,140	644,075	472,065	663,004
Training expenses during the period of mine construction	10	421,507	84,301	337,206	358,281
		2,240,140	983,699	1,256,441	1,508,252
Fixed assets:					
Land and natural resources	10	131,462	-	131,462	131,462
Buildings and other constructions	10	9,149,907	1,236,777	7,913,130	7,671,611
Basic equipment	10	64,314,533	13,858,967	50,455,566	52,667,754
Vehicles and transportation equipment	10	546,556	368,291	178,265	242,421
Tools and dies	10	1,708,465	979,383	729,082	773,962
Administrative equipment	10	997,962	659,458	338,504	379,481
Containers	10	168,962	120,525	48,437	72,487
Other fixed assets	10	43,348	20,514	22,834	27,855
Constrution in progress	10	2,920,444	-	2,920,444	2,900,931
Advances to suppliers of fixed assets	10	47,374	-	47,374	17,420
		80,029,013	17,243,915	62,785,098	64,885,384
CURRENT ASSETS					
Inventories:					
Raw and other materials		2,053,916	-	2,053,916	2,386,241
Finished and semi-finished products		548,679	-	548,679	1,743,930
		2,602,595	-	2,602,595	4,130,171
Short-term receivables:					
Customers, current accounts		6,027,441	-	6,027,441	6,866,942
Advances to suppliers		153,209	-	153,209	605,914
Public entities	50	630,528	-	630,528	1,278,602
Other debtors		33,206	-	33,206	89,138
		6,844,384	-	6,844,384	8,840,596
Securities:					
Other treasury applications		5,366,776	-	5,366,776	2,070,760
		5,366,776	-	5,366,776	2,070,760
Cash and banks:					
Banks		115,692	-	115,692	322,150
Cash		1,434	-	1,434	2,732
		117,126	-	117,126	324,882
DEFERRED COSTS AND PREPAID EXPENSES:					
Prepaid expenses	51	33,934	-	33,934	24,804
Deferred costs	51	2,824,617	-	2,824,617	1,089,723
		2,858,551	-	2,858,551	1,114,527
Total depreciations and amortisation			18,227,614		
Total provisions			-		
Total assets		100,058,585	18,227,614	81,830,971	82,874,572

EQUITY AND LIABILITIES	Notes	1992	1991
EQUITY			
Share Capital	37	14,650,000	14,650,000
Reserves:			
Legal reserves	40	1,868,015	1,399,978
Special reserves	40	874,000	824,000
Free reserves	40	17,214,947	13,866,024
Net profit for the year	40	8,865,293	9,360,736
Total equity		43,472,255	40,100,738
LIABILITIES			
PROVISIONS FOR OTHER RISKS AND COSTS			
Other provisions for risks and costs	34	50,935	444,343
MEDIUM AND LONG-TERM LIABILITIES			
Bank loans	48	27,706,141	29,176,696
Shareholders	27	3,050,000	3,050,00
		30,756,141	32,226,696
SHORT-TERM LIABILITIES			
Bank loans	48	2,473,949	2,552,212
Suppliers current accounts		1,198,827	1,804,303
Suppliers invoices pending approval		299,183	427,197
Shareholders current accounts	27	610,000	610,000
Accounts payable to suppliers of fixed assets		-	33,726
Public entities	50	1,147,756	1,179,188
Other creditors		8,140	13,162
		5,737,855	6,619,788
DEFERRED INCOME AND ACCRUED COSTS:			
Accrued costs	51	884,473	866,161
Deferred income	51	929,312	2,616,846
		1,813,785	3,483,007
Total equity and liabilities		81,830,971	82,874,572

The accompanying notes form an integral part of these balance sheets

DEMONSTRAÇÃO DOS RESULTADOS EM 31 DE DEZEMBRO DE 1992 E 1991
(Valores expressos em milhares de Escudos)

CUSTOS E PERDAS	Notas	1992	1991
Custo das matérias primas consumidas	41	2,505,402	2,477,630
Fornecimentos e serviços externos		8,963,541	9,737,146
Custos com o pessoal:			
Remunerações		2,942,510	2,738,110
Encargos sociais - outros		1,187,265	1,090,943
		4,129,775	3,829,053
Amortizações do imobilizado corpóreo e incorpóreo		4,955,949	4,757,967
Provisões	34	-	388,914
		4,955,949	5,146,881
Impostos		1,047,354	1,167,845
Outros custos operacionais		32,106	62,801
(A)		1,079,460	1,230,646
		21,634,127	22,421,356
Juros e custos similares - outros	45	4,664,939	5,790,255
(C)		26,299,066	28,211,611
Custos e perdas extraordinárias	46	262,948	561,825
(E)		26,562,014	28,773,436
Imposto sobre o rendimento do exercício	6	-	-
(G)		26,562,014	28,773,436
Resultado líquido do exercício		8,865,293	9,360,736
		35,427,307	38,134,172

PROVEITOS E GANHOS	Notas	1992	1991
Vendas de produtos	44	33,215,716	33,651,072
Prestações de serviços		16,935	8,142
		33,232,651	33,659,214
Variação da produção	42	(1,195,251)	1,026,705
Trabalhos para a própria empresa		591,716	818,602
Proveitos suplementares		153,244	217,256
Subsídios à exploração		48,755	38,478
		(401,536)	2,101,041
(B)		32,831,115	35,760,255
Juros e proveitos similares - outros	45	2,391,855	1,984,681
(D)		35,222,970	37,744,936
Proveitos e ganhos extraordinários	46	204,337	389,236
(F)		35,427,307	38,134,172

		1992	1991
Resultados operacionais:	(B) - (A)	11,196,988	13,338,899
Resultados financeiros:	(D-B) - (C-A)	(2,273,084)	(3,805,574)
Resultados correntes:	(D) - (C)	8,923,904	9,533,325
Resultados antes de impostos:	(F) - (E)	8,865,293	9,360,736
Resultados líquido do exercício:	(F) - (G)	8,865,293	9,360,736

As notas anexas fazem parte integrante destas demonstrações

STATEMENTS OF PROFIT AND LOSS FOR THE YEARS ENDED 31 DECEMBER 1992 AND 1991

(Amounts expressed in thousands of Portuguese Escudos)
(Translation of a report originally issued in Portuguese Note 52)

COSTS AND LOSSES	Notes	1992	1991
Cost of inventories sold and used	41		
Raw and other materials		2,505,402	2,477,630
Outside supplies and services		8,963,541	9,737,146
Payroll expenses:			
Salaries and wages		2,942,510	2,738,110
Others		1,187,265	1,090,943
		4,129,775	3,829,053
Depreciation and amortisation	10	4,955,949	4,757,967
Provisions	34	-	388,914
(B)		4,955,949	5,146,881
Taxes		1,047,354	1,167,845
Other operational costs		32,106	62,801
		1,079,460	1,230,646
(A)		21,634,127	22,421,356
Financial expenses - others	45	4,664,939	5,790,255
(C)		26,299,066	28,211,611
Extraordinary costs and losses		262,948	561,825
(E)		26,562,014	28,773,436
Corporation tax	6	-	-
(G)		26,562,014	28,773,436
Net profit for the year		8,865,293	9,360,736
		35,427,307	38,134,772

REVENUES AND GAINS	Notes	1992	1991
Sales - Finished goods	44	33,215,716	33,651,072
Services		16,935	8,142
		33,232,651	33,659,214
Finished products inventory variation	42	(1,195,251)	1,026,705
Works for the company		591,716	818,602
Supplementary income		153,244	217,256
Operating subsidies		48,755	38,478
(B)		(401,536)	2,101,041
		32,831,115	35,760,255
Interest and similar income - Others	45	2,391,855	1,984,681
(D)		35,222,970	37,744,936
Extraordinary gains and income	46	204,337	389,236
(F)		35,427,307	38,134,172

		1992	1991	
Operational results:		11,196,988	13,338,899	(B) - (A)
Financial results:		(2,273,084)	(3,805,574)	(D-B) - (C-A)
Current results:		8,923,904	9,533,325	(D) - (C)
Profit before tax:		8,865,293	9,360,736	(F) - (E)
Net profit for the year:		8,865,293	9,360,736	(F) - (G)

The accompanying notes form an integral part of these statements

DEMONSTRAÇÃO DE ORIGEM E APLICAÇÃO DE FUNDOS PARA OS EXERCÍCIOS FINDOS EM 31 DE DEZEMBRO DE 1992 E 1991
(Montantes expressos em milhares de Escudos)

ORIGEM DE FUNDOS	1992	1991
Internas:		
Resultado líquido do exercício	8,865,293	9,360,736
Amortizações	4,955,949	4.757,967
Variação de provisões	(393,408)	(536,359)
	13,427,834	13,582,344
Diminuição de imobilizações:		
Cessão de imobilizações	86,090	61,954
Total de origens de fundos	13,513,924	13,644,298
Diminuição dos fundos circulantes	-	3,196,116
	13,513,924	16,840,414

APLICAÇÃO DE FUNDOS	1992	1991
Distribuição de fundos:		
Por aplicação de resultados	5,493,776	7,169,560
Diminuição de dívidas a terceiros:		
A médio e longo prazo	1,470,555	2,664,195
Aquisição de imobilizações:		
Imobilizações incorpóreas	26,233	
Imobilizações corpóreas	4,638,544	7,006,659
	4,664,777	7,006,659
Total de aplicações de fundos	11,629,108	16,840,414
Aumento dos fundos circulantes	1,884,816	-
	13,513,924	16,840,414

AUMENTO / DIMINUIÇÃO DOS FUNDOS CIRCULANTES REPRESENTADO POR:

	1992	1991
Variações activas:		
Aumento das existências	-	1,300,938
Aumento das dívidas de terceiros	-	1,804,644
Diminuição das dívidas a terceiros a curto prazo	881,932	103,311
Aumento das disponibilidades	3,088,260	-
Variação dos acréscimos e diferimentos	1,438,412	-
Diminuição dos fundos circulantes	-	3,196,116
	5,408,604	6,405,009

	1992	1991
Variações passivas:		
Diminuição de existências	1,527,576	-
Diminuição das dívidas de terceiros	1,996,212	-
Diminuição das disponibilidades	-	5,921,670
Variação dos acréscimos e diferimentos	-	483,339
Aumento dos fundos circulantes	1,884,816	-
	5,408,604	6,405,009

As notas anexas fazem parte integrante destas demonstrações

STATEMENTS OF SOURCE AND APPLICATIONS OF FUNDS
FOR THE YEARS ENDED 31 DECEMBER 1992 AND 1991

(Amounts expressed in thousands of Portuguese Escudos)

(Translation of a report originally issued in Portuguese Note 52)

SOURCE OF FUNDS	1992	1991	APPLICATION OF FUNDS	1992	1991
From operations:			Distribution of funds		
Net profit for the year	8,865,293	9,360,736	Dividends paid	5,493,776	7,169,560
Depreciation and amortisation	4,955,949	4,757,967			
Change in provisions	(393,408)	(536,359)	Decrease in medium and long-term		
	13,427,834	13,582,344	liabilities	1,470,555	2,664,195
Decrease in fixed assets			Increase in medium and long-term assets:		
Retirements	86,090	61,954	Acquisition of:		
Total source of funds	13,513,924	13,644,298	Intagible assets	26,233	-
			Fixed assets	4,638,544	7,006,659
				4,664,777	7,006,659
			Total application of funds	11,629,108	16,840,414
Net decrease in working capital	-	3,196,116	Net increase in working capital	1,884,816	-
	13,513,924	16,840,414		13,513,924	16,840,414

INCREASE/DECREASE IN WORKING CAPITAL REPRESENTED BY:

	1992	1991		1992	1991
Increase in working capital			**Decrease in working capital**		
Increase in inventories	-	1,300,938	Decrease in inventories	1,527,576	-
Increase in short-term receivables	-	1,804,644	Decrease in short-term receivables	1,996,212	5,921,670
Decrease in short-term liabilities	881,932	103,311	Decrease in cash and banks	-	483,339
Increase in cash and banks	3,088,260	-	Increase in deferred costs	-	-
Increase in deferred costs	1,438,412	-	Net increase in working capital	1,884,816	-
Net decrease in working capital	-	3,196,116			
	5,408,604	6,405,009		5,408,604	6,405,009

The accompanying notes form an integral part of these statements

SOMINCOR - SOCIEDADE MINEIRA DE NEVES CORVO, S.A.

ANEXO AOS BALANÇOS E ÀS
DEMONSTRAÇÕES DOS RESULTADOS
EM 31 DE DEZEMBRO DE 1992 E 1991

NOTES TO FINANCIAL STATEMENTS
AS AT 31 DECEMBER 1992 AND 1991

(Montantes expressos em milhares de Escudos -
mEsc.)

(Amounts expressed in thousands of Portuguese
Escudos - contos)

(Translation of a report originally issued in
Portuguese - See Note 52)

1. NOTA INTRODUTÓRIA

1. INTRODUCTION

A Somincor - Sociedade Mineira de Neves Corvo,
S.A. é uma sociedade anónima, constituída em
24 de Julho de 1980 que tem como actividade
principal a prospecção, extracção,
processamento e comercialização de
concentrados de cobre, estanho e outros
sulfuretos metálicos.

The Company was incorporated on 24 July 1980.
The Company's principal activity is the explora-
tion, extraction, processing and marketing of
copper and tin concentrates and other metalic
sulphides.

No decurso do exercício de 1985, a Sociedade,
os seus Accionistas e o Estado Português
celebraram um contrato de investimento, ao
abrigo do qual a Sociedade poderá beneficiar de
um conjunto de benefícios fiscais e aduaneiros
(Nota 6).

In 1985, the Company, its shareholders, and the
Portuguese Government signed an investment
agreement under which the Company will
receive a number of customs and tax benefits
(Note 6).

As notas que se seguem respeitam a numeração
sequencial definida no Plano Oficial de
Contabilidade (POC). As notas cuja numeração
se encontra ausente deste anexo não são
aplicáveis à Sociedade ou a sua apresentação
não é relevante para a leitura das demonstrações
financeiras anexas.

The notes below follow the numbering defined
by the Oficial Chart of Accounts ("Plano Oficial
de Contabilidade - POC"). Note numbers that are
not included herein are not applicable to the
Company or are not relevant for an appreciation
of the financial statements.

3. BASES DE APRESENTAÇÃO E PRINCIPAIS CRITÉRIOS VALORIMÉTRICOS UTILIZADOS

3. SUMMARY OF PRINCIPAL ACCOUNTING POLICIES AND BASIS OF PRESENTATION

As demonstrações financeiras anexas foram
preparadas a partir dos livros e registos
contabilísticos da Sociedade, mantidos de acordo
com os princípios de contabilidade geralmente
aceites em Portugal.

The accompanying financial statements have
been prepared from the Company's accounting
records maintained in Portuguese Escudos and
in accordance with generally accepted
accounting principles in Portugal.

Os principais critérios valorimétricos utilizados na preparação das demonstrações financeiras foram os seguintes:

The principal accounting polices used in the preparation of the financial statements are as follows:

a) Imobilizações incorpóreas

a) Intangible assets

As imobilizações incorpóreas são constituídas basicamente por:

Intangible assets comprise:

- Despesas de instalação relativas aos custos associados à constituição da Sociedade, aos aumentos de capital, à alteração dos estatutos e outros encargos notariais. São amortizadas segundo o método das quotas constantes durante um periodo de 5 anos que teve início em 1989 (ano de início da actividade comercial) inclusivé;

- Installation and expansion costs incurred with the incorporation of the Company, increases in capital, alterations of statutes and other notarial costs. These costs are being amortised over five years, commencing in 1989 (year of start of commercial activity);

- Despesas de investigação e desenvolvimento incorridas antes do início da construção da mina e despesas relativas a estudos de impacto ambiental incorridas no exercício corrente são amortizadas segundo o método das quotas constantes por um período de 20 anos (período de vida útil estimada da mina), o qual teve início em 1989 (ano de início da actividade comercial) inclusivé e por um período de 5 anos, respectivamente.

- Research and development costs incurred prior to the construction of the mine and costs relating to environmental studies incurred during 1992. The former are being amortised over twenty years (estimated life of the mine), commencing in 1989 (year of start of commercial activity), and the latter over a period of five years;

- Trespasse relativo à obtenção em 1990 do arrendamento de um prédio urbano. Este trespasse não é amortizado.

- Goodwill relating to the acquisition of a building during 1990. This cost is not being amortised by the Company;

- Despesas relativas à fase de arranque e início de actividade da mina. São amortizadas segundo o método das quotas constantes durante um período de 6 anos que teve início em 1989 (ano de início da actividade comercial) inclusivé;

- Expenses relating to the start up of mining operations. These costs are being amortised over a period of six years, on a straight-line basis, commencing in 1989 (year of start of commercial activity);

- Despesas associadas ao treino e formação profissional do pessoal especializado da mina. São amortizadas segundo o método das quotas constantes por um período de 20 anos (período de vida útil estimada da mina) o qual teve início em 1989 (ano de início da actividade comercial) inclusivé.

- Expenses associated with the training and professional education of specialised mining personnel. These costs are being amortised over twenty years (estimated life of the mine), on a straight-line basis, commencing in 1989 (year of start of commercial activity).

b) Imobilizações corpóreas

As imobilizações corpóreas encontram-se reflectidas ao custo de aquisição (que inclui o valor da factura do fornecedor, despesas de compra e montagem e outras de natureza geral directamente associadas à construção e desenvolvimento da mina) acrescidas de encargos financeiros e diferenças cambiais incorridos durante o período de construção (provenientes de empréstimos e outros passivos contraídos para a aquisição do imobilizado corpóreo).

As amortizações são calculadas sobre o valor de custo pelo método das quotas constantes a partir do ano de entrada em funcionamento ou início da utilização dos bens, utilizando-se taxas de amortização determinadas com base na vida útil estimada dos bens ou no período de vida útil esperada da mina (20 anos), os quais se situam entre os limites mínimos e máximos permitidos pela legislação fiscal Portuguesa e de acordo com as seguintes vidas úteis estimadas:

	Anos de vida útil
Edifícios e outras construções (não industriais)	50
Equipamento básico:	
- Construções e equipamento mineiro	15 - 20
- Outros	6 - 10
Equipamento de transporte	4 - 5
Ferramentas e utensílios	3 - 7
Equipamento administrativo	5 - 7
Outras imobilizações corpóreas	7

c) Existências

As mercadorias e as matérias-primas, subsidiárias e de consumo encontram-se valorizadas ao custo médio de aquisição, o qual é inferior ao respectivo valor de mercado, utilizando-se o custo médio como método de custeio das saídas.

Os produtos acabados e intermédios encontram-se valorizados ao custo de produção, o qual é inferior ao seu valor de mercado.

b) Fixed assets

Fixed assets are stated at acquisition cost, which comprises invoice cost (including purchasing, assembly, and other costs associated with the construction and development of the mine), financial expenses and foreign exchange differences associated with borrowings and other debts incurred during the construction period to finance the acquisition of fixed assets.

Depreciation is provided from the date on which fixed assets are brought into use, on a straight-line basis over the estimated useful lives of the assets or the expected life of the mine (twenty years), based on application of annual rates between the minimum and the maximum allowed by Portuguese tax legislation. The following represent the average estimated useful lives:

	Years
Buildings and other constructions (not associated with production)	*50*
Basic equipment:	
- Building and mining equipment	*15 - 20*
- Others	*6 - 10*
Vehicles and transportation equipment	*4 - 5*
Tools and dies	*3 - 7*
Administrative equipment	*5 - 7*
Other tangible fixed assets	*7*

c) Inventories

Raw and other materials are stated at the weighted average cost of purchase (including invoice price, together with the additional expenses associated with the purchase), which is less than net realisable value.

Finished goods are stated at production cost, which is less than net realisable value.

O custo de produção inclui o custo da matéria-prima incorporada, mão-de-obra directa e gastos gerais de fabrico.

Production cost includes the cost of raw materials, labour and overheads.

d) Títulos negociáveis

d) Marketable securities

Os títulos negociáveis são registados ao mais baixo do custo de aquisição ou de mercado. Os juros provenientes são reconhecidos como proveitos no exercício em que ocorrem.

Marketable securities are recorded at cost wich is the lower of cost or market value. The related interest is recognised as profit in the period in which it occurs.

e) Acréscimos e diferimentos

e) Deferred costs and income, and accrued costs and prepaid expenses

Os acréscimos e diferimentos incluem basicamente:

The Company records the following transactions under these headings:

No activo:

Assets:

• Custos diferidos com conservação e reparação de carácter plurienal, os quais são amortizados em seis anos;

• *Maintenance costs incurred prior to commercial production which are amortised over a period of six years on a straight-line basis;*

• Custos de natureza geral incorridos pela Sociedade desde a data da sua constituição até 1 de Janeiro de 1989 (data de início da actividade comercial) e não directamente associados à construção e desenvolvimento da mina, os quais são amortizados em seis anos;

• *General costs incurred by the Company from the date it was established until 1 January 1989 (date of start of commercial activity) and which are not directly associated with the construction and development of the mine. These costs are amortised over a period of six years on a straight-line basis;*

• Custos diferidos incorridos e ainda não totalmente apurados, com a construção de um ramal ferroviário entre a Mina de Neves Corvo e a estação de Ourique cuja utilização plena terá lugar em 1993, iniciando-se então a sua amortização. Nos termos do contrato celebrado entre a CP - Caminhos de Ferro Portugueses, E.P. (CP) e a Sociedade em 16 de Maio de 1991, o ramal ferroviário será entregue à CP para efeitos de exploração passando a constituir bens do domínio público.

• *Costs incurred, and not yet completely quantified, in relation to the construction of the railway between the Neves Corvo Mine and Ourique which will only enter fully into use in 1993 and whose amortisation will only begin at that time. Under the contract signed on 16 May 1991 between the CP - Caminhos de Ferro Portugueses, E.P. (CP) and the Company, the railway will be handed over to CP to be used and will become property of the State.*

• Proveitos relativos a juros a receber no exercício seguinte;

• *Profit relating to interest receivable in the following year.*

No passivo:

Liabilities:

• As remunerações (e respectivos encargos)

• *Holiday pay and bonuses due at the end of the*

devidas por motivo de férias vencidas e não pagas, no fim do exercício;

year but not yet paid;

• As diferenças de câmbio favoráveis não realizadas resultantes de dívidas a médio e longo prazo, uma vez que existem expectativas razoáveis quanto à sua reversibilidade (Nota 48);

• *Unrealised exchange gains relating to the long- -term portion of loans as, in management's opinion, a reversal of the gain may occur prior to repayment (Note 4);*

• Os subsídios recebidos a fundo perdido para financiamento de imobilizações corpóreas (ver alínea g);

• *Cash grants received to finance the acquisition of fixed assets (see Note 3g);*

• Os encargos financeiros incorridos até ao final de cada exercício e com vencimento no exercício seguinte (Nota 48).

• *Interest incurred at the year-end and due for payment in the following year (Note 48).*

f) Reconhecimento dos proveitos

f) Revenue recognition

Os proveitos são registados inicialmente pelo valor das facturas previsionais, estimado no momento do embarque do concentrado. Aquele valor é posteriormente ajustado para os seus valores definitivos quando estes são conhecidos, nomeadamente: quantidade, análises do concentrado à data de desembarque e preço para o período de cotação estabelecido no contrato.

Em 31 de Dezembro de 1992 a Sociedade ajustou o valor estimado das facturas previsionais, ajustando consequentemente as vendas do exercício, com base na cotação média futura do cobre verificada durante o mês de Dezembro no "London Metal Exchange" e em 31 de Dezembro de 1991 com base na cotação futura do cobre àquela data. Adicionalmente, face ao comportamento da cotação do cobre no início de 1993 e de 1992 a Sociedade reconheceu ainda, nos períodos findos em 31 de Dezembro de 1992 e 1991 as perdas resultantes da comparação daquele valor ajustado com o obtido pela cotação futura verificada no "London Metal Exchange" em 19 de Janeiro de 1993 e em 24 de Janeiro de 1992, respectivamente (datas de encerramento das contas relativas ao exercício de 1992 e 1991).

As at 31 December 1992, the Company valued provisional invoices by adjusting sales using the average future copper price during the month of December quoted on the London Metal Ex- change, and as at 31 December 1991 by using the future copper price as at that date. In addi- tion, the Company recognized losses arising as a consequence of the movement of copper prices on the international markets at the beginning of 1993 and 1992. Those losses were determined based on the 19 January 1993 (average of the last five days) and 24 January 1992 future prices for copper on the London Metal Exchange which were the dates that the Company's accounts were closed for the 1992 and 1991 fiscal years respectively.

Em 31 de Dezembro de 1991 este último ajustamento foi registado na rubrica de provisões

As at 31 December 1991 this later adjustment was shown under the heading of provisions for

para riscos e encargos (Nota 34) e em 31 de Dezembro de 1992 foi registado directamente nas rubricas de clientes e de vendas.

g) Subsídios recebidos para financiamento de imobilizacões corpóreas

Os subsídios recebidos a fundo perdido para financiamento de imobilizações corpóreas são registados no passivo, como proveitos diferidos, na rúbrica acréscimos e diferimentos, e reconhecidos na demonstração de resultados proporcionalmente às amortizações das imobilizações corpóreas subsidiadas.

other risks and costs (Note 34) and as at 31 December 1992 was included directly under the heading of customers and sales.

g) Subsidies received to finance the acquisition of fixed assets

Subsidies received to finance the acquisition of fixed assets are recorded as deferred income and are recognised as a profit proportionally to the depreciation of the related fixed assets.

4. ACTIVOS E PASSIVOS EXPRESSOS EM MOEDA ESTRANGEIRA

4. TRANSACTIONS EXPRESSED IN FOREIGN CURRENCIES

Todos os activos e passivos expressos em moeda estrangeira foram convertidos em escudos utilizando as taxas de câmbio vigentes em 31 de Dezembro de 1992 e 1991 publicadas pelo Banco de Portugal.

As diferenças de câmbio, favoráveis e desfavoráveis, originadas pelas diferenças entre as taxas de câmbio em vigor na data das transacções e as vigentes na data das cobranças, pagamentos ou na data do balanço, são registadas como proveitos e custos na demonstração de resultados do exercício, excepto para as diferenças de câmbio favoráveis não realizadas, no montante de mEsc. 683.947 e mEsc. 2.429.345, em 31 de Dezembro de 1992 e de 1991, respectivamente, relativas à parcela a médio e longo prazo dos empréstimos contraídos em moeda estrangeira, as quais foram registadas no balanço na rubrica de proveitos diferidos, uma vez que a Administração da Sociedade considera que a evolução daquelas moedas, face ao Escudo, poderá ser reversível até à data do pagamento dos referidos empréstimos.

All assets and liabilities expressed in foreign currencies have been translated into Portuguese Escudos at the rates of exchange prevailing on 31 December 1992 and 1991.

Realised and unrealised exchange differences arising from changes between historical exchange rates and those prevailing at the repayment date or as at 31 December 1992 and 1991 have been recorded in the profit and loss account for the period, except for unrealised exchange gains as at 31 December 1992 and 1991 of 683,947 contos and 2,429,345 contos respectively, relating to the long-term portion of loans which have been recorded in the balance sheet as deferred income, as in management's opinion, a reversal of the gain may occur before repayment.

6. IMPOSTOS SOBRE LUCROS FUTUROS

6. FUTURE CORPORATION TAX

A Sociedade, de acordo com o contrato de investimento assinado entre a mesma, os seus

In accordance with the investment agreement that the Company signed with the Portuguese

Accionistas e o Estado Português, encontra-se isenta pelo período de cinco anos, o qual se iniciou em 1989 (data de início de exploração), do pagamento do Imposto sobre o Rendimento das Pessoas Colectivas (IRC). Caso a Sociedade não usufruísse deste benefício fiscal o montante deste imposto a pagar relativo aos resultados dos exercícios de 1992 e 1991 seria de, aproximadamente, mEsc. 3.200.000 e mEsc. 3.400.000, respectivamente. Adicionalmente estipula este contrato que a Sociedade fica obrigada a efectuar durante o período de vigência do contrato as reavaliações do activo imobilizado corpóreo, segundo o autorizado pela lei vigente e de acordo com os critérios administrativos pertinentes.

O Decreto-Lei nº 49/91 de 25 de Janeiro e o Decreto-Lei nº 264/92 de 24 de Novembro vieram permitir às empresas a reavaliação do seu activo imobilizado corpóreo através de coeficientes de desvalorização monetária, referindo como multiplicadores máximos os constantes da Portaria nº 240/90 de 4 de Abril e na Portaria nº 395/92 de 12 de Maio, respectivamente.

Tendo em atenção que é deixado ao livre arbítrio das empresas que decidirem utilizar a faculdade permitida pela lei, um amplo campo de decisão, consoante os seus legítimos interesses de acordo com o melhor critério de gestão, a Administração da Sociedade decidiu não efectuar a reavaliação, informando de tal o ICEP - Instituto do Comércio Externo de Portugal. Assim, a Administração da Sociedade considera que pelo facto de não ter efectuado a reavaliação permitida pelos Decretos-Lei atrás indicados não incorreu em qualquer incumprimento contratual.

Government, the Company is exempt from paying Corporation Tax (IRC) for a period of five years, commencing with and including the year in which exploration begins. As a result of certain benefits granted under this contract, the Company was exempted from the payment of corporation tax for 1992 and 1991 of approximately 3,200,000 contos and 3,400,000 contos respectively. In addition, under the terms of this contract, the Company is obliged to revalue its fixed assets, during the period of the contract, as permitted by law and in accordance with the legal administrative criteria.

Decree-Law 49/91 of 25 January and Decree-Law 264/92 of 24 November permits that companies revalue their fixed assets by the application of rates of monetary devaluation, by reference to the maximum rates published in Portaria 240/90 of 4 April and Portaria 395/92 of 12 May, respectively.

As companies are left to decide whether or not to make use of these legal provisions by management considering whether or not it is in the best interests of the company, the Board of Directors of the Company decided not to revalue its fixed assets and accordingly, informed ICEP - Instituto do Comércio Externo de Portugal. The Board of Directors of the Company considers that the decision not to revalue the fixed assets, as permitted by the Decree-Law mentioned above, will not result in the Company being considered as not having fulfilled the conditions of the contract conditions.

7. NUMERO MÉDIO DE PESSOAL

O número médio de pessoal foi o seguinte:

Empregados:	**1992**	**1991**
Efectivos	961	859
A prazo	109	230
	1.070	1.089

A 31 de Dezembro de 1992 e 1991, o número total de pessoal empregado ao serviço da Empresa era de, respectivamente, 1.073 e 1.062.

7. AVERAGE NUMBER OF PERSONNEL

In 1992 and 1991, the average number of personnel was as follows:

Employees:	*1992*	*1991*
On long-term contracts	961	859
On short-term contracts	109	230
	1.070	1.089

As at 31 December 1992 and 1991, the total number of personnel was 1,073 and 1,062, respectively.

10. MOVIMENTO DO ACTIVO IMOBILIZADO

Durante o exercício, o movimento ocorrido no valor de custo das imobilizações incorpóreas e corpóreas, bem como nas respectivas amortizações acumuladas foi o seguinte:

	Activo bruto				
Rubricas	Saldo inicial	Adições	Alienações	Transferências e abates	Saldo final
Imobilizações incorpóreas:					
Despesas de instalação	238.112	-	-	-	238.112
Despesas de investigação e de desenvolvimento	368.148	26.233	-	-	394.381
Trespasses	70.000	-	-	-	70.000
Despesas de instalação e arranque da mina	1.116.140	-	-	-	1.116.140
Despesas de treino e formação profisional	421.507	-	-	-	421.507
	2.213.907	26.233	-	-	2.240.140
Imobilizações corpóreas:					
Terrenos e recursos naturais	131.462	-	-	-	131.462
Edifícios e outras construções	8.557.198	-	-	592.709	9.149.907
Equipamento básico	62.901.694	-	(139.406)	1.552.245	64.314.533
Equipamento de transporte	540.483	-	(81.613)	87.686	546.556
Ferramentas e utensílios	1.515.683	-	(13.925)	206.707	1.708.465
Equipamento administrativo	823.779	-	(2.152)	176.335	997.962
Taras e vasilhame	168.879	-	-	83	168.962
outras imobilizações corpóreas	43.348	-	-	-	43.348
Imobilizações em curso	2.900.931	4.610.112	-	(4.590.599)	2.920.444
Adiantamentos por conta de imobilizações corpóreas	17.420	29.954	-	-	47.374
	77.600.877	4.640.066	(237.096)	(1.974.834)	80.029.013

10. FIXED ASSETS MOVEMENT

During 1992, the movements in the intangible assets, fixed assets and construction in progress accounts and in the related accumulated amortisation and depreciation accounts, were as follows:

	Cost				
Captions	Initial balance	Additions	Retirements	Transfers and write-offs	Final balance
Intangible assets:					
Installation costs	238.112	-	-	-	238.112
Expenses related with research and development	368.148	26.233	-	-	394.381
Goodwill	70.000	-	-	-	70.000
Expenses related with the start-up of mining operations	1.116.140	-	-	-	1.116.140
Training expenses during the period of mining construction	421.507	-	-	-	421.507
	2.213.907	26.233	-	-	2.240.140
Fixed assets:					
Land and natural resources	131.462	-	-	-	131.462
Buildings and other construction	8.557.198	-	-	592.709	9.149.907
Basic equipment	62.901.694	-	(139.406)	1.552.245	64.314.533
Vehicles and transportation equipment	540.483	-	(81.613)	87.686	546.556
Tools and dies	1.515.683	-	(13.925)	206.707	1.708.465
Administrative equipment	823.779	-	(2.152)	176.335	997.962
Containers	168.879	-	-	83	168.962
Other fixed assets	43.348	-	-	-	43.348
Construction in progress	2.900.931	4.610.112	-	(4.590.599)	2.920.444
Advances to suppliers of fixed assets	17.420	29.954	-	-	47.374
	77.600.877	4.640.066	(237.096)	(1.974.834)	80.029.013

Rubricas	Saldo inicial	Amortizações Amortizações do exercício	Regu- larizações	Abates	Saldo final
Imobilizações incorpóreas:					
Despesas de instalação	134.071	47.622	-	-	181.693
Despesas de investigação e de desenvolvimento	55.222	18.408	-	-	73.630
Trespasses	-	-	-	-	-
Despesas de instalação e arranque da mina	453.136	190.939	-	-	644.075
Despesas de treino e formação profissional	63.226	21.075	-	-	84.301
	705.655	278.044	-	-	983.699
Imobilizações corpóreas:					
Terrenos e recursos naturais					
Edifícios e outras construções	885.587	351.190	-	-	1.236.777
Equipamento básico	10.233.940	3.712.381	1.523	(88.877)	13.858.967
Equipamento de transporte	298.062	128.654	-	(58.425)	368.291
Ferramentas e utensílios	741.721	239.490	-	(1.828)	979.383
Equipamento administrativo	444.298	217.036	-	(1.876)	659.458
Taras e vasilhame	96.392	24.133	-	-	120.525
Outras imobilizações corpóreas	15.493	5.021	-	-	20.514
	12.715.493	4.677.905	1.523	(151.006)	17.243.915

Amortisation and depreciation

Captions	Initial balance	Amortisation depreciation	Transfers	Retirements	Final balance
Intangible assets:					
Instalation costs	134.071	47.622	-	-	181.693
Expenses related with research and development	55.222	18.408	-	-	73.630
Goodwill	-	-	-	-	-
Expenses related with the start-up of mining operations	453.136	190.939	-	-	644.075
Training expenses during the period of mining construction	63.226	21.075	-	-	84.301
	705.655	278.044	-	-	983.699
Fixed assets:					
Land and natural resources					
Buildings and other constructions	885.587	351.190	-	-	1.236.777
Basic equipment	10.233.940	3.712.381	1.523	(88.877)	13.858.967
Vehicles and transportation equipment	298.062	128.654	-	(58.425)	368.291
Tools and dies	741.721	239.490	-	(1.828)	979.383
Administrative equipment	444.298	217.036	-	(1.876)	659.458
Containers	96.392	24.133	-	-	120.525
Other fixed assets	15.493	5.021	-	-	20.514
	12.715.493	4.677.905	1.523	(151.006)	17.243.915

14. IMOBILIZAÇÕES CORPÓREAS E EM CURSO (Informação adicional)

A repartição do imobilizado corpóreo (valores brutos) e em curso em 31 de Dezembro de 1992 e 1991, por actividade é como segue:

	1992	1991
Cobre	63.560.469	60.150.217
Estanho	12.181.673	11.530.687
Comuns	4.286.871	5.919.973
	80.029.013	77.600.877

Em 31 de Dezembro de 1992 o imobilizado em curso tem a seguinte composição:

Projecto de aprofundamento da mina	1.302.729
Prospecção e sondagens	677.229
Projecto da prospecção de minérios complexos	323.508
Outros projectos em curso	616.978
	2.920.444

14. FIXED ASSETS AND CONSTRUCTION IN PROGRESS

The analysis of the fixed assets and construction in progress accounts by activity, as at 31 December 1991, is as follows:

	1992	*1991*
Copper production	*63.560.469*	*60.150.217*
Tin production	*12.181.673*	*11.530.687*
Others	*4.286.871*	*5.919.973*
	80.029.013	*77.600.877*

As at 31 December 1992, construction in progress comprise:

Mine deepening project	*1.302.729*
Exploration and drilling	*677.229*
Exploration of complex minerals	*323.508*
Other construction in progress	*616.978*
	2.920.444

Em 31 de Dezembro de 1992 e 1991, a Sociedade não possuía imobilizações corpóreas em poder de terceiros, reversíveis, localizadas no estrangeiro ou implantadas em propriedade alheia, com excepção do imobilizado corpóreo implantado no porto de Setúbal no montante de m Esc. 925.410.

The Company did not have any fixed assets held by third parties, except for fixed assets located at the port of Setúbal valued at 925,410 contos, not did it have any held abroad as at 31 December 1992 and 1991.

16. SALDOS E TRANSACÇÕES COM EMPRESAS ASSOCIADAS	*16. GROUP COMPANIES*

Os saldos em 31 de Dezembro de 1992 e 1991 e as transacções efectuadas com empresas associadas, nos exercícios findos naquelas datas, são os seguintes:

At a 31 December 1992 and 1991, balances with related companies and the related transaction during the years ended on those dates were as follows:

	1992	1991
EDM - Empresa de Desenvolvimento Mineiro, S.A. (conta a receber)	14.829	51.652
RTZ Metals, Ltd. (conta a pagar)	(37.148)	-

	1992	*1991*
EDM - Empresa de Desenvolvimento Mineiro, S.A. (account receivable)	*14.829*	*51.652*
RTZ Metals, Ltd. (account payable)	*(37.148)*	

22. EXISTÊNCIAS EM TRÂNSITO OU À GUARDA DE TERCEIROS	*22. GOODS IN TRANSIT AND WAREHOUSED WITH THIRD PARTIES*

Em 31 de Dezembro de 1992 e de 1991 existiam fora da Sociedade, as seguintes existências:

As at 31 December 1992 and 1991, the following inventories were held by third parties:

	1992	1991
Produtos acabados e intermédios em poder de terceiros	25.019	14.940
Matérias e materiais em trânsito	41.194	73.566
	66.213	88.506

	1992	*1991*
Finished goods stored in third party warehouses outside Portugal	*25.019*	*14.940*
In transit (raw materials and others)	*41.194*	*73.566*
	66.213	*88.506*

25. DÍVIDAS ACTIVAS E PASSIVAS COM O PESSOAL	*25. EMPLOYEES ACCOUNTS RECEIVABLE AND PAYABLE*

Em 31 de Dezembro de 1992 e 1991, a Sociedade tinha as seguintes dívidas activas e passivas com o pessoal:

As at 31 December 1992 and 1991, the Company had the following balances with its employees:

	1992	1991
Saldos devedores	28.379	26.968
Saldos credores	5.254	2.165

	1992	*1991*
Accounts receivable	*28.379*	*26.968*
Accounts payable	*5.254*	*2.165*

27. TÍTULOS DE PARTICIPAÇÃO

A Sociedade, durante o exercício de 1989, procedeu à emissão de 3.050.000 títulos de participação com o valor unitário de mEsc. 1 cada. Os mesmos foram integralmente subscritos pelos Accionistas, na proporção do capital social (Nota 37).

Os títulos são remunerados com base numa parte fixa, a qual será calculada aplicando a 60% do valor nominal uma taxa de juro igual a 85% da taxa de referência das obrigações em vigor no início do ano a que a remuneração respeita; e uma parte variável, a qual será calculada atribuindo a 40% do valor nominal o valor correspondente ao coeficiente entre o resultado líquido de impostos e o somatório do capital social com o montante de títulos de participação. Contudo, a remuneração anual não será inferior a 75% da taxa de referência das obrigações em vigor no início do ano a que a remuneração respeita nem superior a 125% da mesma.

A remuneração dos títulos será paga anualmente, por uma só vez, no mês seguinte ao da aprovação das contas da Sociedade. O pagamento no montante de mEsc. 610.000, relativo ao exercício de 1992, ocorrerá em 1993, encontrando-se este montante reflectido no Balanço na rubrica Accionistas (dívidas a terceiros - curto prazo).

Os títulos podem ser reembolsados ao par, decorridos dez anos sobre a sua emissão, por iniciativa da Sociedade, ou dos detentores dos mesmos, com o acordo daquela.

27. PARTICIPATING SHARES

In 1989, the Company issued 3,050,000 participating shares with a nominal value of 1 conto. These shares were purchased by current shareholders in direct proportion to their shareholding (Note 37).

Interest on these shares is paid based on a fixed and a variable portion. The payment on the fixed portion is calculated by applying to 60% of the nominal value of each bond an interest rate equal to 85% of the reference rate for Portuguese shares, applicable at the beginning of the year in which the payment is due. The payment on the variable portion is calculated by applying to 40% of the nominal value a rate which corresponds to the coefficient between the profits (or losses), net of taxes, divided by the sum of equity and the total amount of the participating shares. The annual payment, however, cannot be either less than 75% or more than 125% of the reference rate for government bonds, applicable at the beginning of the year.

Payments related to participating shares will be made annually in the month following the approval of the Company's accounts. The payment amounting to 610,000 contos, which applies to 1992, will be made in 1993 (the Company has shown this amount under the heading of shareholders current accounts-short term liabilities).

Participating shares can be redeemed at par value, ten years after issue, either at the request of the Company or at the request of the participation shareholders with the prior agreement of the Company.

29. DÍVIDAS A TERCEIROS A MAIS DE CINCO ANOS

Em 31 de Dezembro de 1992 e 1991, a Sociedade tinha as seguintes dívidas a terceiros a mais de cinco anos:

Empréstimos a médio e longo prazo:	1992	1991
Empréstimos bancários (Nota 48)	17.804.716	18.769.963
Títulos de participação (Nota 27)	3.050.000	3.050.000

29. ACCOUNTS PAYABLE AFTER MORE THAN FIVE YEARS

As at 31 December 1992 and 1991, the Company had the following accounts payable after more than five years:

Medium an long-term:	1992	1991
Bank Loans (Note 48)	17.804.716	18.769.963
Participating shares (Note 27)	3.050.000	3.050.000

32. GARANTIAS PRESTADAS

Em 31 de Dezembro de 1992 e 1991, a Sociedade tinha assumido responsabilidades, com garantias prestadas, como segue:

	1992	1991
Garantias bancárias a terceiros:		
EDP - Electricidade de Portugal	206.999	228.443
Direcção-Geral das Contribuições		
e Impostos	30.000	30.000
Câmara Municipal de Almodôvar	57.163	57.163
Alfândega de Lisboa	35.512	55.512
Ministério da Indústria e Energia	12.000	12.000
IAPMEI - Instituto de Apoio		
às Pequenas e Médias Empresas	250.000	250.000
Concedidas por:		
Crédit Lyonnais Portugal	500.716	536.419
Banco Totta & Açores	61.887	67.727
Banco de Comércio e Indústria	29.071	28.972

O empréstimo concedido pelo Banco Europeu de Investimento no montante equivalente a ECU's 135 milhões à Sociedade está garantido em 51% pela E.D.M. - Empresa de Desenvolvimento Mineiro, S.A., contragarantido em partes iguais por um consórcio de bancos formado pelo Barclays Bank PLC e pelo Deutsche Bank AG, e em 49% por RTZ Limited.

32. GUARANTEES PROVIDED BY THIRD-PARTIES

As at 31 December 1992 and 1991, the following guarantees have been provided by third parties in relation to certain obligations of the Company:

	1992	1991
Bank guaranties given to third parties:		
EDP - Electricidade de Portugal	206.999	228.443
Direcção-Geral das Contribuições		
e Impostos	30.000	30.000
Câmara Municipal de Almodôvar	57.163	57.163
Alfândega de Lisboa (Portuguese		
Customs)	35.512	55.512
Ministério da Indústria e Energia	12.000	12.000
IAPMEI - Instituto de Apoio		
às Pequenas e Médias Empresas	250.000	250.000
Guaranties provided by:		
Crédit Lyonnais Portugal	500.716	536.419
Banco Totta & Açores	61.887	67.727
Banco de Comércio e Indústria	29.071	28.972

Fifty one percent of the loan granted to the Company by the European Investment Bank (equivalent to Ecu 135,000,000) is guaranteed by EDM - Empresa de Desenvolvimento Mineiro, S.A., with a secondary guarantee in equal parts by a consortium of banks that includes Barclays Bank PLC and the Deutsche Bank AG. The remaining 49% is guaranteed by the RTZ Limited.

34. MOVIMENTO OCORRIDO NAS PROVISÕES

Durante o exercício realizaram-se os seguintes movimentos nas contas de provisões:

	Saldo inicial	Aumento	Redução	Saldo final
Provisões para riscos e encargos:				
Para perdas potenciais na cotação do cobre	149.907		(149.907)	
Para processos judiciais em curso	2.300	-	(240)	2.060
Outros riscos e encargos	292.136	-	(243.261)	48.875
	444.343	-	(393.408)	50.935

34. MOVEMENT IN PROVISIONS

The movement in the provision accounts during 1992 was as follows:

	Opening balance	Increases	Decreases	Closing balance
Provision for other risks:				
For fluctuations in the copper price	149.907		(149.907)	
For litigation and and claims	2.300	-	(240)	2.060
Other risks	292.136	-	(243.261)	48.875
	444.343	-	(393.408)	50.935

36. COMPOSIÇÃO DO CAPITAL

Conforme deliberado pelos Accionistas na Assembleia Geral de 21 de Março de 1990, foram convertidas em acções preferenciais, sem direito a voto, acções ordinárias representativas de 20% das respectivas participações sociais pelo que o capital da Sociedade, em 31 de Dezembro de 1992 tinha a seguinte composição:

Categoria	Número	%	Valor nominal
Acções ordinárias	11.720.000	80	mEsc. 1
Acções preferenciais	2.930.000	20	mEsc. 1

As acções preferenciais sem voto conferem direito a um dividendo prioritário, 5% do seu valor nominal.

36. SHARE CAPITAL

As at 31 December 1992, the Company's share capital was constituted as follows:

Category	Number	%	Nominal value
Ordinary shares	11.720.000	80	mEsc. 1
Preference shares	2.930.000	20	mEsc. 1

The preferences shares, which are without voting right, are entitled to a priority dividend of 5% of their nominal value.

37. IDENTIFICAÇÃO DE PESSOAS COLECTIVAS DETENTORAS DO CAPITAL SUBSCRITO E REALIZADO

O capital em 31 de Dezembro de 1992 e 1991 encontrava-se totalmente subscrito e realizado e é detido pelas seguintes entidades:

	Montante		%	
	1992	1991	1992	1991
EDM - Empresa de Desen-volvimento Mineiro, S.A.	7.471.500	7.471.500	51.0	51.00
Tinto Investments Europe, Ltd.	7.178.427	7.178.427	48.99	48.99
RTZ Metals, Ltd.	73	73	0.001	00.01
	14.650.000	14.650.000	100.0	100.00

37. SHAREHOLDERS

The Company's share capital as at 31 December 1992 and 1991, fully subscribed and paid up, was held as follows:

	Amount		%	
	1992	1991	1992	1991
EDM - Empresa de Desen-volvimento Mineiro, S.A.	7.471.500	7.471.500	51,0	51,00
Tinto Investments Europe, Ltd.	7.178.427	7.178.427	48,99	48,99
RTZ Metals, Ltd.	73	73	0,001	00,01
	14.650.000	14.650.000	100,0	100,00

40. VARIAÇÃO DE OUTRAS CONTAS DO CAPITAL PRÓPRIO

As outras contas do capital próprio tiveram o seguinte movimento durante o exercício de 1992:

Rubrica	Saldo inicial	Aumentos	Diminuições	Saldo final
Reservas legais	1.399.978	468.037		1.868.015
Reservas especiais	824.000	50.000		874.000
Reservas livres	13.866.024	3.348.923		17.214.947
Resultado líquido do exercício	9.360.736	8.865.293	(9.360.736)	8.865.293
	25.450.738	12.732.253	(9.360.736)	28.822.255

40. MOVEMENT IN OTHER EQUITY ACCOUNTS

The following movements in equity accounts occurred during 1992:

	Opening balance	Increases	Decreases	Final balance
Legal reserve	1.399.978	468.037		1.868.015
Special reserve	824.000	50.000		874.000
Free reserve	13.866.024	3.348.923		17.214.947
Net profit for the year	9.360.736	8.865.293	(9.360.736)	8.865.293
	25.450.738	12.732.253	(9.360.736)	28.822.255

A reserva legal foi constituída de acordo com a legislacão comercial que estabelece que pelo menos 5% do resultado líquido anual tem de ser destinado ao seu reforço, até que esta represente pelo menos 20% do capital. Esta reserva não é distribuível, a não ser em caso de liquidação da Sociedade, podendo ser utilizada para absorver prejuízos depois de esgotadas todas as outras reservas.
A reserva especial foi constituída por força do contrato de investimento celebrado entre o Estado Português e os seus Accionistas, em 1985, que estabelece que a Sociedade e os seus Accionistas assegurarão uma política de constituição de reservas destinadas a fazer face aos seus compromissos de natureza financeira assumidos no referido contrato e, mais geralmente, de desenvolvimento e exploração da pirite complexa de zinco e à valorização dos minérios exploráveis nas concessões da Sociedade.
A aplicação dos resultados relativos aos exercícios de 1991 e 1990 foi a seguinte:

Portuguese law provides that at least 5% of net profit each year must be appropriated to a legal reserve until the reserve equals the statutory minimum requirement of 20% of share capital. This reserve is not avaiable for distribution.
In accordance with the Investiment Agreement, signed by the Company, its Shareholders and the Portuguese Governement and its Shareholders will create special reserves, the Company to enable the Company to comply with its financial commitements under the Investment Agreement and, more generally, to develop the zinc project and the natural resources avaiable on the Company's concessions.

The net profit for the year ended 31 December 1991 and 1990 was appropriated as follows during 1992 and 1991:

	1992	1991		1992	1991
- Dividendos	5.335.619	7.000.000	- *Dividends*	*5.335.619*	*7.000.000*
- Reservas livres	3.348.923	9.125.752	- *Free reserve*	*3.348.923*	*9.125.752*
- Reservas especiais	50.000	124.000	- *Special reserve*	*50.000*	*124.000*
- Reservas legais	468.037	864.174	- *Legal reserve*	*468.037*	*864.174*
- Resultados distribuídos aos trabalhadores	150.000	164.193	- *Distributed to the employees*	*150.000*	*164.193*
- Resultados atribuídos ao Conselho de Administração	8.157	5.367	- *Distributed to the Board of Directors*	*8.157*	*5.367*
	9.360.736	17.283.486		*9.360.736*	*17.283.486*

41. CUSTO DAS MATÉRIAS CONSUMIDAS

41. COST OF INVENTORIES SOLD AND USED

O custo das matérias consumidas no exercício de 1992 e 1991, foi determinado como segue:

The cost of inventories sold and used in 1992 and 1991 was as follows:

Matérias-primas subsidiárias e de consumo	1992	1991	*Raw Materials*	*1992*	*1991*
Existências iniciais	2.386.241	2.112.008	*Opening inventories*	*2.386.241*	*2.112.008*
Compras	2.173.077	2.751.863	*Purchases*	*2.173.077*	*2.751.863*
Regularização de existências	-	-		*-*	*-*
Existências finais	(2.053.916)	(2.386.241)	*Closing inventories*	*(2.053.916)*	*(2.386.241)*
Custo no exercício	2.505.402	2.477.630	*Cost of goods sold and used*	*2.505.402*	*2.477.630*

42. VARIAÇÃO DA PRODUÇÃO

A demonstração da variação da produção ocorrida no exercício de 1992 é como segue:

Produtos acabados e intermédios	1992	1991
Existências finais	548.679	1.743.930
Existências iniciais	(1.743.930)	(717.225)
Aumento/(Diminuição) no exercício	(1.195.251)	1.026.705

42. INVENTORY MOVEMENT

The inventory movements for 1992 and 1991 were as follows:

Finished goods	1992	1991
Closing inventories	548.679	1.743.930
Opening inventories	(1.743.930)	(717.225)
Increase / (Decrease) in the period	(1.195.251)	1.026.705

43. REMUNERAÇÃO DOS MEMBROS DOS ORGÃOS SOCIAIS

As remunerações atribuídas aos membros dos orgãos sociais nos exercícios de 1992 e 1991, foram respectivamente, mEsc. 47.909 e mEsc. 41.562.

43. REMUNERATION OF THE BOARD OF DIRECTORS AND AUDIT COMMITTEE

The remuneration of the Board of Directors and the Audit Committee (Conselho Fiscal) during 1992 and 1991 amounted to 47,909 contos, and 41,562 contos respectively.

44. VENDAS POR ACTIVIDADE E MERCADOS GEOGRÁFICOS

As vendas efectuadas no exercício de 1992 distribuem-se da seguinte forma:

Mercado geográfico Actividade	Cobre	Estanho	Total
- Europa	22.047.810	154.535	22.202.345
- América	5.372.291	247.679	5.619.970
- Asia	3.938.278	1.455.123	5.393.401
Vendas de produtos			33.215.716

44. SALES BY ACTIVITY AND BY MARKET

Sales by activity and by market are as follows:

	Copper	Tin	Total
- Europe	22.047.810	154.535	22.202.345
- America	5.372.291	247.679	5.619.970
- Asia	3.938.278	1.455.123	5.393.401
Sales of finished goods			33.215.716

45. DEMONSTRAÇÃO DOS RESULTADOS FINANCEIROS

Os resultados financeiros têm a seguinte composição:

Custos e perdas	1992	1991
Juros suportados	2.707.527	3.301.235
Remuneração de títulos de participação	610.000	610.000
Diferenças de câmbio desfavoráveis	1.111.052	1.728.648
Outros custos e perdas financeiras	106.874	26.615
Despesas com avales	129.486	123.757
Proveitos e ganhos	4.664.939	5.790.255
Juros obtidos	592.467	779.909
Diferenças de câmbio favoráveis	1.790.577	1.203.636
Descontos de pronto pagamento obtidos	8.811	1.136
	2.391.855	1.984.681
Resultados financeiros	2.273.084	3.805.574
	4.664.939	5.790.255

45. ANALYSIS OF FINANCIAL EXPENSES AND INCOME

Financial expenses and income are as follows:

Financial expenses	1992	1991
Interest payable	2.707.527	3.301.235
Participating shares remuneration	610.000	610.000
Foreign exchange losses	1.111.052	1.728.648
Other financial costs	106.874	26.615
Expenses relating to guarantees	129.486	123.757
Financial income	4.664.939	5.790.255
Interest receivable	592.467	779.909
Foreign exchange gains	1.790.577	1.203.636
Cash discounts obtained	8.811	1.136
	2.391.855	1.984.681
Net financial expenses	2.273.084	3.805.574
	4.664.939	5.790.255

46. DEMONSTRAÇÃO DOS RESULTADOS EXTRAORDINÁRIOS

Os resultados extraordinários têm a seguinte composição:

Custos e perdas:	1992	1991
Donativos	9.817	6.238
Apoio ao desenvolvimento regional	99.740	104.912
Perdas em existências	1.190	188
Perdas em imobilizações	15.410	23.898
Multas e penalidades	199	140
Correcções relativas a exercícios anteriores	136.592	210.257
Correcções em vendas	-	185.532
Outros custos e perdas extraordinários	-	30.660
	262.948	561.825

Proveitos e Ganhos		
Ganhos em imobilizações	27.720	12.400
Reduções de amortizações e de provisões	1.828	94.684
Correcções relativas a exercícios anteriores	127.727	258.392
Correcções em vendas	-	23.760
Outros proveitos e ganhos extraordinários	47.062	-
	204.337	389.236
Resultados extraordinários	58.611	172.589
	262.948	561.825

46. EXTRAORDINARY ITEMS

Extraordinary items are as follows.

Costs and losses	1992	1991
Donations	9.817	6.238
Regional development aid	99.740	104.912
Inventories losses	1.190	188
Fixed assets losses	15.410	23.898
Fines and penalties	199	140
Corrections relating to prior years	136.592	210.257
Corrections relating to sales	-	185.532
Other costs and extraordinary losses	-	30.660
	262.948	561.825

Gains and income		
Fixed assets gains	27.720	12.400
Decrease in amortisation and provisions	1.828	94.684
Corrections relating to prior years	127.727	258.392
Corrections relating to sales	-	23.760
Other	47.062	-
	204.337	389.236
Net extraordinary losses	58.611	172.589
	262.948	561.825

48. DÍVIDAS A INSTITUIÇÕES DE CRÉDITO

As dívidas a instituições de crédito em 31 de Dezembro de 1992 e de 1991, tinham a seguinte composicão, correspondendo os primeiros à parcela de curto prazo dos empréstimos a médio e longo prazo:

48. BANK LOANS

Bank loans as at 31 December 1992 and 1991 comprise:

Curto Prazo	1992	1991		Short-term	1992	1991
Empréstimos em moeda estrangeira				Loans in foreign currency		
- Banco Português do Atlântico	653.564	597.565		- Banco Português do Atlântico	653.564	597.565
- Banco Pinto & Sotto Mayor	1.521.079	1.402.979		- Banco Pinto & Sotto Mayor	1.521.079	1.402.979
- Banco Fonsecas & Burnay	245.087	224.089		- Banco Fonsecas & Burnay	245.087	224.089
- Consórcio de Bancos Franceses	54.219	52.579		- Consortium of French Banks	54.219	52.579
	2.473.949	2.277.212			2.473.949	2.277.212
Empréstimos em Escudos				Loans in Portuguese Escudos		
- Banco Português de Investimento		125.000		- Banco Português de Investimento		125.000
- Banco Internacional de Crédito e Espírito Santo Sociedade de Investimentos	-	150.000		- Banco Internacional de Crédito and Espírito Santo Sociedade de Investimentos		150.000
	-	275.000			-	275.000
Total a curto prazo	2.473.949	2.552.212		Total short-term	2.473.949	2.552.212

Médio e Longo Prazo	1992	1991		Medium and long-term	1992	1991
Empréstimos em moeda estrangeira				Loans in foreign currency		
- Banco Europeu de Investimento	23.936.603	22.745.321		- European Investment Bank	23.936.603	22.745.321
- Banco Pinto & Sotto Mayor	2.067.669	3.299.597		- Banco Pinto & Sotto Mayor	2.067.669	3.299.597
- Banco Português do Atlântico	1.307.129	1.792.692		- Banco Português do Atlântico	1.307.129	1.792.692
- Banco Fonsecas & Burnay	367.630	560.217		- Banco Fonsecas & Burnay	367.630	560.217
- Consórcio de Bancos Franceses	27.110	78.869		- Consortium of French Banks	27.110	78.869
	27.706.141	28.476.696			27.706.141	28.476.696
Empréstimos em Escudos				Loans in Portuguese Escudos		
- Banco Internacional de Crédito e Espírito Santo Sociedade de Investimentos		450.000		- Banco Internacional de Crédito and Espírito Santo Sociedade de Investimentos	-	450.000
- Banco Português de Investimento	-	250.000		- Banco Português de Investimento	-	250.000
	-	700.000			-	700.000
Total a médio e longo prazo	27.706.141	29.176.696		Total medium and long-term	27.706.141	29.176.696
Total geral	30.180.090	3.1728.908		Total	30.180.090	3.1728.908

A parcela de médio e longo prazo em 31 de Dezembro de 1992 e 1991 tinha os seguintes prazos de reembolso:

The medium and long-term portion is repayable as follows:

	1992	1991		1992	1991
1993	-	2.552.208	*1993*	-	*2.552.208*
1994	3.105.493	3.149.462	*1994*	*3.105.493*	*3.149.462*
1995	3.063.985	3.010.031	*1995*	*3.063.985*	*3.010.031*
1996	1.783.887	1.695.032	*1996*	*1.783.887*	*1.695.032*
1997	1.948.060	1.851.053	*1997*	*1.948.060*	*1.851.053*
Anos seguintes	17.804.716	16.918.910	*After 1997*	*17.804.716*	*16.918.910*
	27.706.141	29.176.696		*27.706.141*	*29.176.696*

Os empréstimos bancários contraídos em moeda estrangeira em 31 de Dezembro de 1992, estão convertidos em Escudos às taxas de câmbio em vigor naquela data. Em 31 de Dezembro de 1992 a parcela a médio e longo prazo daqueles financiamentos era representada pelas seguintes divisas:

	Em milhares				
	1994	1995	1996	1997	Anos seguintes
Dólares dos Estados Unidos	18.278	16.719	7.633	8.334	76.114
Marcos Alemães	1.174	-	-	-	-
Ecu's	1596	3.407	3.722	4.066	37.209
Francos Franceses	1.015	-	-	-	-

The amount of bank loans stated in foreign currency as at 31 December 1992 and 1991 has been translated into Portuguese Escudos at the applicable exchange rate in effect on those dates. As at 31 December 1992, the long-term portion of these loans was made up of the following currencies:

	In thousands				
	1994	*1995*	*1996*	*1997*	*After 1997*
US Dollars	*18.278*	*16.719*	*7.633*	*8.334*	*76.114*
Deutche Marks	*1.174*	*-*	*-*	*-*	*-*
ECU	*1596*	*3.407*	*3.722*	*4.066*	*37.209*
French Francs	*1.015*	*-*	*-*	*-*	*-*

Os encargos financeiros incorridos até 31 de Dezembro de 1992 e de 1991, mas não vencidos naquelas datas, no montante de mEsc. 159.910 e mEsc. 187.361, respectivamente, encontram-se reflectidos no Balanço na rubrica de Acréscimos de Custos (Nota 51).

Financial charges incurred but unpaid as at 31 December 1992 and 1991 amounting to 159,910 contos and 187,361 contos respectively are included in the balance sheet under the heading of deferred costs (Note 51).

49. OBRIGAÇÕES DA SOCIEDADE DECORRENTES DA CONCESSÃO MINEIRA

49. COMPANY OBLIGATIONS RESULTING FROM THE MINING CONCESSION

De acordo com a legislação em vigor a propriedade dos jazigos de substancias minerais pertence ao Estado Português, podendo o aproveitamento dos mesmos ser alvo de concessão. Deste modo, o Ministério da Indústria e Energia atribuiu em 1981 à Sociedade um conjunto de concessões mineiras por tempo indeterminado às quais corresponde o actual "Couto Mineiro de Neves Corvo". No âmbito daquelas concessões a Sociedade tem, de entre outras, as seguintes obrigações:

- A Sociedade fica obrigada a ter a concessão em constante estado de lavra activa, condicionando o ritmo da exploração ao custo da exploração e às possibilidades de transformação e venda de minérios extraídos, não se aproveitando do regime de suspensão de lavra para manter inexploradas reservas que largamente excedam as normais reservas estratégicas;

- Para além dos encargos tributários legais, a Sociedade terá como encargo de exploração a obrigação de:

In accordance with Portuguese legislation, the Portuguese Government owns all underground minerals in the country. Their exploration, however, can be licensed in the form of a concession. Accordingly, in 1981, the Government granted to the Company a number of mining concessions for an indeterminate period of time. These concessions constitute the "Couto Mineiro de Neves Corvo". As a result of these concessions, the Company has, among others, the following obligations:

- The Company is obliged to explore the mineral reserves under concession, varying its pace depending on the cost and the possibilites for the transformation and the sale of the extracted minerals. This obligation exists to avoid any suspention of exploration activities which could result in unexplored reserves exceeding normal strategic reserves;

- The Company has the following additional obligations:

a) Pagar ao Estado Português uma percentagm de 3% sobre o valor, à boca da mina, dos produtos mineiros ou concentrados expedidos ou utilizados, com excepção dos provenientes do tratamento de sulfuretos complexos maciços, para os quais aquela percentagem será de 2%;

b) Pagar ao Fundo de Desenvolvimento Mineiro uma percentagem de 0,5% do valor à boca da mina dos produtos mineiros ou concentrados expedidos ou utilizados;

c) Em substituição do quantitativo resultante da aplicação da alínea a), a Sociedade pagará ao Estado Português 10% dos lucros líquidos da exploração, deduzidos de todos os encargos tributários inerentes, sempre que este valor seja superior àquele quantitativo.

A Sociedade registou na rubrica de Impostos nas Demonstrações de Resultados dos exercícios de 1992 e de 1991, os montantes de mEsc. 1.035.891 e de mEsc. 1.083.891 respectivamente, relativos aos encargos anteriormente referidos, os quais se encontram também reflectidos no balanço anexo na rubrica Estado e outros entes públicos (Nota 50).

a) To pay the Portuguese Governement a 3% tax on the value of the products or concentrates which are extracted from the mine, with the exception of those which originate from the treatment of complex sulphides; in this case, the tax will be 2%;

b) To pay the Fund for Mining Development an amount equal to 0.5% of the value of the mining products or concentrates which are produced at the mine;

c) In substitution of the amount which results from the application of a) above, the Company will pay the Portuguese Government 10% of net profits resulting from the exploration of the mine, after deduction of all other taxes involved, whenever this amount is greater than the calculated above.

During 1992 and 1991 the Company included expenses amounting to 1,035,891 contos and 1,083,891 contos respectively resulting from the above in taxes and other operational costs. These amounts are also shown under the balance sheet heading of public entities and other creditors for 1992 and 1991 respectively (Note 50).

50. ESTADO E OUTROS ENTES PÚBLICOS

50. PUBLIC ENTITIES

Em 31 de Dezembro de 1992 e 1991, esta rubrica tinha a seguinte composição:

As at 31 December 1992 and 1991, balances with public entities comprise:

Rubrica	1992 Saldo devedor	1992 Saldo credor	1991 Saldo devedor	1991 Saldo credor
IVA a recuperar	479.260	-	619.486	-
IVA reembolsos pedidos	83.589	-	293.904	-
IVA regularizações	-	-	249.421	-
Direcção Geral de Geologia e Minas (Nota 49)	-	1.035.891	-	1.083.891
Segurança Social	-	73.331	-	63.309
Outros	67.679	38.534	115.791	31.988
	630.528	1.147.756	1.278.602	1.179.188

	1992 Debtor balances	1992 Creditor balances	1991 Debtor balances	1991 Creditor balances
VAT receivable	479.260	-	619.486	-
VAT payments request	83.589	-	293.904	-
VAT regularisations	-	-	249.421	-
Direcção Geral de Geologia e Minas (Note 49)	-	1.035.891	-	1.083.891
Social security	-	73.331	-	63.309
Other	67.679	38.534	115.791	31.988
	630.528	1.147.756	1.278.602	1.179.188

51. ACRÉSCIMOS E DIFERIMENTOS

51. DEFERRED COSTS AND INCOME AND PREPAID EXPENSES AND ACCRUED COSTS

Em 31 de Dezembro de 1992 e 1991, esta rubrica tinha a seguinte composição:

As at 31 December 1992 and 1991, these comprise:

Rubrica	1992	1991
Acréscimos de proveitos:		
Juros a receber	33.934	24.804
Custos diferidos:		
Ramal ferroviário	1.974.834	-
Conservação e reparação	683.801	1.025.702
Outros	165.982	64.021
	2.824.617	1.089.723
Acréscimos de custos:		
Férias e subsídio de férias vencidas		
e não pagas	452.142	482.939
Juros a liquidar	159.910	187.361
Outros	272.421	195.861
	884.473	866.161
Proveitos diferidos:		
Subsídio ao investimento	245.365	187.500
Diferenças de câmbio favoráveis	683.947	2.429.346
	929.312	2.616.846

Description	1992	1991
Prepaid expenses:		
Interest receivable	33.934	24.804
Deferred costs:		
Railway project	1.974.834	-
Repairs and maintenance	683.801	1.025.702
Other	165.982	64.021
	2.824.617	1.089.723
Accrued costs:		
Holiday pay and bonuses due		
but not yet paid	452.142	482.939
Interest payable but not yet paid	159.910	187.361
Other	272.421	195.861
	884.473	866.161
Deferred income:		
Subsidies to finance the acquisition		
of fixed assets	245.365	187.500
Unrealised exchange gains	683.947	2.429.346
	929.312	2.616.846

Os custos relativos ao ramal ferroviário foram tratados durante o exercício como imobilizado em curso e transferidos para esta rubrica no fim do exercício (ver Nota 3 e), tendo sido classificados na Demonstração de Origem e Aplicação de Fundos como imobilizações corpóreas.

The costs related to the railway project were accounted during 1992 as construction in progress and transfered to this balance sheet heading at the end of the period (Note 3 e). They have been classified in the Statement of Source and Application of Funds as fixed assets.

52. EXPLANATION ADDED FOR THE ENGLISH TRANSLATION

These financial statements are presented in accordance with generally accepted accounting principles in Portugal and with the disclosures required by the Official Chart of Accounts, some of which may not conform with or be required by generally accepted accounting principles in other countries.

RELATÓRIO E PARECER DO CONSELHO FISCAL	*AUDIT COMMITTEE'S REPORT AND OPINION*

SENHORES ACCIONISTAS:

TO THE SHAREHOLDERS

De acordo com as disposições legais e estatutárias, o Conselho Fiscal da SOMINCOR - Sociedade Mineira de Neves Corvo, S.A, apresenta à apreciação de V.Exas. o seu Relatório e Parecer sobre o Relatório do Conselho de Administração referentes ao exercício findo em 31 de Dezembro de 1992.

As required by the law and the Articles of Association the Audit Committee of SOMINCOR - Sociedade Mineira de Neves Corvo, SA has pleasure in presenting its report and opinion on the Report and Accounts of the Board of Directors for the financial year ending December 31, 1992.

1. ACTUAÇÃO DO CONSELHO FISCAL / *1. AUDIT COMMITTEE ACTIVITY*

No desempenho das suas funções estabeleceu contactos regulares com o Conselho de Administração e com os Serviços da Empresa, tendo obtido todas as informações e esclarecimentos solicitados.

In the exercise of its functions the committee monitored the company's activities through regular contacts with the Directors and the departments of the company, from whom we obtained all necessary information and explanations.

Procedeu, como vem sendo habitual, à elaboração de relatórios trimestrais enviados aos accionistas e à tutela.

We made quarterly reports as is normal practice which were sent to the shareholders.

Examinou, também, regularmente e por amostragem, a contabilidade da empresa e a documentação que lhe serve de suporte, tendo contado com a franca colaboração dos Auditores Externos.

During the year we also regularly examined the accounting ledgers, records and supporting documentation on a sample basis and we received the full support of the External Auditors.

2. RELATÓRIO DE GESTÃO E CONTAS / *2. MANAGEMENT REPORT AND ACCOUNTS*

O Relatório de Gestão, contendo uma exposição clara sobre a evolução da actividade desenvolvida e a situação da Sociedade no exercício, encontra-se elaborado de acordo com os preceitos legais e estatutários.

The Management Report, which contains full details of past performance and relates how the company has performed during the year in question, has been prepared as required by law and the Articles of Association.

Também o Balanço, a Demonstração dos Resultados e o respectivo Anexo reflectem a situação da Empresa e encontram-se elaborados em conformidade com as disposições legais em vigôr.

The Balance Sheet and Profit and Loss Account and respective footnotes, reflecting the company's position are drawn up in conformity with the law as currently applied.

No decorrer do exercício em que atingiu um máximo de vendas de cobre metal, em quantidade, há a registar os seguintes factos mais relevantes:

- apuramento de um Resultado Líquido de 8,9 milhões de contos, traduzindo um decréscimo de 5,3% comparativamente ao ano anterior, justificado, fundamentalmente, pela quebra das cotações do cobre e do dólar.

- continuação do esforço de investimento que se cifrou em 4,3 milhões de contos;

- início dos transportes pelo ramal ferroviário de Ourique, cuja utilização plena a partir de 1993, se traduzirá certamente, em consideráveis benefícios.

- não realização, no exercício, da permitida reavaliação do activo imobilizado, de acordo com o Decreto-Lei n° 264/92, de 24 de Novembro, como se refere na nota n° 6 do Anexo ao Balanço e Demonstração dos Resultados.

The following developments were noted during a year in which the quantity of copper metal sold was maximised:

- *The net profit for the year was Esc 8.9 billion, which is 5.3% lower than last year, caused principally by lower copper prices and the weaker dollar;*

- *Esc 4.3 billion was spent on capital expenditure;*

- *Concentrate began to be shipped via the rail link to Ourique, and once this is fully utilised in 1993 considerable cost savings will be realised;*

- *During the year the opportunity to revalue its fixed assets, which was available to the company under Decree-Law No. 264/92 of November 24th, was not utilised, as referred in Note 6 of the Notes to the Accounts.*

3. RELATÓRIO ANUAL DA FISCALIZAÇÃO EFECTUADA PELA SOCIEDADE DE REVISORES OFICIAIS DE CONTAS

3. AUDIT BY THE STATUTORY AUDITOR

De acordo com o disposto no n° 1 do art° 453 do Código das Sociedades Comerciais (CSC), o Conselho Fiscal apreciou o Relatório Anual da Sociedade de Revisores Oficiais de Contas, vogal deste Conselho.

We have also examined the annual report of the Statutory Auditor (as stipulated in paragraph 1 of Article 453 of the Companies Act). The Statutory Auditor is a member of this Audit Committee.

4. CERTIFICAÇÃO LEGAL DAS CONTAS

4. LEGAL CERTIFICATION OF ACCOUNTS

Examinámos, nos termos do n° 2 do art° 453° do CSC, a Certificação Legal das Contas emitida pela Sociedade de Revisores Oficiais de Contas, membro deste Conselho, a qual mereceu a nossa concordância, ficando parte integrante deste Relatório.

In accordance with paragraph 2 of Article 453 of the Companies Act, we have examined the legal certification of accounts given by the Statutory Auditor, a member of this Audit Committee, and this is approved by us.

5. APRECIAÇÃO DA GESTÃO

5. ACKNOWLEDGEMENTS

O Conselho Fiscal, no desempenho das suas funções, apreciou a forma meritória, dedicada e competente como o Conselho de Administração conduziu os negócios da empresa e recomenda à Assembleia Geral que aprove um voto de confiança ao mesmo.

The Audit Committee, in the exercise of its functions, has noted the dedicated, competent and meritorious way in which the Board of Directors has handled the affairs of the Company and recommends that the General Meeting passes a vote of confidence in the said Board of Directors.

6. PARECER

6. OPINION

Face ao exposto nos números anteriores somos de parecer que merecem a vossa aprovação:

- O Relatório de Gestão, Balanço e Contas do exercício de 1992;
- A proposta de Aplicação de Resultados;

In the light of the above we are of the opinion that:

- *The Report, Balance Sheet and Accounts for 1992 be approved*
- *The Proposed Appropriation of Profits be approved*

Lisboa, 3 de Março de 1993

Lisbon, March 3, 1993

O CONSELHO FISCAL

AUDIT COMMITTEE

Presidente - Rui da Silva Rodrigues
Vogal - Patrício, Mimoso e Mendes Jorge (SROC)
representada por João Fernandes Mendes Jorge
Vogal - José Alberto da Silva Jorge

Chairman - Rui da Silva Rodrigues
Member - Patrício, Mimoso e Mendes Jorge (SROC)
represented by João Fernandes Mendes Jorge
Member - José Alberto da Silva Jorge

CERTIFICAÇÃO LEGAL DAS CONTAS   *LEGAL CERTIFICATION OF ACCOUNTS*

- Exercício de 1992 -

Examinámos as contas da "SOMINCOR - Sociedade Mineira de Neves Corvo, S.A.", que compreendem o Balanço em 31 de Dezembro de 1992, a Demonstração dos Resultados do exercício de 1992 e o respectivo Anexo, documentos que foram preparados a partir dos livros, registos contabilísticos e documentos de suporte, mantidos em conformidade com os preceitos legais.

We have examined the accounts of SOMINCOR - Sociedade Mineira de Neves Corvo, SA. consisting of the Balance Sheet as at December 31, 1992, the Profit and Loss Account for 1992 and their respective footnotes. These documents were prepared from the accounting ledgers, records and supporting documentation maintained in accordance with the law.

O nosso exame foi efectuado de acordo com as Normas Técnicas de Revisão Legal de Contas aprovadas pela Câmara dos Revisores Oficiais de Contas com a profundidade considerada necessária nas circunstâncias.

Our examination was made in accordance with the technical norms approved by the Association of Statutory Auditors with all the thoroughness deemed necessary.

É nossa convicção que os citados documentos de prestação de contas apresentam, de forma verdadeira e apropriada, a situação financeira da "SOMINCOR", em 31 de Dezembro de 1992, bem como os resultados das suas operações referentes ao exercício findo naquele data, de acordo com os princípios contabilísticos geralmente aceites.

It is our opinion that the accounts are a true and adequate reflection of the company's financial position as at December 31, 1992 and of the results of its operations for the 1992 financial year, and have been prepared in accordance with generally accepted accounting principles applied in a manner consistent with the previous year.

Lisboa, 3 de Março de 1993

Lisbon, March 3, 1993

PATRICIO, MIMOSO E MENDES JORGE - Sociedade de Revisores Oficiais de Contas n° 42 - representada por João Fernandes Mendes Jorge (ROC n° 546)

PATRICIO MIMOSO E MENDES JORGE -Statutory Auditors n° 42 Represented by João Fernandes Mendes Jorge (ROC n° 546)

RELATÓRIO DOS AUDITORES ARTHUR ANDERSEN

EXTERNAL AUDITORS' REPORT

Ao Conselho de Administração e Accionistas da SOMINCOR - Sociedade Mineira de Neves Corvo, S.A.

To the Board of Directors and Sareholders of SOMINCOR - Sociedade Mineira de Neves Corvo, S.A.

(Translation of a report originally issued in Portuguese - See Note 52)

Examinámos os balanços da Somincor-Sociedade Mineira de Neves Corvo, S.A. em 31 de Dezembro de 1992 e 1991 e as demonstrações dos resultados e de origem e aplicação de fundos para os exercícios findos naquelas datas. Os nossos exames foram efectuados de acordo com normas de auditoria geralmente aceites e, consequentemente, incluiram as provas dos livros e documentos de contabilidade e outras técnicas e procedimentos de comprovação que considerámos necessários nas circunstâncias. Em nossa opinião, as demonstrações financeiras acima referidas, reflectem adequadamente a situação financeira da Somincor - Sociedade Mineira de Neves Corvo, S.A., em 31 de Dezembro de 1992 e 1991, bem como os resultados das suas operações e a origem e aplicação dos seus fundos para os exercícios findos naquelas datas, de acordo com princípios de contabilidade geralmente aceites (Nota 3), aplicados numa base consistente entre exercícios.

We have examined the accompanying balance sheets of Somincor - Sociedade Mineira de Neves Corvo, S.A. (a Portuguese shareholder company) as at 31 December 1992 and 1991 and the related statements of profit and loss and source and application of funds for the years then ended. Our audits were performed in accordance with generally accepted auditing standards and, accordingly, included such tests of the accounting records and such other auditing procedures as we considered necessary in the circumstances. In our opinion, the financial statements referred to above present fairly the financial position of Somincor - Sociedade Mineira de Neves Corvo, S.A. as at 31 December 1992 and 1991 and the results of its operations and the source and application of its funds for the years then ended, in conformity with generally accepted accounting principles (Note 3) applied on a consistent basis.

5 de Fevereiro de 1993

5 February 1993

Arthur Andersen

Appendix B
Differences in financial reporting – the UK, US and IAS

Abbreviations **APB** Opinion of the Accounting Principles Board of the American Institute of Certified Public Accountants, **ARB** *Accounting Research Bulletin* of the American Institute of Certified Public Accountants, **CSC** Código das Sociedades Comerciais (Companies Act), **FASB** Statement of the US Financial Accounting Standards Board, **GAAP** Generally accepted accounting principles, **POC** Plano Oficial de Contabilidade (Official Accounting Plan), **SEC** US Securities and Exchange Commission, **SSAP** Statement of Standard Accounting Practice

	Portugal	*UK*	*US*
1 ACCOUNTING CONCEPTS			
1 *Taxes*	Accounting rules have been largely influenced by tax regulations: however, efforts are now being made to separate accounting and financial reporting tax rules. Examples are accounting for goodwill depreciation, leasing contracts, etc. (see Part II of this book for details).	Tax rules are separate from financial accounting regulation.	As for the UK except that LIFO is permitted.
2 *Historical cost*	The valuation system is based on the historical cost method and free revaluation is not permitted. Adjustments of assets that lead to value increases are permitted only under special laws, designed essentially for tax purposes and only for fixed tangible assets. The last approved decree to permit revaluation made the authorization effective for 1990 balance sheets but depreciation of the year was calculated over the revalued values only for 1991 and subsequent years. (POC, 4.4, and decree law 49/91)	Revaluation permitted with the surplus being credited to a revaluation reserve. (4 sch. 34 (2) CA)	Upward revaluations may not be incorporated into the accounts other than as supplementary information.

	Portugal	UK	US

3   *Financial accounts*

The following financial statements must be prepared: balance sheet, profit and loss account, notes on the accounts, proposal of profit and loss allocation, report of the board of directors, report of the statutory audit board. (See Part II and Appendix A of this book for details.) (POC, 2.1, 2.2, 2.4, 6, 7 and 8) Companies may voluntarily present a statement of profit and loss in vertical formats and according to sales turnover procedure. Also the statement of the sources and applications of funds and of working capital changes is voluntary. (POC, 2.3, 2.6, 7 and 9)

The Companies Act requires the same as Portugal except that a funds statement is not required by law but by SSAP 10.

No general requirement in state or federal law. Publically owned corporations and listed companies must prepare financial statements. (SEC S-X)

4   *Accounting principles*

Going concern
Consistency
Accruals
Historical cost
Prudence
Substance over form
Materiality
(POC, chapter 4, points 4.1–7, in the above order)

The POC also refers the qualitative characteristics of the financial information, i.e.:
Relevance
Reliability
Comparability
(POC, 3.2)

As for Portugal, although prudence is not a preferential criterion.
(4 sch. 15 CA, SSAP 2, para. 14)

As for the UK.

2   BALANCE SHEET

(A)   General

(i)   Format: horizontal format is obligatory for all companies. (POC. 2.1 and 6)

Usually vertical (under 4 sch. 1(1) CA a company may adopt the alternative format, but formats cannot be changed without justification).

Vertical.

(ii)   Valuation rules: assets are generally valued at historical cost, except for inventories and listed investments and negotiable securities, which can be valued at market price when that is lower than historical cost; also, the equity method is optional for investments in group and associated companies. (POC, 5.4.3)

State rules for valuation where fixed assets are revalued and when valuing work-in-progress (Sec. 275 CA 85). CA provides for historical cost (4 sch. sec. 8) and alternative accounting rules (4 sch. sec. C). SSAPs 1, 9, 19, 22 and 23, have an input on these matters.

Value assets at historical cost except for inventories which are stated at the lower of cost or market value (not defined as net realizable value).

(B)   Capital stock

(i)   Types of shares: shares may be common, preference, non-voting (CSC, 345, etc.)

Shares may be categorized and allocated different votes (4 sch. 38 (1)(b) CA 85). Shares may

As for the UK.

	Portugal	UK	US
	Shares may be bearer and registered (CSC, 299) Foreigners may generally acquire shares.	be purchased by foreigners.	
(ii)	Capital issues: shares may be issued at par value or with a premium (CSC, 298); in the latter case, the premium must be reflected in the 'Share premium account' and its payment cannot be postponed (CSC, 277)	Premium on shares should be transferred to the share premium account. (Sec. 130 para. 1 CA 85)	Disclosed as paid-in capital in excess of par or stated value.
(iii)	Own shares: in no circumstances may a company subscribe for its own shares. It may acquire and hold its own shares only in relevant legal situations, which stipulate, namely, that the par value of the shares acquired must not exceed 10 per cent of the capital stock and the purchase is possible only if there are free reserves amounting at least to the cash payment which corresponds to the purchase of the own shares. (CSC, 316, 317 and 324)	May purchase and cancel own shares. (Sec. 160(4), 162(2) CA)	May purchase and either cancel or hold as treasury stock. ARB No. 43, Chapter 18, an APB Opinion 6, para 13. State laws vary and where they differ from GAAP, state laws are followed.
(C) Reserves			
(i)	Legal reserve: 5 per cent of the profit of the year must be transferred to the legal reserve account until it reaches at least 20 per cent of capital stock (nominal value).The statutes of the company may impose higher percentages for the legal reserve. (CSC 218 for Ldas and 295, 296 for SAs)	No equivalent concept.	As for the UK.
(ii)	Other reserves: unrestricted reserves and restricted reserves must be reflected in separate accounts. (POC, 6)	No equivalent concept.	As for the UK.
(iii)	Dividends: can be distributed out of the profit of the year after tax and provision to the legal reserve and other statutory or contractual appropriations, but only if net worth is not lower than the capital stock plus the legal reserve, if capitalized R&D expenses and formation costs have not been completely written off. (CSC, 32 and 33) Fifty per cent of the profit for the year that can be distributed as dividends must be distributed as dividends unless the annual general meeting resolves otherwise through a majority of 75 per cent of the votes cast. (CSC, 217 and 294, respectively, for Ldas and for SAs)	Dividends may be paid out of distributable reserves. (Sec. 261(1) CA)	Dividends may be paid out of retained earnings but subject to any other restrictions. For example, restrictions placed on distributions by lenders. State laws determine the amount of dividends permitted.

Portugal	*UK*	*US*
Interim dividends may be distributed only when authorized by the statutes of the company and only during the second half of the financial year and may not exceed half the expected profit for the year. (CSC, 297)		

(D) Deferred taxes

The notes on the accounts must disclose deferred tax, but in practice such disclosure is not very frequent. (POC, note 6, chapter 8)	Partial provision based on the liability method for timing differences. Provision is required where a liability is expected to crystallize. (SSAP 15)	Comprehensive method based on the liability method for all short-term and long-term timing differences. (FASB No. 96)

(E) Long-term debt

(i) Disclosure: the notes must disclose debts with maturities longer than five years. (POC, note 29, chapter 8) Breakdown as for current liabilities. See detailed balance sheet format, Chapter 8. Disclosure of nominal value and related rights of bonds and *titulos de participação* issued by the company. (POC, note 27, chapter 8) Disclosure of currency exchange rates used for conversion into PTE of debts originally expressed in foreign currency. (POC, note 4, chapter 8)	Show the aggregate amount for each category split between amounts owing in excess of five years and amounts owing less than five years. (Sch. 4 Para. 1 CA)	For each issue or obligation: (i) the rate of interest; (ii) date of maturity; (iii) any contingencies; (iv) priority; (v) convertibility; (vi) aggregate amount or maturities and sinking fund requirements. (FASB No. 5, paras 18–19, and No. 47, para. 106; S-X 5.02(22))

(F) Current liabilities

(i) Classification: see detailed balance sheet formats, Chapter 8 of this book. (ii) Breakdown: of advances and loans from employees, members of the board of directors and audit board, debts to public entities in delay, arrears, debts with collateral. (POC, notes 24, 25, 26, 28, 29 and 30, chapter 8) (iii) Other disclosures: disclosure of currency exchange rates used for conversion into escudos of debts originally expressed in foreign currency. (POC, note 4, chapter 8)	Disclose separately Debenture loans Bank loans and overdrafts Payments received on account Trade creditors Bills of exchange payable Amounts owed to related companies Other creditors including taxation and social security Accruals and deferred income. (Sch. 4 Part I CA)	Disclose separately amounts payable to: Short-term borrowing Factors Holders of commercial paper Trade creditors Parent and subsidiaries Other affiliates Underwriters, directors, employees, officers, promoters and all amounts for Payroll, taxes, interest, other material items Dividends declared, current portion of bonds, mortgages and similar debt Any other item in excess of 5 per cent of current liabilities (Regulation S-X 5-02) Amounts payable to related parties (FASB No. 57)

Portugal	UK	US

(G) Contingencies

Disclosure of contingencies not included in the balance sheet. Disclosure of pension fund commitments. (POC, note 30, chapter 8)

Disclose the amount or estimated amount of that liability, its legal nature and whether any valuable security has been provided by the company in connection with that liability and if so, what. (4 sch. 50 (2) CA 85)

The treatment of contingent losses depends upon the probability of the loss and ability to estimate it reasonably. Where a loss is considered remote no provision and no disclosure is provided. In other situations the contingency is disclosed in the notes to the accounts. Contingent gains are recognized on realization. (FASB No. 5)

(H) Fixed Assets

(i) Classification: broken down into intangibles, tangibles and investments with specific subdivisions. (POC, chapters 6, 10 and 11) Broken down by activities to which these assets have been allocated during the year, by location (within the company or located abroad), reversible, leased assets, etc. (POC, note 14, chapter 8)

Split between intangibles, tangibles and investment with specified subdivision. (Sch. 4 CA 85)

Split by major class – for example, land, buildings, machinery and equipment, leasehold or functional grouping such as revenue producing equipment or industry categories. Subdivide intangibles. (APB 12 and APB 22)

(ii) Disclosure of variations: Opening balance Additions Increases due to revaluations Disposals, retirements or reductions Closing balance (POC, note 10, chapter 8)

Disclose opening and closing balances and revisions, acquisitions, disposals and transfers during the year. (Para. 42 Sch. 4 CA 85)

Disclose carrying value and depreciation and cost for each major class of tangible assets. (APB 12 and APB 22)

(iii) Disclosure of valuation method: cost and accumulated depreciation must be shown separately. Disclosure of the depreciation rates used is not necessary. (POC, notes 3 and 10, chapter 8)

Disclose purchase price or production cost. (Para. 17 Sch. 4 CA 85) Alternative accounting rules. (Sec. C Sch. 4 CA 85)

Disclose carrying basis, method and period of amortization and accumulated amortization of intangibles. (S-X 5.02-15)

(iv) Revaluation: revaluations are permitted by decree law only of the operating tangible fixed assets. Disclosure of decree laws permitting the revaluation must be done. (POC, note 12, chapter 8) Disclosure of the aggregate amount at year end of the net restatements pursuant to a restatement law, and of the effect of such restatements on annual depreciation and the period depreciation charge; a table including the historical cost, revaluation increases for the year and revalued book values of the assets must be disclosed. (POC, note 13, chapter 8)

Revaluations permitted. (Sch. 4, 34 CA 85)

Not permitted. (APB 6; ARB 43 chapter 9B)

	Portugal	UK	US

(I) Intangibles

(i) Types:
    Formation expenses
    Research and development
    expenses
    Patents and other rights
    Goodwill
    (POC, chapters 6, 10 and 11)

Types:
    Development costs
    Concessions, patents,
    licences, trade marks
    Goodwill
    Payments on account
    (Sch. 4 CA)

Classify by type.
(S-X 5.02-15)
(APB 17)

(ii) Disclosure of valuation method: intangibles must be valued and amortized by the same standards as those used to depreciate tangible fixed assets. The amortization period goodwill cannot exceed five years; if the amortization exceeds that period, the reasons for that must be stated in the notes on the accounts.
(POC, notes 3, 8 and 9, chapter 8)

Write-off goodwill to reserves on acquisition or amortize over its useful life.
(SSAP 22)

Amortize goodwill over its useful life, not exceeding forty years.
(APB 7)

(iii) Disclosure of variations:
    Opening balance
    Additions
    Disposals, retirements or
    reductions
    Closing balance
    (POC, note 10, chapter 8)

(J) Subsidiary companies

(i) Disclosure: of names and addresses of group companies, percentage of capital stock owned (directly or indirectly), amount of capital stock, reserves and result for the previous financial year, book value of the investments.

Disclose the name of each subsidiary:
    Where incorporated
    Identity of each class and
    proportion of the nominal
    value or the alloted shares
    of that class.
(Sch. 5 CA)

Disclose the name of each subsidiary.
(ARB 51)

(ii) Valuation rules: acquisition cost or market value (in the case of listed shares), if the latter is lower than the former. Equity method is optional, with goodwill calculated at the date of first use of equity method, beginning of the year balance.
(POC, 5.4.3 and note 3, chapter 8)

(iii) Disclosure of variations: if the market value is used, according to prudence accounting principle, disclosure of provisions has to be done, namely:
    Opening balance
    Additions
    Reductions
    Closing balance
(POC, note 34, chapter 8)

(K) Associated companies

(i) Definition: associated company is a company in which the shareholder (quotaholder) owns at least 20 per

(Related company) any body corporate in which there is a long-term capital interest and

Significant influence.
(APB 18)

Portugal	*UK*	*US*
cent of the voting capital but not more than 50 per cent of it. (CSC, title VI and POC, 2.7)	the company exercises control or influence. Generally at least 20 per cent and up to 50 per cent of the equity voting rights and significant influence. (SSAP 1)	
(ii) Disclosure: of names and addresses of group companies, percentage of capital stock owned (directly or indirectly); amount of capital stock, reserves and result for the previous financial year, book value of the investments may in some cases be omitted. (POC, note 16, chapter 8)	Amount attributable to listed shares. The aggregate market value of listed investments where it differs from the amount stated. (Para. 45 Sch. 4 CA)	Carry at the lower of cost of market value segregated between current and non-current portfolios. (FASB 12)
(iii) Valuation rules: acquisition cost or market value (in the case of listed shares), if the latter is lower than the former. Equity method is optional, with goodwill calculated at the date of first use of equity method, beginning of the year balance. (POC, 5.4.3 and note 3, chapter 8)		
(iv) Disclosure of variations: if the market value is used, according to prudence accounting principle, disclosure of provisions has to be done, namely: Opening balance Additions Reductions Closing balance (POC, note 34, chapter 8)		
(L) Inventories		
(i) Classification: raw materials, goods and merchandise, work in progress, finished goods, by-products and waste must be reflected in separate inventory accounts. (See detailed balance sheet format, Chapter 8 of this book.) (POC, 6, 10 and 11)	Subheading required as follows: raw materials and consumables; work in progress; finished goods and goods for resale; payments on account. (Sch. 4 CA) Classification appropriate to the business. (SSAP 9)	Disclose different classes and basis on which determined. (S-X 5.02-6(a) and ARB 43 chapters 3A and 4)
(ii) Allocation of indirect costs: allocation of indirect variable costs is allowed: so is allocation of indirect fixed costs according to normal capacity use. But distribution costs, administrative costs and financial costs may not be capitalized. (POC, 5.3.3)	Required the inclusion of overhead costs. (SSAP 9)	Include related production overheads. (ARB 43 chapters 3A and 4) Normally apply percentage or completion method. (ARB 45)
(iii) Valuation method: the rule is valuation by historical cost accounting, but when the market value is lower than the historical	Lower of cost and net realizable value. (SSAP 9)	Lower of cost or market value. Market value is usually current replacement cost but market value cannot exceed net

Portugal	UK	US
cost, the related provision must be recorded. (POC, 5.3)		realizable value. Mid-point of net realizable value, replacement cost and net realizable value less normal profit margin. (ARB 43 chapters 3A and 4)

(M) Debtors

(i)   Types: see detailed balance sheet format, Chapter 8 of this book. Short-term and medium and long-term debts must be disclosed separately.

(ii) Breakdown: breakdown of advances and loans to employees, members of the board of directors and audit board, debts to public entities in arrears, debts with bills of exchange, doubtful debts, etc.
(POC, notes 23, 24 and 25; chapter 8)

(iii) Other disclosures: disclosure of currency exchange rates used for conversion into PTE of debts originally expressed in foreign currency.
(POC, note 4, chapter 8)
Disclosure of discounted receivables not shown in the balance sheet.
(POC, note 26, chapter 8)

Portugal	UK	US
(i) Types... (see above)	Debtors is a main heading on the balance sheet. Subdivision required. (Sch. 4 CA 85)	Classify by source, segregating notes from accounts receivable and unusual receivables such as tax refunds. (S-X 5.02-3)

3   PROFIT AND LOSS ACCOUNT

(A) Sales

Portugal	UK	US
Breakdown by activity and geographical area (domestic and exports). (POC, note 44, chapter 8)	Disclose amount divided by different business classes. (Para. 55 Sch. 4 CA)	Disclose for each significant type, defined as 10 per cent of sales. Disclose method of recognizing sales. (APB 22 and 13)

(B) Other income

Portugal	UK	US
Breakdown according to format of the profit and loss account outlined in Chapter 8. (POC, chapter 7)	Disclose the amount of income from listed investments. (Para. 53 Sch. 4 CA)	Disclose amounts earned from dividends, interest income and sale of securities. (FASB 12, S-X 5.03-7)

(C) Wages, salaries and other benefits

Portugal	UK	US
Breakdown by annual gross wages, social security costs and pension costs. (POC, chapter 7)	Wages and salaries, social security costs, other pension costs. (Para. 56 Sch. 4 CA)	No requirement to disclose.

(D) Auditors' fees

Portugal	UK	US
Disclosure not required. Auditors may not be paid any other compensation or receive any benefit from the company being audited other than the legal fee, established according to the size of the company (total assets and income for the year) and set before the start of the	Required. (Para. 53 Sch. 4 CA)	Not required.

	Portugal	UK	US

auditors' work and for the entire period.
(*Portaria* 231/85, 24 April)

(E) Lease expenses

| Lease payments must be disclosed separately in the notes on the accounts. Leased assets including book values must be disclosed in the notes on the accounts. (POC, note 15, chapter 8) | Required. (Para. 53 Sch. 4 CA) | Disclose operating lease rental expenses. (APB 15.70) |

(F) Income distribution

| The profit and loss account does not disclose the income distribution. Changes in net equity accounts must be disclosed in the notes on the accounts. (POC, note 40, chapter 8) | Dividends may only be paid out of distributable profits. (Sec. 253 CA) Directors' Report should recommend the dividend. (Sec. 235 CA) | Dividends paid and declared on a per share basis. (APB 15.70) |

(G) Segmented information

| Breakdown by: sales by activity and geographical area and purchases, sales and services, currency to/from group companies, associated companies and others, to/from managers, directors, employees, etc. (POC, various notes, chapter 8) | State turnover and profit or loss for each different class of business. (Para. 55 Sch. 4 CA) Geographical analysis of profit. (SE) | Split sales, revenues, cost of sales and expenses by type (10 per cent of sales). (APB 22) Income before tax should be split between domestic and foreign. (FASB 14 and FASB 21) |

4   GENERAL

(A) Disclosure of parent company's name

| Disclosure of the name of any company which owns, directly or indirectly, 20 per cent or more of the capital stock. (POC, note 37 on the accounts) | Disclose the name of the ultimate holding company. (Para. 20 Sch. 5 CA) | Disclose the name of the ultimate holding company. (ARB 51) |

(B) Disclosure of subsidiary and associated companies' names

| The names and addresses of these companies must be disclosed in the notes, stating the percentage of their capital stock owned, amount of capital stock, reserves, approved results for the previous year, net book value of the holding, dividends received and closing market price of the shares, if listed. However, information about equity and results for the year may be omitted for associated companies whenever such companies are not obliged to publish their financial statements. In the case of parent companies exempted from presenting group accounts, the reasons for the exemption must be disclosed. | Disclose names, where incorporated, shares of each class held and the proportion of the nominal value of the allotted shares of that class represented by the shares held. (Para. 1 Sch. 5 CA) | Disclose names, shares held and proportion owned. (ARB 51.01) |

	Portugal	UK	US
	If the company is included in any consolidated accounts, it is necessary to state with the name and address of the company in which consolidated accounts it is included. In the case of excluded companies, disclosure of name and address is necessary. (POC, note 16 on the accounts)		

(C) Management report

	Portugal	UK	US
	This report must include a true and fair view of the company's operations and position, stating major events subsequent to year end, the outlook, R&D activities, market conditions, investments, costs, provisions for the immediate future and acquisitions, disposals and ownership of treasury stock. Also a proposal of disposition for the result of the year must be included in the report and the authority, if any, given to the members of the board of directors to enter into contracts on the company's behalf. (CSC, arts. 66 and 324, No. 2)	Required (sec. 239 CA) to contain a fair review of the development of the business and amount of dividend to be paid (Sec. 235 CA). State directors, principal activities of the company and any significant changes. Disclose changes in values, directors' shareholdings and other interests, contributions for political and charitable purposes, etc. (Sec. 235 CA)	Publicly owned companies must provide information on operations in different industries, foreign operations, export sales and its major customers. (SEC)

(D) Standard auditors' report

	Portugal	UK	US
	A standard auditors' report must be issued pursuant to CROC technical auditing standards. (CSC 452)	Standard report issued by the Auditing Practices Committee.	Standard report for SEC registrants only.

(E) Statement of changes in financial position

	Portugal	UK	US
	Not required, but the POC provides a model. (POC, 2.6 and 9)	Required for companies with a turnover in excess of £25,000. (SSAP 10)	Required for all profit-oriented businesses.

(F) Earnings per share

	Portugal	UK	US
	Not required.	To be shown in the profit and loss account of listed companies. (SSAP 3) Not required for banking, insurance and certain other companies.	Disclose if a publicly traded corporation provided it is not a wholly owned subsidiary. (APB 15 and FASB 21)

Appendix C
EC directives and Portuguese legislation

Appendix C summarizes the main accounting options included in the Fourth and Seventh Directives and indicates the articles of the directives where they are referred to. The purpose is to show the extent of adoption in Portuguese legislation of such options. The left-hand side gives the text of the articles of the EC directives; the right-hand side, the Portuguese options.

THE FOURTH DIRECTIVE

Article	Option	Portuguese legislation
4.3.b	Member states may require balance sheet and income statement items to be regrouped for clarity purposes.	Not adopted.
4.4	Member states may require that where the amounts in the balance sheet and profit and loss account are not comparable with the amounts of the preceding year, the latter figures must be adjusted.	Adopted. Note 2 of the notes on the accounts must disclose any adjustment of the figures that have been made.
6	Member states may authorize or require that the balance sheet and the income statement be adapted to include the distribution of income.	Not adopted. The appropriation of profit or the treatment of loss must be included in the managers'/board of directors' annual report and has to be submitted to the annual general meeting for approval, under the Companies Act (and article 50 of the Fourth Directive).
8	Member states may authorize that the balance sheet be presented as an account or in a vertical format or allow companies to choose between the two forms.	Not adopted. The balance sheet must be prepared in the account format (article 9 of the Fourth Directive).
9.A. 9.D.II.5	Member states may permit the 'Uncalled subscribed capital' account to be reflected on the liability side as a deduction, under A.I.	Not adopted. This head is recorded on the asset side of the balance sheet, as a receivable, under D.II.5 ('Debtors').

Article	Option	Portuguese legislation
9.B	Member states may permit the recording of 'Formation expenses' as the first item of intangibles.	Adopted. By the terms of the Companies Act, if such expenses have not been completely written off there are restrictions on the distribution of profits. The notes on the accounts must explain the 'formation expenses'.
9.C.I.2(b)	Concessions, patents, licences, trade marks and similar rights and assets may be shown as assets even if they are created by the undertaking itself.	Adopted.
9.C.1 37.1	Member states may permit 'Research and development expenses' to be recorded on the asset side of the balance sheet and they must be amortized over a period of five years or over a longer peiod in exceptional cases.	Adopted. Under the Companies Act, if such expenses have not been completely written off there are restrictions on the distribution of profits. The notes on the accounts must explain these expenses and the reasons for the write-off over a period longer than five years.
37.2	Member states may authorize goodwill to be amortized over a period of more than five years.	Adopted. The notes on the accounts must disclose expenses which have been written off over a period longer than five years. The depreciation of goodwill is not tax-deductible.
9.C.III.7 13.2	Own shares may be shown as an asset, recorded either as investments or as current assets, but must not be recorded under headings not intended for that purpose.	Not adopted. 'Own shares' are shown in the net equity, as negative capital and reserves. The old POC presented them as prescribed in the option.
9.D.II.6 18	Member states may require that pre-payments and accrued income are included under 'Debtors'.	Not adopted. They are presented at the foot of the asset side of the balance sheet under an appropriate heading ('Acréscimos e diferimentos').
9.C.9/I.9 21	Member states may require that accruals and deferred income are included under 'Creditors'.	Not adopted. They are presented at the foot of the liabilities side of the balance sheet under an appropriate heading ('Acréscimos e diferimentos').
9.A.6 9.L.VI	A loss for the year may be included on the asset side or recorded on the liabilities side under 'Capital and reserves'	Not adopted. Losses may be included only on the liabilities side, under the same heading that is used to record the profit for the financial year.
9.E 9.A.VI 9.L.VI	Profit of the year may be shown under a heading on the liabilities side of the balance sheet, either under E or under 'Capital and reserves'.	Not adopted. Profits may be included only on the liabilities side, under the same heading that is used to record the losses for the financial year.
9.B.1/J.1 43.1.7	Double classification is permitted for provisions for pensions, either on the liabilities side of the balance sheet or in the notes on the accounts.	Adopted. Disclosure must be in both places (in some cases, under various notes).
14	Member states may require any guarantees covering the commitments of the company to be disclosed by category at the foot of the balance sheet or in the notes on the accounts.	Adopted. Disclosure must be made in the notes on the accounts. Portuguese legislation does not mention notes on the balance sheet.
6 15.3(a)	Movements in the various fixed asset items may be disclosed either in the balance sheet, as a separate deduction under the head, or in the notes.	Adopted. Adjusted values must be disclosed in the balance sheet. The notes on the accounts include statements to break down the year's movements, e.g. by depreciation,

Article	Option	Portuguese legislation
		revaluation, disposals, acquisitions, as well as movements in the intangible fixed assets.
17	Member states may set the percentage required for the presumption of a participating interest lower than a share of 20 per cent of the capital of another undertaking.	Adopted. The percentage was set at its maximum (20 per cent).
43.1.2	Member states may permit that as regards some presumed participating interests companies are not to be obliged to disclose details of such undertakings in the notes on the accounts.	Adopted. If the company in which a participation is held is not obliged to disclose and publish its accounts, the participating company may omit the disclosure of that information from the notes on the accounts.
20.2	Member states may authorize the recording of provisions for expenses, provided that as of the date of the financial statements the expenses comply with the condition of being probable or certain.	Adopted, provided that at the date of the balance sheet the expenses comply with the condition of being probable but not certain.
22–6	Member states shall establish one of various formats as per articles 23–6 for income statement presentation purposes, and may empower companies to choose between them.	Not adopted. The horizontal layout by the nature of the item (article 24) is compulsory and the vertical format by functions (article 25) is optional; it cannot be substituted for the former.
30	Member states may authorize that tax on ordinary and extraordinary income may be grouped under a single heading.	Adopted. The notes on the accounts must disclose the extent to which the taxes affect the results for the financial year.
33	Exceptions to the historical cost principle of article 33.	Adopted. Revaluation is permitted of tangible fixed assets, using the equity method for participations of at least 20 per cent and replacement cost in some cases defined by special laws.
35.1(c)(aa)	Value adjustments may be made to financial fixed assets so that they are valued at a lower figure on the balance sheet date.	Adopted. The lower value must be a market value and the difference between that value and the higher one is to be shown in the balance sheet and also in the notes on the accounts, and is to be charged to the profit and loss account.
35.1(d) 39.1(e)	Exceptional value adjustments permissible for tax purposes in respect of fixed and current assets.	Adopted. Not according to the POC, but mainly owing to companies' income tax coding.
35.3(b)	Production cost may be increased by a reasonable fraction of the costs indirectly allocable to the product.	Financial and marketing costs may not be allocated to the product.
35.4	Fixed asset production costs may include interest on loans used to finance their production. This interest must be disclosed in the notes on the accounts.	Adopted.
39.2	Member states may permit the current asset production costs to include the interest on loans used to finance their production.	Not adopted.
39.1(c)	Member states may authorize exceptional value adjustments if on the basis of sound commercial judgement they are considered necessary.	Adopted.

Article	Option	Portuguese legislation
39.2 43.1.1 40.2	Member states may permit the average prices used to value inventories to be calculated by FIFO, LIFO or any similar method.	Adopted. The method employed must be disclosed in the notes on the accounts.
41	If the amount payable for debts is higher than the amount collected, the difference may be reflected on the asset side and disclosed in the notes.	Adopted. Disclosure to be made under note 33 on the accounts.
1.2	Application to banks and insurance companies.	Not adopted. Banks, insurance companies and other financial institutions use sectoral accounting plans drawn up by the Banco de Portugal and the Instituto de Seguros de Portugal.
33	Value adjustments to marketable securities set off directly against equity investment companies.	Not adopted.
	Investment companies may value their securities at market value.	Adopted. When the market price is lower than the acquisition price at the balance sheet date.
2.6	Member states may authorize or require the annual accounts to include reports other than those envisaged in the Fourth Directive.	Adopted. It is optional to present the statement of the sources and applications of funds. Also further information not required by this Directive is to be disclosed in the notes.
1.2	Member states may require companies in certain economic sectors to adapt the items in their annual accounts.	Adopted.
3/31.2 4.2	Exceptionally, companies may be permitted not to apply the general principles.	Adopted.
5.3	Grouping of items preceded by arabic numbers if the amount is not material, and other departures from the materiality principle.	Adopted. Not the arabic-numbered grouping but other departures.
11	Member states may permit the presentation of an abridged balance sheet.	Adopted. Permission is based on the company's size – the limits are the following: assets, PTE 180 million; net turnover, PTE 370 million; employees, fifty.
27	Member states may permit the presentation of an abridged income statement	Adopted. Permission is based on the company's size – the limits are the following: assets, PTE 180 million; net turnover, PTE 370 million; employees, fifty.
44	Member states may permit the presentation of abridged notes on the accounts.	Adopted. Permission is based on the company's size – the limits are the following: assets, PTE 180 million; net turnover, PTE 370 million; employees, fifty.
45.1(b)	Omission from the notes of the names and registered offices of companies less than 20 per cent-owned.	Adopted. This information may be omitted if the companies in which a participation is held are not bound by the disclosure requirements of company law.
47.1	Member states may permit the management report not to be published.	Not adopted. Companies' Act requires the annual accounts and the report to be deposited with the Commercial Register.
	Until it has been determined, the residual value of an asset may be deemed to be its cost.	Adopted.

THE SEVENTH DIRECTIVE

Article	Option	Portuguese legislation
1.1(c)	The controlling company need not be a shareholder if it has right to exercise a dominant influence over a subsidiary pursuant to a contract or by-law clause.	Not adopted.
1.1(d)(aa)	To make the obligation to consolidate dependent on the ownership of 20 per cent of the voting rights and on the right to appoint a majority of the directors.	Adopted.
1.2	To require the consolidation of investee companies if the controlling company exercises a dominant influence over them and manages them on a unified basis.	Not adopted.
4.2	To exempt from the obligation to consolidate if the controlling company is not established as a specified type of company.	Adopted. The controlling company must be a corporation, a private limited company or a limited partnership with shares.
5.1	To exempt from the obligation to consolidate financial holding companies.	Not adopted.
6.2	To exempt from consolidation on the basis of quantitative thresholds for assets, sales or number of employees.	Adopted. Exemption unless two of the following three limits are exceeded (except for listed companies): assets, PTE 1.5 million; net turnover and other revenues, PTE 3 million; average number of employees, 250.
6.2	To calculate the asset and sales limits before elimination.	Adopted. Not mentioned in Portuguese legislation.
6.5	To increase the economic limits temporarily by 150 per cent and the number of employees by 100 per cent.	Not adopted.
7.1	To exempt from the obligation to consolidate subsidiaries of wholly or 90 per cent-owned foreign parent companies with the approval of the minority shareholders.	Adopted.
7.2(a)(bb)	To require a subsidiary of a foreign parent company in the EC which heads a national sub-group to publish its consolidated accounts in the member state's official language.	Adopted.
7.3	Not to exempt from consolidation the subsidiary of a foreign parent company in the EC which heads a national sub-group whose shares are listed.	Adopted.
8.1	To exempt from consolidation the subsidiary of a foreign parent company in the EC which heads a national sub-group, unless the shareholders request consolidation.	Not adopted.
9	To make the exemption from consolidation of the subsidiary of a foreign parent company in the EC which heads a national sub-group dependent on the publication of certain data.	Adopted. Disclosure of the following data is required in the notes on the annual accounts of the exempted company: assets; net turnover and other revenues; profit or loss during the financial year; capital and reserves; average number of employees during the year.

Article	Option	Portuguese legislation
11	To exempt the subsidiary of a foreign parent company outside the EC which heads a sub-group from preparing consolidated accounts.	Not adopted.
12.1	To require consolidation if there is a management contract between two companies when a majority of the directors, management or members of the supervisory board are common to both companies.	Not adopted.
13.1	Not to include an undertaking in consolidated accounts where it is not material to the 'true and fair view'.	Adopted. The notes must disclose some data about the excluded companies.
13.3(a)(aa)	Not to include an undertaking in consolidated accounts where severe long-term restrictions substantially hinder the parent undertaking in the exercise of its rights over the assets or management of that undertaking.	Adopted.
13.3(b)	Not to include an undertaking in consolidated accounts where the information necessary for the preparation of consolidated accounts in accordance with the Seventh Directive cannot be obtained without disproportionate expense or undue delay.	Not adopted.
13.3(c)	Not to include an undertaking in consolidated accounts where the shares of that undertaking are held exclusively with a view to their subsequent resale.	Adopted. These undertakings are classified in the balance sheet under the item 'Short-term investments'.
15.1	To exclude from consolidation a parent company which does not carry out industrial and commercial activities and which holds shares in a subsidiary undertaking on the basis of a joint arrangement with one or more undertakings not included in the consolidated accounts.	Not adopted.
16.5	To exempt from and derogate the regulations in order to comply with the 'true and fair view' precept.	Adopted.
16.6	To require or permit the disclosure in the consolidated accounts of other information as well as that which must be disclosed in accordance with the Seventh Directive.	Adopted. Consolidated statement of the sources and applications of funds is recommended. Also some additional notes on the consolidated accounts are foreseen.
17.2	To combine inventories if consolidation would entail undue expense.	Not adopted.
19.1(b)	To authorize or require investments to be offset against equity on the basis of the item values at the date of acquisition or of initial consolidation.	Not adopted.
19.1(c)	To offset positive and negative differences arising from the elimination of investments against equity.	Not adopted.
20	To offset against capital but not against reserves if a share exchange has taken place.	Not adopted.

Article	Option	Portuguese legislation
26.1(c)	To partially eliminate unrealized gains/losses on the basis of the percentage of capital held.	Not adopted.
26.2	To permit the non-elimination of unrealized gains/losses if elimination would entail undue costs or the transactions were on an arm's-length basis.	Adopted.
26.3	To permit non-elimination where the amounts concerned are not material to the 'true and fair view' precept.	Adopted.
27.2	To require or permit the consolidated financial statements to be as of a date different from that of the parent company's annual accounts.	Adopted as permissible rather than as a requirement.
28	To require or permit the preparation of an adjusted opening balance sheet and an adjusted income statement if the consolidated group as a whole has changed significantly.	Adopted as permissible rather than as a requirement.
29.2(a)	To permit or require the use of asset and liability valuation methods on consolidation different from those used in the annual accounts.	Adopted as permissible rather than as a requirement.
29.3	To permit the valuation of assets and liabilities by undertakings included in the consolidation by methods different from those used in the consolidated accounts.	Adopted.
29.5	To permit or require assets to be included in the annual accounts without prior elimination of tax value adjustments.	Adopted. Not mentioned in Portuguese legislation.
30.2	To permit a positive difference on consolidation to be immediately and clearly deducted from reserves.	Not adopted.
32.1	To authorize or require the use of the proportional integration method of consolidation.	Adopted. The proportional consolidation method is optional. When not applied, the equity method must be used.
33.2(c)	To include the accounts of an associated company (when included for the first time) at book value or by the equity method.	Adopted.
33.3	To require uniform valuation before calculating the difference arising from the use of the equity method.	Adopted.
33.9	Not to apply where the participating interest in the capital of the associated undertaking is not material for the purposes of Article 16.3.	Adopted.
34.5	To disclose holdings of less than 10 per cent in the capital of other companies.	Adopted.
34.11	To disclose the difference between the tax charged to the consolidated profit and loss account for the financial year and to those for earlier financial years and the amount of tax payable in respect of those years in the balance sheet.	Adopted. Disclosure is also required in the income statement and in the notes.
34.12	To require disclosure of the compensation of,	Not adopted.

Article	Option	Portuguese legislation
	and pension commitments to, the controlling company's directors from or by associated and multi-group companies.	
34.13	To require disclosure of loans and guarantees to the controlling company's directors from associated and multi-group companies.	Not adopted.
35	To permit disclosure in the notes of companies included in or excluded from consolidation to take the form of Mercantile Register entries to be omitted.	Not adopted.
36(d)	To require or permit disclosure of the group's treasury stock in the notes rather than in the annual report.	Not adopted. Disclosure of sales and purchases of the group's treasury stock is also required in the annual report.
39.1–2	To authorize or require that account should be taken of the results of previous consolidations of groups which already existed before the entry into force of the directive, for group, multi-group or associated companies.	Not adopted.
39.3(a)	To authorize existing groups to amortize the positive differences on consolidation as from the date of the entry into force of the legislation implementing the directive.	Adopted.
39.3(b)	To authorize the positive differences on consolidation to be deducted from reserves at the date of the first consolidation of already existing groups.	Adopted.
40.1	To derogate from the consolidated accounts format, valuation methods and content of the notes in the case of banks, financial entities and insurance companies.	Not adopted. Consolidated accounts are now compulsory for banks and other financial institutions whose financial year begins on or after 1 January 1992 (decree law 36/92 of 28 March 1992, drafted by the Bank of Portugal). Insurance companies are not yet required to prepare consolidated accounts. The Insurance Institute of Portugal is preparing a new Chart of Accounts for insurance companies in line with EC directives.
40.2(a)	To suspend until 1993 the obligation for banks, financial entities and insurance companies to consolidate.	Not adopted. Consolidated accounts are now compulsory for banks and other financial institutions whose financial year begins on or after 1 January 1992 (decree law 36/92 of 28 March 1992, drafted by the Bank of Portugal). Insurance companies are not yet required to prepare consolidated accounts. The Insurance Institute of Portugal is preparing a new Chart of Accounts for insurance companies in line with EC directives.
40.2(b)	To omit from consolidation until 1993 subsidiaries that are banks, financial entities and insurance companies.	Adopted. They are included in the consolidated accounts by the equity method.

Article	Option	Portuguese legislation
41.3	To include as group companies those controlled by contract, or by-law provision, or by virtue of the right to appoint a majority of directors, or by a management contract.	Not adopted.
41.5	To exclude from the group companies which are parent companies or which are established as companies of a type other than that required for limited liability companies.	Adopted. State-owned companies, co-operatives and sole proprietors are not obliged to prepare consolidated accounts.

For options included in articles 43–6, see the comments on the Fourth Directive

Article	Option	Portuguese legislation
43 (57 of Fourth Directive)	To exempt the subsidiaries of parent companies in the EC, with the prior agreement of all the shareholders, from the obligations concerning the content, audit and publication of the annual accounts.	Not adopted.
44 (58 of Fourth Directive)	To exempt parent companies carrying out a consolidation from the obligation to have their income statements audited and published.	Not adopted.
45 (59.1 of Fourth Directive)	To include holdings in associated and group companies in the individual balance sheet as sub-item accounts.	Adopted.
45 (59.2(d) of Fourth Directive)	To use alternative valuation methods for the above-mentioned items.	Adopted. Valuation follows the IAS suggestion, rather than the EC directive.
45 (59.5 of Fourth Directive)	Treatment in the individual financial statements of the portion of income allocable to holding in companies recorded by the equity method.	Adopted.
46	To exempt a consolidating company from the obligation to disclose its holdings in its individual financial statements.	Adopted. Note 16 to the individual accounts of the mother company must identify the group where the company appears to be consolidated.

Appendix D
Useful information

MINISTRIES AND OTHER PUBLIC BODIES
Ministries

Ministério da Administração Interna (Ministry of Internal Affairs)
Praça do Comércio
1100 Lisboa
Tel. 01-346 4521, fax 01-342 8279

Ministério da Agricultura, Alimentação e Pescas (Ministry of Agriculture, Fisheries and Food)
Praça do Comércio
1100 Lisboa
Tel. 01-342 7597, fax 01-347 0356

Ministério do Ambiente e Recursos Naturais (Ministry of the Environment and Natural Resources)
Rua do Século 51
1200 Lisboa
Tel. 01-347 5512, fax 01-346 0150

Ministério do Comércio e Turismo (Ministry of Trade and Tourism)
Avenida da República, 79 – 6º
1000 Lisboa
Tel. 01-793 4049, fax 01-793 0508

Ministério da Defesa (Ministry of Defence)
Avenida Ilha da Madeira
1400 Lisboa
Tel. 01-301 0001, fax 01-301 5293

Ministério da Educação (Ministry of Education)
Avenida 24 de Julho, No. 142, 3º
1000 Lisboa
Tel. 01-609500, fax 01-607003

Ministério do Trabalho (Ministry of Labour)
Praça de Londres 2
1091 Lisboa
Tel. 01-847 0430, fax 01-805823

Ministério da Economia e das Finanças (Ministry of Economic Affairs and Finance)
Rua da Alfândega 5
1100 Lisboa
Tel. 01-288 1222, fax 01-877580

Ministério da Justiça (Ministry of Justice)
Praça do Comércio
1100 Lisboa
Tel. 01-347 4780, fax 01-346 0028

Ministério dos Negócios Estrangeiros (Foreign Ministry)
Largo Rilvas
1300 Lisboa
Tel. 01-396 5041, fax 01-605927

Ministério das Construções Públicas, Transportes e Comunicações (Ministry of Public
Works, Transport and Communications)
Praça do Comércio
1100 Lisboa
Tel. 01-886 8441, fax 01-870650

Ministério do Planeamento e da Administração do Território (Ministry of Planning and
Territorial Administration)
Praça do Comércio
1100 Lisboa
Tel. 01-342 0593, fax 01-3464539

Ministério da Saúde (Ministry of Health)
Avenida João Crisóstomo 9
1000 Lisboa
Tel. 01-544560, fax 01-522861

Ministério da Indústria e Energia (Ministry of Industry and Energy)
Rua Horta Seca 15
1200 Lisboa
Tel. 01-346 3091, fax 01-347 5901

Direcção-Geral das Contribuições e Impostos (Directorate General of Taxes, DGCI)
Rua da Alfândega 2
1100 Lisboa
Tel. 01-879961, fax 01-888 1534

Direcção-Geral do Turismo (Directorate General of Tourism)
Avenida António Augusto de Aguiar 86
1000 Lisboa
Tel. 01-575086, fax 01-355 6917

Secretaria Regional da Economia e do Plano dos Açores (Regional Board for Study and Planning, DREPA)
Caminho do Meio 58
São Carlos
9700 Angra do Heroismo
Tel. 096-31146

Official organization responsible for planning and studying the region. It provides excellent information on labour, salaries and matters related to employment.

Secretaria Regional da Economia (Açores) (Regional Economy Secretary)
Rua Caetano de Andrade 11
9500 Ponta Delgada
Tel. 09-626999

Official government department responsible for the economy, like the Ministry of the Economy but on a regional scale.

Other public bodies

Instituto do Emprego e da Formação Profissional (Employment and Vocational Training Institute, IEFP)
Avenida José Malhoa 11/11E
1000 Lisboa
Tel. 01-727 2536, fax 01-726 4414

Employment and vocational training institute – the local employment centre which provides assistance in labour legislation and vocational training programmes.

Instituto de Apoio às Pequenas e Médias Empresas e ao Investimento (Institute for SME and Investment Support, IAPMEI)
Rua Rodrigo da Fonseca 73/73A
1200 Lisboa
Tel. 01-386 4333, fax 01-386 3161

Official organization responsible for examining the economic and financial feasibility of industrial projects and for co-ordinating EC support, PEDIP funds. Can provide technical and administrative assistance; much information of this sector is available.

Instituto do Comércio Externo de Portugal (Department of Foreign Trade, ICEP)
Avenida 5 de Outubro, 101/3
1000 Lisboa
Tel. 01-793 0103, fax 01-793 5023

Secretaria da Integração Europeia (Secretariat of European Integration)
Avenida Visconde Valmor, 66 – 6º
1000 Lisboa
Tel. 01-760530

Departamento dos Assuntos do Fundo Social Europeu (Department of European Social
Fund Programmes)
Avenida Almirante Reis 72 – 3º/7º
1100 Lisboa
Tel. 01-814 1450, fax 01-820063

Investimentos e Participações do Estado SA (State Financial Participation and
Investment Institute, IPE)
Avenida Júlio Dinis 9–11
1000 Lisboa
Tel. 01-793 0103, fax 01-793 5028

Managed as a financial company, the institute is the holding company for all share-
holdings and investments held by the state. It manages and administers various
companies indirectly.

Operação Integrada de Desenvolvimento da Península de Setúbal (OIDPS)
Avenida 5 de Outubro 114 – 5º
2900 Setúbal
Tel. 065-22452

Câmara do Comércio e Indústria dos Açores (Azores Chamber of Commerce and
Industry, CCIA)
Rua dos Mercadores 63
9500 Ponta Delgada
Tel. 096-22427

Instituto para o Investimento e Participações dos Açores (Institute for Investment and
Privatization in the Açores, IIAP)
Avenida Infante D. Herique, Lote 1 – 5º D
9500 Ponta Delgada
Tel. 096-24146

Supervises all investment projects in the region and co-ordinates related activity.

Sociedade de Desenvolvimento Regional da Ilha de Santa Maria (Santa Maria Island
Free Zone Development Society, ZOFRAM)
Avenida Infante D. Henrique – Edifício Solmar, 10º Frente
9500 Ponta Delgada
Tel. 096-25573

Responsible for all matters related to the free zone; provides information on tax,
financial and commercial incentives in the zone.

STOCK EXCHANGES (BOLSES DE VALORES)

Lisbon Stock Exchange
Praça do Comércio
1100 Lisboa
Tel. 01-888 2735, fax 01-888 3034

Rua dos Fanqueiros 10
1100 Lisboa
Fax 01-864231, 01-877402

Oporto Stock Exchange
Palácio da Bolsa
Rua Ferreira Borges
4000 Porto
Tel. 02-318546/318624/318631/318656, fax 01-200 2475

UNIVERSITIES, TECHNICAL INSTITUTES AND ACCOUNTING SCHOOLS

The list below includes state and private institutions, identified by (S) and (P) respectively.

Universities

The universities listed below are business schools that include the teaching of accounting as independent courses.

University of Trás-os-Montes and Alto Douro (S)
Apartado 202
5000 Vila Real
Tel. 059-321631, fax 059-74480

University of the Algarve (S)
Estrada da Penha
8000 Faro
Tel. 089-803561, fax 089-818560

University of the Azores (S)
Rua Mãe de Deus
9500 Ponta Delgada
Tel. 096-653130, fax 096-653070

University of Oporto (S)
Rua D. Manuel II
4000 Porto
Tel. 02-694462, fax 02-698736

University of Coimbra (S)
Palácio dos Grilos
3000 Coimbra
Tel. 039-22033, fax 039-314935

University of Évora (S)
Rua Cardeal do Rei
7000 Évora
Tel. 066-25572, fax 066-20775

University of Aveiro (S)
Rua Pires Barbosa 67 R/C Dto
3800 Aveiro
Tel. 034-381977, fax 034-28975

University of Beira Interior (S)
Rua Marquês d'ávila e Bolema
6200 Covilhã
Tel. 075-314207, fax 075-26198

Universidade Portucalense (P)
Avenida Rodrigues de Freitas 349
4000 Porto
Tel. 02-577823, fax 02-575127

Universidade Aberta (P)
Rua da Escola Politécnica 147
1200 Lisboa
Tel. 01-397 2334, fax 01-397 3229

Universidade Internacional (P)
Estrada de Benfica 275
1500 Lisboa
Tel. 01-727 2231, fax 01-726 7422

Instituto Superior de Gestão (P)
Estrada da Ameixoeira 112/4/6
1700 Lisboa
Tel. 01-757 0053

Universidade Lusíada (P)
Rua da Junqueira 194
1300 Lisboa
Tel. 01-363 9944, fax 01-363 8307

Universidade Autónoma de Lisboa (P)
Rua de Santa Marta 56
1000 Lisboa
Tel. 01-526701, fax 01-533702

Universidade Nova de Lisboa (S)
Travessa Estevão Pinto
1000 Lisboa
Tel. 01-388 1364, fax 01-387 1105

Instituto Superior de Economia e Gestão (S)
(part of the Universidade Técnica de Lisboa, Lisbon University of Technology)
Rua Miguel Lupi 20
1200 Lisboa
Tel. 01-607099, fax 01-397 4153

Universidade Catolica Portuguesa (P)
Caminho Palma de Cima
1600 Lisboa
Tel. 01-726 5550, fax 01-727 0256

Rua Paraíso da Foz
4100 Porto
Tel. 02-677 0666, fax 02-610 1618

Rua Bela S. Tiago 23 – 1º
9000 Funchal
Tel. 091-25774

Estrada da Circunvalação
3500 Viseu
Tel. 032-27745

Instituto Superior de Ciências do Trabalho e da Empresa (ISCTE) (S)
Avenida das Forças Armadas
1600 Lisboa
Tel. 01-793 5000

Technical Institutes

The technical institutes listed below are business schools that include the teaching of accounting on independent courses.

Technical Institute of Castelo Branco (S)
Rua de S. João de Deus 25 – 3º
6000 Castelo Branco
Tel. 072-23394

Technical Institute of Guarda (S)
Rua Comandante Salvador Nascimento
6300 Guarda
Tel. 071-21634

Technical Institute of Bragança (S)
Rua 1º de Dezembro 6
5300 Bragança
Tel. 073-23082

Technical Institute of Setubal (S)
Largo Defensores da República
2900 Setúbal
Tel. 065-35301

Accounting schools

Instituto Superior de Contabilidade e Administração de Lisboa (ISCAL) (S)
Avenida Miguel Bombarda 20
1000 Lisboa
Tel. 01-769915

Instituto Superior de Contabilidade e Administração de Aveiro (ISCAA) (S)
Rua do Ilhavo
Apartado 58
3800 Aveiro
Tel. 034-381972/381911

Instituto Superior de Contabilidade e Administração do Porto (ISCAP) (S)
Rua Entreparedes 48
4000 Porto
Tel. 02-319009/200 4676

Instituto Superior de Contabilidade e Administração de Coimbra (ISCAC) (S)
Rua Luis de Camões
3000 Coimbra
Tel. 039-71042/72752

REPRESENTATIVE OFFICES IN OTHER EC COUNTRIES
Portuguese Chambers of Commerce abroad

Portuguese Chamber of Commerce and Industry in the United Kingdom
Fourth floor 1–5 New Bond Street House
New Bond Street
London W1Y 9EP
United Kingdom

Chambre de Commerce Franco-Portugaise
97 Boulevard Haussmann
75008 Paris
France

Chambre de Commerce du Portugal
Rue Joseph II 3, 6 étage
1040 Bruxelles
Belgium

Portugal–US Chamber of Commerce Inc.
5 West 45th Street, New York, N.Y. 10036
United States of America

Portuguese–Canadian Chamber of Commerce
1350 Dundas Street West
Toronto
Ontario M6J IY2
Canada

Câmara de Comércio Uruguayo–Portuguesa
Mariano Moreno 2629
Montevideo
Uruguay

Offices of the Portuguese Foreign Trade Institute abroad

Belgium
Institute du Commerce Extérieur du Portugal (ICEP)
Rue Joseph II 5, Bte 3
1040 Bruxelles
Tel. 32-2-2309625, telex 046 24570 ICEP B

Denmark
Det Portugisiske Handelsbureau (ICEP)
Frederiksborggade 1 MZ
1360 Copenhagen K
Tel. 45-1-127632/127613, telex 055 22936 ICEP DK, fax 45-1-938885

France
Institut du Commerce Extérieur du Portugal (ICEP)
135 Boulevard Haussmann
750088 Paris
Tel. 33-1-45639330, telex 042 644594 ICEP F, fax 33-1-42893074

The Netherlands
Portuguese Handelsafdeling (ICEP)
Paul Gabrielstraat 70
2596 NG Den Haag
Tel. 31-70-264371, telex 044 34132 ICEP NL, fax 070-280025

Italy
Ufficio Commerciale del Portogallo (ICEP)
Piazzale Giovanni de Agostini
320146 Milano
Tel. 39-2-470659/4223214, telex 043 321280 Fexpor I, fax 39-2-4122893

Via Flaminia
5600196 Roma
Tel. 39-6-3605284/3603443, telex 043 626331 ICEPRO I, fax 39-6-3613163

Spain
Instituto do Comércio Externo de Portugal (ICEP)
Paseo de la Castellana 141, 17 D
28046 Madrid
Tel. 34-1-5711424/5710442/5713126, telex 052 23618 ICEP E, fax 34-1-5711424

United Kingdom
Portuguese Trade Office (ICEP)
Fourth floor, New Bond Street House
1–5 New Bond Street
London W1Y 9PE
Tel. 44-01-4930212, telex 051 918089 ICEP G, fax 44-01-4934772

Germany
Portugiesisches Handelsburo (ICEP)
Zentrale Bonn
Ubierstrasse 78
5300 Bonn 2
Tel. 49-228-351066/67, telex 41 889620/8869275 ICEP D, fax 49-228-362076

Zweigstelle Hamburg
Am Gaensemarkt 21-23, II
2000 Hamburg 36
Tel. 49-40-344214, telex 41 2163807 ICEP D

PROFESSIONAL ASSOCIATIONS
Accounting associations

Comissão de Normalização Contabilística (CNC)
Rua Angelina Vidal 41
1196 Lisboa Codex
Tel. 01-847978

Câmara dos Técnicos de Contas (CTC)
Rua do Loreto 16 – 3º Dir.
1200 Lisboa
Tel. 01-347 1610/1322/1323

Associação Portuguesa de Contabilistas (APC)
Rua dos Douradores No. 20 1º
1100 Lisboa
Tel. 01-878509

Associação Portuguesa de Técnicos de Contas (APOTEC)
Rua Rodrigues Sampaio 50 – 3º E
1100 Lisboa
Tel. 01-576038, fax 576038

Sociedade Portuguesa de Contabilidade (SPC)
Rua Barata Salgueiro 1 – 2º Esq.
1100 Lisboa
Tel. 01-571844

Financial associations

Câmara dos Revisores Oficiais de Contas (CROC)
Rua Filipe Folque 26 – 4º
1000 Lisboa
Tel. 01-352 9029

Associação Portuguesa dos Analistas Financeiros (APAF)
Largo Eng. António Almeida 70–10º
Sala 432
4100 Porto
Tel. 02-6064810, fax 6003633

Instituto Português dos Executivos Financeiros (IPEF)
Avenida Estados Unidos da América 97 – 1º Esq.
1700 Lisboa
Tel. 01-848 7794/8451, fax 806127

Management associations

Associação Nacional de Gestores das Empresas Portuguesas (ANGEP)
Alameda D. Afonso Henriques 72 R/C E
1000 Lisboa
Tel. 01-890635

Associação Portuguesa de Economistas (APEC)
Rua da Estrela 8
1200 Lisboa
Tel. 01-396 1584

Associação Portuguesa dos Gestores e Técnicos de Recursos Humanos (APGTRH)
Avenida do Brasil 194 – 7º
1700 Lisboa
Tel. 01-899766

Associação Portuguesa de Management (APM)
Rua Rodrigo da Fonseca 182 – 2º Esq.
1000 Lisboa
Tel. 01-682653/683266

Movimento Católico de Empresários e Gestores
Rua dos Douradores 57
1100 Lisboa
Tel. 01-524557

Sindicato dos Economistas
Rua Rodrigo da Fonseca 76 – 1º
1200 Lisboa
Tel. 01-355 7830

ARBITRATION PANELS

Confederação dos Agricultores de Portugal (CAP)
Calçada Ribeiro Santos 19 – R/C
1200 Lisboa
Tel. 01-674063/675171/676820

Confederação do Comércio Português (CCP)
Rua Saraiva de Carvalho 1 – 2º
1200 Lisboa
Tel. 01-396 8539

Confederação da Indústria Portuguesa (CIP)
Avenida 5 de Outubro 35 – 1º
1000 Lisboa
Tel. 01-547454

Federação do Comércio Grossista Português (FCG)
Rua dos Correeiros 79
1100 Lisboa
Tel. 01-347 7689

Portuguese Industrial Association (AIP)
Praça das Indústrias
1399 Lisboa
Tel. 01-645341

Oporto Industrial Association (AIP)
Avenida da Boavista 2671
Apartado 1092
4102 Porto
Tel. 02-672275

AIP European Information Bureau
Praça das Indústrias
1399 Lisboa
Tel. 01-362 0100

JOURNALS, MAGAZINES AND NEWSPAPERS

Cadernos de economia (quarterly journal)
Rua Francisco Rodrigues Lobo 2 R/C Dto
1000 Lisboa
Tel. 01-659950/659959

Comércio de Lisboa (monthly magazine)
Rua Castilho 14
1200 Lisboa
Tel. 01-574778, fax 01-352 0907

Exame (monthly magazine)
Rua Marcos Portugal 16-A
1495 Lisboa
Tel. 01-410 5823/5873, fax 01-410 7050

Fisco (monthly journal)
Rua José Ricardo 5 – 2º Esq.
1900 Lisboa
Tel. 01-815 3540/44, fax 01-815 3545

Vida economica (weekly newspaper)
Rua Gonçalo Cristovão 111 – 6º
4000 Porto
Tel. 02-200 3661, fax 02-318098

APOTEC (monthly journal)
Rua Rodrigues Sampaio 19 – 1º Dir.
1100 Lisboa
Tel. 01-540034, fax 01-576038

Diário de notícias (weekly newspaper)
Avenida da Liberdade 266
1200 Lisboa
Tel. 01-561151/562505/548104, fax 01-536627

Expresso (weekly newspaper)
Rua Duque de Palmela 37 – 3º Dir.
1296 Lisboa Codex
Tel. 01-352 6141

JTCE – Jornal do Técnico de Contas e da Empresa (monthly magazine)
Largo Jean Monet 1 – Piso Menos Um, Fracção A
1200 Lisboa
Tel. 01-534356, fax 01-524446

Informador fiscal (fortnightly magazine)
Rua Santo Ildefonso 42 – 1º
4000 Porto
Tel. 02-200 1006

Revista de contabilidade e finanças (quarterly magazine)
Rua dos Douradores 20 – 1º
1100 Lisboa
Tel. 01-364509

Semanário ecónomico (weekly newspaper)
Rua Santa Marta 47 – 2º Dir.
1100 Lisboa
Tel. 01-352 8071, fax 01-352 8515

Diário económico (daily newspaper)
Rua Santa Marta 47 – 2º Dir.
1100 Lisboa
Tel. 01-352 8171, fax 01-352 8515

Revista das empresas (monthly magazine)
Rua Francisco Rodrigues Lobo 2 – R/C Dto
1000 Lisboa
Tel. 01-659950/659959/692440, fax 01-651430

Pequena e média empresa (fortnightly magazine)
Rua Rodrigo da Fonseca 73
1297 Lisboa Codex

Revista de contabilidade e comércio (trimestrial journal)
Rua Júlio Dinis 778 – 2º DTO
4000 Porto
Tel. 02-6000042, fax 02-6000044

Glossary

PORTUGUESE–ENGLISH

In addition to this glossary, financial statement terminology may be found in the following tables in this book:

- Chapter 3, Table 3.2 (Credit instruments)
- Chapter 5, Table 5.8 (Chart of Accounts)
- Chapter 8, Table 8.1 (Detailed balance sheet)
- Chapter 8, Table 8.2 (Abridged balance sheet)
- Chapter 8, Table 8.3 (Detailed profit and loss account)
- Chapter 8, Table 8.4 (Abridged profit and loss account)
- Chapter 8, Table 8.6 (Vertical layout of the profit and loss account)
- Chapter 8, Table 8.7 (Statement of the sources and application of funds)
- Chapter 9, Table 9.1 (Consolidated balance sheet)
- Chapter 9, Table 9.2 (Consolidated profit and loss account)
- Chapter 9, Table 9.3 (Vertical layout of the consolidated profit and loss account)

A

a curto prazo	short-term
a longo prazo	long-term
acção	share
acção ao portador	bearer share
acção convertível	convertible share
acção nominativa	registered share
acção ordinária	ordinary share
accionista	shareholder
accionista minoritário	minority shareholder

acções e/ou obrigações	securities
acções novas/nova emissão	new (share) issue
acções preferenciais	preference shares
acordo de dupla tributação	double taxation agreement
acréscimos	accruals
acréscimos e diferimentos	accrued expenses
actas	minutes
activo corrente/activo circulante	current assets
activo fixo	fixed asset
activo incorpóreos	intangible assets
activo total	capital employed
activos	assets
activos líquidos	liquid assets
activos não monetários	non-monetary assets
activos tangíveis/corpóreos	tangible assets
adiantamentos	prepayments
admissão a cotação	go public
admissão a cotação na bolsa	introduction to the stock exchange
advogado	lawyer
ajustamento à inflação	inflation adjustment
ajustamentos de consolidação	consolidation adjustments
alavancagem	leverage
alugar	hire
amortização	amortization; depreciation
amortização /depreciação linear/quotas constantes	straight-line depreciation
amortização acelerada	accelerated depreciation
amortização acumulada	accumulated depreciation
amortização contabilística	depreciation as recorded in the books
amortização degressiva	declining balance depreciation
amortização do exercício (regular)	depreciation 'according to plan'
amortização extraordinária	additional depreciation; excess depreciation
amortizar (depreciar/reintegrar)	depreciate
análise por idades	age analysis
anexo ao balanco e à demonstração de resultados	notes on the accounts
ano de atribuição	year of assessment
ano financeiro/exercício económico	financial year
ano fiscal	fiscal year
aplicação de lucros	appropriation of profits; profit allocation
aquisição	acquisition
aquisição de capital	stocktaking
arrendamento de imóvel	lease agreement
arrendar	let, rent out

arrendatário	leasehold
assembleia geral anual	annual general meeting (AGM)
Associação Portuguesa de Analistas Financeiros (APAF)	Portuguese Society of Financial Analysts
Associação Portuguesa de Contabilistas (APC)	Portuguese Society of Accountants
Associação Portuguesa de Economistas (APE)	Portuguese Society of Economists
Associação Portuguesa de Técnicos de Contas (APOTEC)	Portuguese Society of Registered Accountants
auditor das contas consolidadas	group auditor
auditoria	audit
auditor, revisor de contas	auditor
avaliação/valorimetria	valuation

B

badwill	negative goodwill
balanço	balance sheet
balanço consolidado	consolidated balance sheet
balanço social	social audit
banco	bank
Banco de Portugal (*banco central*)	central bank (of Portugal)
base de afectação	allocation basis
base de avaliação	valuation basis
base de tributação/matéria colectável	tax assessment value
base do exercício/especialicação	accrual basis
bens imobiliários/imóveis	property, real estate
bolsa de valores	business community's stock exchange; stock exchange, stock market
bruto	gross

C

caixa	cash
Câmara do Comércio	Board of Commerce
Câmara dos Revisores Oficiais de Contas	National Audit Bureau; Chamber of Official Auditors
Câmara dos Técnicos de Contas (CTC)	Chamber of Chartered Accountants
Câmara Municipal	town hall
câmbio	exchange (foreign)
capital	capital; stock
capital alheio	loan capital
capital próprio	shareholders' equity; equity
capital social (por acções)	share capital

capitalização bolsista	market capitalization
capitalização de despesas (no activo)	capitalize (expenses to assets)
características qualitativas da informação	fundamental accounting concept
certificação legal de contas	report of independent auditor; qualified audit report
cessão de imobilizado	disposal (fixed assets)
cheque	cheque
classificação de contas	account classification
clientes	trade debtors
cobranças duvidosas	doubtful receivables
Código Civil	Civil Code
Código Comercial	Commercial Code
Código das Sociedades Comerciais	Companies Act
Comissão de Normalização Contabilística (CNC)	Accounting Standards Board
Comissão de Normas Internacionais de Contabilidade (IASC)	International Accounting Standards Committee (IASC)
comissão de trabalhadores	board representation (for employees)
Comissão do Mercado de Valores Mobiliários (CMVM)	the business community's stock exchange committee
companhia multinacional	multinational company (MNC)
compra	purchase
comprador	buyer
comprar a prestações	hire-purchase
conceito	concept
conceito contabilístico	accounting concept
conceito de materialidade	concept of materiality
conceito de rendimento	income concept
concentreção de empresas	business combination
Confederação da Agricultura Portuguesa	Confederation of Portuguese Agriculture
Confederação da Indústria Portuguesa	Confederation of Portuguese Industry
Confederação do Comércio Português	Confederation of Portuguese Commerce
Confederação Geral de Trabalhadores Portugueses (CGTP)	General Confederation of Portuguese Workers
conselho de administração/conselho de gerência	board (of directors)
consistente	consistent
consolidação	consolidation
consolidação proporcional	proportional consolidation
consolidado	consolidated
conta	account
conta bancária congelada	blocked (bank) account
conta de lucros e perdas consolidada	consolidated profit and loss accounts
contabilidade	accountancy, accounting
contabilidade a preços correntes	price-level accounting

contabilidade ajustada a inflação	inflation accounting
contabilidade ao custo corrente	current cost accounting
contabilidade ao custo de aquisição (histórica)	acquisition accounting
contabilidade como profissão	accountancy profession
contabilidade das fusões	merger accounting
contabilidade das sociedades	equity accounting
contabilidade de custos/contabilidade analítica	cost accounting
contabilidade do exercício (anual)	accrual accounting
contabilidade externa	financial accounting
contabilidade financeira	financial accounting
contabilidade geral	financial accounting
contabilidade social	social accounting
contabilista	accountant
contas anuais	annual accounts
contas consolidadas	consolidated accounts, group accounts
contas de ordem; contas extra-patrimoniais	off-balance sheet
contas intercalares	interim accounts
contingente	contingent
contrato	contract
contrato de arrendamento (imóveis) ou aluguer (móveis)	lease contract
contrato social/estatutos da sociedade/ pacto social	articles of association
contribuições para a previdência	pension scheme
conversão	conversion, translation (currency)
conversão (de divisas/moedas)	translation (of currencies)
conversão de moeda estrangeira	foreign currency translation
convertível	convertible
corpo contabilístico	accountancy body
corrector	broker/dealer
cotada	listed (on the stock exchange)
cotada (em bolsa de valores)	quoted (on the stock exchange)
cotada na bolsa	public
crédito	credit
crédito de imposto	tax credit
crédito incobrável	bad debt loss
credor	creditor
custo	cost
custo das vendas	cost of sales
custo de aquisição	acquisition cost, cost of acquisition
custo das mercadorias vendidas	cost of goods sold
custo de reposição	replacement cost
custo histórico	historical cost

custo real	actual cost
custos de exploração/operacionais	operating costs
custos/despesas de investigação e desenvolvimento	research and development costs/expenses
custos diferidos	deferred charge/deferred credit
custos fixos	fixed costs
custos indirectos	indirect costs

D

dar contas; prestar contas	account for
débito	debit
declaração de rendimentos	income tax return
dedutível (para efeitos fiscais)	deductible (for tax purposes)
democracia industrial	industrial democracy
demonstração consolidada de resultados	consolidated income statement
demonstração de resultados	income statement
demonstração de resultados líquidos	profit and loss account
descoberto bancário	bank overdraft
descoberto bancário	overdraft
desconto	discount
desembolso	disbursement
despesa/gasto	expenditure/expenses
despesa de investimento	capital expenditure
despesas	costs
despesas antecipadas	pre-paid expenses
despesas de exploração	operating expenses
desvio	variance
devedor	debtor
diário	day book
diferença de consolidação	reserve against consolidated assets
diferença de consolidação	goodwill on consolidation
diferença de tradução/conversão	translation difference
dinheiro	money
Direcção-Geral das Contribuições e Impostos	National Tax Board
director/administrador	director
director executivo	managing director
disponibilidades	cash and bank balance
distribuição de dividendos	distribution (dividend)
dívida	debt
dívida a pagar	liability
dívidas a receber	receivables
dívidas de cobrança duvidosa	doubtful debts

dívidas incobráveis (ou de cobrança duvidosa)	bad debts
dividendo	dividend
dividendo antecipado	interim dividend
divisa	currency
dos dois o mais baixo (custo ou mercado)	lower of cost or market value
dos dois o mais baixo (custo ou valor realizável líquido)	lower of cost or net realizable value

E

edifícios	buildings
emissão de acções	issue of share capital
empregado por conta de outrem	employee
empregador/patrão	employer
empresa/sociedade	company
empresa associada	associated company
empresa cotada em bolsa	listed company
empresa do grupo	group company
empresa locadora	lessor company
empresa locatária	lessee company
empresa multinacional	multinational enterprise
empréstimo convertível	convertible loan
empréstimo por livranças	promissory note loan
empréstimos	borrowings; loans
empréstimos com garantia	secured loan
encargo diferido	deferral expenditure
equipamentos e maquinaria	machinery and equipment
escritório	office
escritório de contabilidade	accounting firm
escrituração/contabilidade	bookkeeping
escrituração anual de contas/livros	annual accounts book
especialização dos exercícios	matching concept
estrutura conceptual	conceptual framework
estrutura financeira	financial structure
exercício anterior	prior period
exigências/requisitos estatutários	statutory requirements
exigências de prestação de contas	disclosure requirements
exígivel a curto prazo	current liabilities
existências	inventories
exportações	exports
exposição ao risco cambial	foreign exchange exposure
exposição cambial	currency exposure
exposição (cambial) transacção	transaction exposure
extraordinário	extraordinary

F

fábrica	factory
factura	invoice
FAS	Financial Accounting Standards (FAS)
FASB	Financial Accounting Standards Board (FASB)
Federação Internacional de Contabilidade (IFAC)	International Federation of Accountants (IFAC)
ferramentas	tools
FIFO	first in, first out (FIFO)
filial	affiliated company
fisco/administração fiscal/Direcção-geral das contribuições e impostos	tax authority
(fluxo de caixa líquido) cash flow	cash flow
fornecedores	trade creditors
fraude fiscal	tax fraud
fundo de maneio	working capital
fundo de pensões	pension fund
fusão	merger

G

ganho cambial	exchange gain
ganho comercial	trading profit
ganho extraordinário	extraordinary income
ganhos	earnings
ganhos de conversão/perdas de conversão	translation gains/losses on consolidation
garantia	guarantee
gastos gerais	overheads
gastos gerais directos	direct overheads
gestão	management
gestor	manager
goodwill negativo	negative goodwill
goodwill, trespasse, chave	goodwill
grupo	group

H

hipoteca	mortgage

I

idade das dívidas, ageing	ageing of debts
imagem verdadeira e apropriada	true and fair view

imposto	tax
imposto a pagar	income tax liability
imposto a pagar (diferido)	deferred tax liability
imposto de retenção na fonte	withholding tax
imposto de selo	stamp duty
imposto diferido	deferred tax
imposto municipal (derrama)	municipal tax
imposto sobre as mais-valias (ganhos de capital)	capital gains tax (CGT)
imposto sobre o rendimento	income tax
imposto sobre o rendimento das pessoas colectivas (IRC)	corporation tax
imposto sobre o valor acrescentado (iva)	value-added tax (VAT)
imposto sobre os dividendos	profit-sharing tax
impostos antecipados	pre-paid tax
indicador de rendimento	income measure
índice de precos no consumidor	consumer price index
'insider trading'	insider trading
instalações	plant; fixtures and fittings
Instituto de Apoio as Pequenas e Medias Empresas e ao Investimento (IAPMEI)	
Instituto do Comércio Externo de Portugal (ICEP)	Portuguese Foreign Trade Institute
Instituto do Emprego e Formação Profissional (IEFP)	Institute of Employment and Professional Training
Instituto Português de Executivos Financeiros (IPEF)	Portuguese Institute of Financial Executives
interesse minoritário	minority interest
interesses minoritários	minorities
inventariação física	physical stocktaking
inventário	inventory
inventário	list of assets and liabilities
investimentos	investments

J

juro	interest

L

lease-back	lease-back
lei	law
lei/convenção	Act/law
letra de câmbio	bill of exchange
LIFO	last in, first out (LIFO)

liquidação do passivo	discharge from liability
liquidez	liquidity
líquido	net
Lista de Contas	Chart of Accounts
livrança	promissory note
livro de caixa	cash book
livros de escrituração	books of account
livros selados	statutory books
locação financeira	finance lease
locador	lessor
locatário	lessee
loja	shop
lucro	profit
lucro/prejuizo anual	profit/loss for the year
lucro bruto	gross profit
lucro cambial	exchange profit
lucro de exploração	operating income
lucro distribuível	distributable earnings, profit available for distribution
lucro líquido/prejuízo anual	net profit/loss for the year
lucro ou prejuízo consolidado	consolidated profit or loss for the year
lucros anteriores a aquisição	pre-acquisition profits
lucros por acção	earnings per share (EPS)
lucros retidos/reservas	revenue reserve

M

mais-valia	capital gain
mapa de fluxos/mapa de origens e aplicações de fundos (MOAF)	funds statement
mapa de origens e aplicações de fundos	sources and application of funds statement
mapas financeiros anuais	annual financial statements
mapas financeiros consolidados	consolidated financial statements
marca	brand
marca comercial	trade mark
material de transporte	motor vehicles
materialidade	materiality
matérias-primas	raw materials
melhorias no terreno	land improvements
membro do conselho de administração	board member, member of the board (of directors)
menos-valia	capital loss
mercado de capitais	capital market
mercado de listagem/sem cotações	unlisted securities market (USM)
mercado de títulos	securities market

mercado não oficial	over-the-counter (OTC) market
mercadorias	goods
mesa da assembleia geral	general meeting of shareholders
método da percentagem de acabamento	percentage of completion method
método da equivalência patrimonial	equity method
método da soma dos dígitos	sum of the digits method
método de amortização	depreciation method
método de avaliação	valuation method
método da concentração de capital	pooling of interests method
método de reporte/diferimento	deferral method
Ministério das Finanças	Ministry of Finance
mobiliário	movable
modelo de balanço	balance sheet format
modelos de demonstração de resultados	profit and loss account formats
moeda estrangeira/divisa	foreign currency
monopólio	monopoly

N

não cotada (na bolsa de valores)	unquoted
negócio; actividade	business
nominal	nominal
nominal/par	par
norma contabilística	accounting standard
normas de auditoria	auditing standards
Normas Internacionais de Contabilidade (IAS)	International Accounting Standards (IAS)
Normas Técnicas de Revisão de Contas	Generally Accepted Auditing Standards (GAAS)
notário	public notary
número, cifra	figure

O

obrigação	bond
obrigação (título de dívida)	debenture
oferta de compra	take-over bid
parecer ser reservas	unqualified opinion
órgãos sociais	governing bodies

P

pacto social	certification of incorporation
pagamento em dinheiro	cash payment
pagar; a pagar; pago	pay; payable; paid

parecer 'com reservas'	'except for' opinion
parecer do conselho fiscal	audit of management's administration
parecer favorável	clear (from of) audit report
participação dos empregados	employee participation
participação maioritária	majority shareholding
participações financeiras (em filiais e associadas)	investments in subsidiary and associated companies
passivo condicional	contingent liabilities
passivo de longo prazo	long-term liabilities
passivos	liabilities
patente	patent
pedir a admissão a cotação	make public
pensão	pension
pensões de reforma	pension costs
per/rácio cotação/lucro por acção	p/e ratio (price–earnings ratio)
perda	loss
perda cambial	exchange loss
perda comercial	trading loss
período de amortização	depreciation period
pessoal	personnel
poder de compra	purchasing power
política contabilística	accounting policy
política de dividendos	dividend policy
portofólio, carteira	portfolio
situação financeira consolidada	consolidated financial position
situação financeira do grupo/situação financeira do grupo	financial position of group
práticas contabilísticas	accounting practices
prática comercial geralmente aceite	accepted business practice
prática negocial	business practice
preço	price
preço de reposição	replacement price
preço de transferência (no grupo)	transfer price, intra-group
prejuízo acumulado	accumulated deficit
prémio	premium
prémio de emissão	share premium
prémios (de pensões)	pension obligation
presidente	chairman
presidente do conselho de administação	chairman of the board
princípio da conservação do capital	capital maintenance concept
princípio da continuidade da empresa	'going concern' concept
princípio da especialização dos exercícios	accrual concept
princípio da materialidade	materiality concept
princípio da prudência	prudence concept
princípio da realização	realization concept

princípio de continuidade	consistency concept
princípio de valorimetria	valuation principle
princípios contabilísticos	accounting principles
princípios contabilísticos geralmente aceites	Generally Accepted Accounting Principles (GAAP)
princípios de consolidação	consolidation principles
procuração	proxy
produção	production
produtos acabados	finished goods
prospecto de emissão	issue prospectus
proveito(s)/receita(s)	revenue
provisão	provision
provisão para depreciação de existências	provision for depreciation
provisão para devedores de cobrança duvidosa	provision for doubtful debts/receivables
provisão para imposto diferido	deferred tax provision

R

rácio de endividamento	gearing
rácio de liquidez geral	current ratio
realização/liberação/pagamento	realization
realizável	realizable
realizável a curto prazo	current receivables
reavaliação	revaluation
reavaliar	revalue
recebimento em dinheiro	cash receipt
recibo	receipt
reconciliação de contas	reconciliation of accounts
reconhecimento	recognition
reconhecimento do proveito	revenue recognition
reembolso	redemption
registo comercial	commercial register centre
registo de accionistas da sociedade	shareholders' register
registo de acções	share register
Registo Nacional de Marcas e Patentes	Portuguese Patent and Registry Office
Registo Nacional de Pessoas Colectivas (RNPC)	National Register of Companies
registos contabilísticos/lançamentos/ assentos	accounting records
relações intra-grupo	parent–subsidiary relationship
relatório	report
relatório anual	annual report
relatório da administração	administration report; directors' report, management report

relatório de auditoria	audit option
relatório do conselho de administração	statutory administration report
relatório do emprego	employment report
relatório dos auditores	auditors' report
relatório e contas	report and accounts
relatório interino	interim report
relatório semestral	half-yearly report
relatórios financeiros interinos	interim financial statements
remuneração	remuneration
remunerações	payroll
rendibilidade	profitability
rendibilidade do activo total	return on capital employed
rendimento	yield, income
rendimento ajustado	adjusted income
rendimento anual	annual income
rendimento obtido	earned income
representação paritária dos sindicatos e accionistas	co-determination
representante dos empregados	employee representative
reserva	reserve
reserva de inventário	inventory reserve
reserva de reavaliação	revaluation reserve
reserva de reposição	replacement reserve
reserva especial para investimentos	special investment reserve
reserva legal	legal reserve
reserva para investimento	fixed assets acquisition reserve
reservas livres	non-restricted reserves
reservas não tributadas	untaxed reserves
reservas obrigatórias (legal, estatutária, contratuais)	compulsory reserves
reservas ocultas	secret reserves
responsabilidade	accountability
responsabilidade ilimitada	unlimited liability
resultado antes de imposto	profit/loss before tax
resultado líquido	net profit
resultados	results
revisor oficial de contas (ROC)	official auditor
risco cambial	currency risk
rotação de pessoal	employee turnover
royalty	royalty
rubricas extraordinárias	extraordinary items
rubricas monetárias	monetary items

S

salário	salary
salários	wages
saldo (de uma conta)	balance (on an account)
sede social	registered office
seguro	insurance
sindicatos	trade union
situação líquida	equity capital
situação líquida consolidada	consolidated shareholders' equity
sociedade anónima	public limited company (PLC)
sociedade cotada em bolsa	quoted company
sociedade de controlo; sociedade-mãe	parent company
sociedade de responsabilidade limitada (por quotas)	limited (liability) company
sociedade em comandita	limited partnership
sociedade em nome colectivo	partnership
sociedade gestora de fundos de pensões	pension management company
sociedade gestora de participações sociais (SGPS)	holding company
sociedade não cotada	close company
sociedade participada	related company
sociedade por quotas	private company
Sociedade Portuguesa de Contabilidade (SPC)	Portuguese Accounting Society
solvibilidade/solvabilidade	solvency
subsidiária/filial	subsidiary company
sucursal	branch

T

take-over/aquisição	take-over
tangíveis/corpóreos	tangibles
taxa	rate
taxa/percentagem	percentage
taxa de admissão a cotação	floating charge
taxa de câmbio	exchange rate
taxa de câmbio corrente	current (exchange) rate
taxa de imposto	tax rate
taxa efectiva de imposto	effective tax rate
técnico de contas	chartered accountant, authorized public accountant
técnico de contas responsável	registered accountant
terrenos e recursos naturais	land
título de conta	account heading

título; existências	stocks
totalmente pago/liquidado realizado	paid up/fully paid
trabalhos em curso/produtos em vias de fabrico	work in progress
transação em moeda estrangeira	foreign currency transaction
tribunal de trabalho	labour court
tribunal tributário	fiscal appeal court

U

União Geral de Trabalhadores (UGT)	General Workers' Union

V

valor	value
valor atribuído	assessed value
valor contabilístico	book value
valor de mercado	market value
valor de reposição	replacement value
valor nominal/par	par value
valor nominal/valor ao par	nominal value/par value
valor realizável	realizable value
valor realizável líquido	net realizable value
valorimetria das existências	inventory valuation
valorimetria do activo	asset valuation
valorização	appreciation in value
variável	variable
venda a prestações	instalment sale
vendas	sales
verificação interina de contas (auditoria interina)	interim audit
vida ainda não decorrida	remaining life
vida económica	economic life
vida útil	working life
vida útil estimada	estimated useful life
volume de negócios	turnover

ENGLISH–PORTUGUESE

A

accelerated depreciation	*amortização acelerada*
accepted business practice	*prática comercial geralmente aceite*
account	*conta*
account classification	*classificação de contas*
account for	*dar contas; prestar contas*
account heading	*título de conta*
accountability	*responsabilidade*
accountancy	*contabilidade*
accountancy body	*corpo contabilístico*
accountancy profession	*contabilidade como profissão*
accountant	*contabilista*
accounting	*contabilidade*
accounting concept	*conceito contabilístico*
accounting firm	*escritório de contabilidade*
accounting policy	*política contabilística*
accounting practices	*prácticas contabilísticas*
accounting principles	*princípios contabilísticos*
accounting records	*registos contabilísticos/lançamentos/ assentos*
accounting standard	*norma contabilística*
Accounting Standards Board	Comissão de Normalização Contabilística (CNC)
accrual accounting	*contabilidade do exercício (anual)*
accrual basis	*base do exercício*
accrual concept	*princípio da especialização dos exercícios*
accruals	*acréscimos*
accrued expenses	*acréscimos de custos*
accumulated deficit	*prejuízo acumulado*
accumulated depreciation	*amortização acumulada*
acquisition	*aquisição*
acquisition accounting	*contabilidade ao custo de aquisição (histórica)*
acquisition cost	*custo de aquisição*
act/law	*lei/convenção*
actual cost	*custo real*
additional depreciation	*amortização extraordinária*
adjusted income	*rendimento ajustado*
administration report	*relatório da administração*
affiliated company	*filial*
age analysis	*análise por idades*
ageing of debts	*idade das dívidas, ageing*
allocation basis	*base de afectação*

amortization	*amortização*
annual accounts	*contas anuais*
annual accounts book	*escrituração anual de contas/livros*
annual financial statements	*mapas financeiros anuais*
annual general meeting (AGM)	*assembleia geral anual*
annual income	*rendimento anual*
annual report	*relatório anual*
appreciation in value	*valorização*
appropriation of profits	*aplicação de lucros*
articles of association	*contrato social/estatutos da sociedade/ pacto social*
assessed value	*valor atribuído*
asset valuation	*valorimetria do activo*
assets	*activos*
associated company	*empresa associada*
audit	*auditoria*
audit of management's administration	*parecer do conselho fiscal*
audit opinion	*relatório de auditoria*
auditing standards	*normas de auditoria*
auditor	*auditor; revisor de contas*
auditor's report	*relatório dos auditores*
authorized public accountant	*técnico de contas*

B

bad debt loss	*crédito incobrável*
bad debts	*dívidas incobráveis (ou de cobrança duvidosa)*
balance (on an account)	*saldo (de uma conta)*
balance sheet	*balanço*
balance sheet format	*modelo de balanço*
bank	*banco*
bank overdraft	*descoberto bancário*
bearer share	*acção ao portador*
bill of exchange	*letra de câmbio*
blocked (bank) account	*conta bancária congelada*
board member	*membro do conselho de administração*
board of commerce	*câmara do comércio*
board (of directors)	*conselho de administração/conselho de gerência*
board representation (for employees)	*comissão de trabalhadores*
bond	*obrigação*
bookkeeping	*escrituração/contabilidade*
books of account	*livros de escrituração*
book value	*valor contabilístico*

borrowings	*empréstimos*
branch	*sucursal*
brand	*marca*
broker/dealer	*corrector*
buildings	*edifícios*
business	*negócio; actividade*
business combination	*concentreção de empresas*
business community's stock exchange	*bolsa de valores*
business practice	*prática negocial*
buyer	*comprador*

C

capital	*capital*
capital employed	*activo total*
capital expenditure	*despesa de investimento*
capital gain	*mais-valia*
capital gains tax (CGT)	*imposto sobre as mais-valias (ganhos de capital) (irc e/ou irs)*
capital loss	*menos-valia*
capital maintenance concept	*princípio da conservação do capital*
capital market	*mercado de capitais*
capitalize (expenses to assets)	*capitalização de despesas (no activo)*
cash	*caixa*
cash and bank balance	*disponibilidades*
cash book	*livro de caixa*
cash flow	*(fluxo de caixa líquido)*
cash payment	*pagamento em dinheiro*
cash receipt	*recebimento em dinheiro*
central bank (of Portugal)	*banco de Portugal (banco central)*
certification of incorporation	*pacto social*
chairman	*presidente*
chairman of the board	*presidente do conselho de administração*
Chamber of Chartered Accountants	Câmara dos Técnicos de Contas (CTC)
chamber of official auditor	Câmara dos Revisores Oficiais de Contas
Chart of Accounts	*Lista de Contas*
chartered accountant	*técnico de contas*
cheque	*cheque*
Civil Code	*Código Civil*
clear (from of) audit report	*parecer favorável*
close company	*sociedade não cotada*
co-determination	*representação paritária dos sindicatos e accionistas nos conselhos de administração*
Commercial Code	*Código Comercial*

Commercial Register	*Registo Comercial*
Companies Act	*Código das Sociedades Comerciais*
company	*empresa/sociedade*
compulsory reserves	*reservas obrigatórias (legal, estatutária, contratuais)*
concept	*conceito*
concept of materiality	*conceito de materialidade*
conceptual framework	*estrutura conceptual*
Confederation of Portuguese Agriculture	Confederação da Agricultura Portuguesa
Confederation of Portuguese Commerce	Confederação do Comércio Português
Confederation of Portuguese Industry	Confederação da Indústria Portuguesa
consistency concept	*princípio da continuidade*
consistent	*consistente*
consolidated	*consolidado*
consolidated accounts	*contas consolidadas*
consolidated balance sheet	*balanço consolidado*
consolidated financial position	*situação financeira consolidada*
consolidated financial statements	*mapas financeiros consolidados*
consolidated income statement	*demonstração consolidada de resultados*
consolidated profit and loss account	*conta de lucros e perdas consolidada*
consolidated profit or loss for the year	*lucro ou prejuízo consolidado*
consolidated shareholders' equity	*situação líquida consolidada*
consolidation	*consolidação*
consolidation adjustments	*ajustamentos de consolidação*
consolidation principles	*princípios de consolidação*
consumer price index	*índice de preços no consumidor*
contingent	*contingente*
contingent liabilities	*passivo condicional*
contract	*contrato*
conversion	*conversão*
convertible	*convertível*
convertible loan	*empréstimo convertível*
convertible share	*acção convertível*
corporate income tax	*imposto sobre o rendimento das pessoas colectivas (IRC)*
cost	*custo*
cost accounting	*contabilidade de custos/contabilidade analítica*
cost of acquisition	*custo de aquisição*
cost of goods sold	*custo das mercadorias vendidas*
cost of sales	*custo das vendas*
costs	*despesas*
credit	*crédito*
creditor	*credor*
currency	*divisa*

currency exposure	*exposição cambial*
currency risk	*risco cambial*
current assets	*activo corrente/activo circulante*
current cost accounting	*contabilidade ao custo corrente*
current (exchange) rate	*taxa de câmbio corrente*
current liabilities	*exigível a curto prazo*
current ratio	*rácio de liquidez geral*
current receivables	*realizável a curto prazo*

D

day book	*diário*
debenture	*obrigação (título de dívida)*
debit	*débito*
debt	*dívida*
debtor	*devedor*
declining balance depreciation	*amortização degressiva*
deductible (for tax purposes)	*dedutível (para efeitos fiscais)*
deferral expenditure	*encargo diferido*
deferral method	*método de reporte/diferimento*
deferred charge/deferred credit	*custos diferidos*
deferred tax	*imposto diferido*
deferred tax liability	*imposto a pagar (diferido)*
deferred tax provision	*provisão para imposto diferido*
depreciate	*amortizar (depreciar/reintegrar)*
depreciation	*amortização*
depreciation 'according to plan'	*amortização do exercício (regular)*
depreciation as recorded in the books	*amotização contabilística*
depreciation method	*método de amortização*
depreciation period	*período de amortização*
direct overheads	*gastos gerais directos*
director	*director/administrador*
directors' report	*relatório da administração*
disbursement	*desembolso*
discharge from liability	*liquidação do passivo*
disclosure requirements	*exigências de prestação de contas*
discount	*desconto*
disposal (fixed assets)	*cessão de imobilizado*
distributable earnings	*lucro distribuível*
distribution (dividend)	*distribuição de dividendos*
dividend	*dividendo*
dividend policy	*política de dividendos*
double taxation agreement	*acordo de dupla tributação*
doubtful debts	*dívidas de cobrança duvidosa*
doubtful receivables	*cobranças duvidosas*

E

earned income	*rendimento obtido*
earnings	*ganhos*
earnings per share (EPS)	*lucros por acção*
economic life	*vida económica*
effective tax rate	*taxa efectiva de imposto*
employee	*empregado por conta de outrém*
employee participation	*participação dos empregados*
employee representative	*representante dos empregados*
employee turnover	*rotação de pessoal*
employer	*empregador/patrão*
Employment and Professional Training Institute	Instituto do Emprego e Formação Profissional (IEFP)
employment report	*relatório do emprego*
equity	*capital próprio*
equity accounting	*contabilidade das sociedades*
equity capital	*situação líquida*
equity method	*método de equivalência patrimonial*
estimated useful life	*vida útil estimada*
'except for' opinion	*parecer 'com reservas'*
excess depreciation	*amortização extraordinária*
exchange (foreign)	*câmbio*
exchange gain	*ganho cambial*
exchange loss	*perda cambial*
exchange profit	*lucro cambial*
exchange rate	*taxa de câmbio*
expenditure/expenses	*despesa/gasto*
exports	*exportações*
extraordinary	*extraordinário*
extraordinary income	*ganho extraordinário*
extraordinary items	*rubricas extraordinárias*

F

factory	*fábrica*
figure	*número, cifra*
finance lease	*locação financeira*
financial accounting	*contabilidade financeira, contabilidade geral, contabilidade externa*
Financial Accounting Standards (FAS)	*FAS*
Financial Accounting Standards Board (FASB)	*FASB*
financial position of group	*posição financeira do grupo/situação financeira do grupo*

financial structure	*estrutura financeira*
financial year	*ano financeiro/exercício económico*
finished goods	*produtos acabados*
first in, first out (FIFO)	*FIFO*
fiscal year	*ano fiscal*
fixed asset	*activo fixo*
fixed assets acquisition reserve	*reserva para investimento*
fixed costs	*custos fixos*
fixtures and fittings	*instalações*
floating charge	*taxa de admissão à cotação*
foreign currency	*moeda estrangeira/divisa*
foreign currency transaction	*transação em moeda estrangeira*
foreign currency translation	*conversão de moeda estrangeira*
foreign exchange exposure	*exposição ao risco cambial*
fundamental accounting concept	*características qualitativas da informação*
funds statement	*mapa de fluxos/mapa de origens e aplicações de fundos (MOAF)*

G

gearing	*rácio de endividamento*
General Confederation of Portuguese Workers	Confederação Geral de Trabalhadores Portugueses (CGTP)
general meeting of shareholders	*mesa da assembleia geral*
Generally Accepted Accounting Principles (GAAP)	*Princípios Contabilísticos Geralmente Aceites*
Generally Accepted Auditing Standards (GAAS)	*Normas Técnicas de Revisão de Contas*
go public	*admissão a cotação*
'going concern' concept	*princípio da continuidade da empresa*
goods	*mercadorias*
goodwill	*goodwill, trespasse, chave*
goodwill on consolidation	*diferença de consolidação*
governing bodies	*órgãos sociais*
gross	*bruto*
gross profit	*lucro bruto*
group	*grupo*
group accounts	*contas consolidadas*
group auditor	*auditor das contas consolidadas*
group company	*empresa do grupo*
guarantee	*garantia*

H

half-yearly report	*relatório semestral*
hidden reserves	*reservas ocultas*
hire	*alugar*
hire-purchase	*comprar a prestações*
historical cost	*custo histórico*
holding company	*sociedade gestora de participações sociais (SGPS)*

I

income	*rendimento*
income concept	*conceito de rendimento*
income measure	*indicador de rendimento*
income statement	*demonstração de resultados*
income tax	*imposto sobre o rendimento*
income tax liability	*imposto a pagar*
income tax return	*declaração de rendimentos*
indirect costs	*custos indirectos*
industrial democracy	*democracia industrial*
inflation accounting	*contabilidade ajustada à inflação*
inflation adjustment	*ajustamento à inflação*
insider trading	*'insider trading'*
instalment sale	*venda a prestações*
insurance	*seguro*
intangible assets	*activos incorpóreos*
interest	*juro*
interim accounts	*contas intercalares*
interim audit	*verificação interina de contas (auditoria interina)*
interim dividend	*dividendo antecipado*
interim financial statements	*relatórios financeiros interinos*
interim report	*relatório interino*
International Accounting Standards (IAS)	Normas Internacionais de Contabilidade (IAS)
International Accounting Standards Committee (IASC)	Comissão de Normas Internacionais de Contabilidade (IASC)
International Federation of Accountants (IFAC)	Federação Internacional de Contabilidade (IFAC)
introduction to the stock exchange	*admissão à cotação na bolsa*
inventories	*existências*
inventory	*inventário*
inventory reserve	*reserva de inventário*
inventory valuation	*valorimetria das existências*
investments	*investimentos*

investments in subsidiary and associated companies	*participações financeiras (em filiais e associadas)*
invoice	*factura*
issue of share capital	*emissão de acções*
issue prospectus	*prospecto de emissão*

L

labour court	*tribunal de trabalho*
land	*terrenos e recursos naturais*
land improvements	*melhorias no terreno*
last in, first out (LIFO)	*LIFO*
law	*lei*
lawyer	*advogado*
lease agreement	*arrendamento de imóvel*
lease-back	*'lease-back'*
lease contract	*contrato de arrendamento (imóveis) ou aluguer (móveis)*
leasehold	*arrendatário*
legal reserve	*reserva legal*
lessee	*locatário*
lessee company	*empresa locatária*
lessor	*locador*
lessor company	*empresa locadora*
leverage	*alavancagem*
liabilities	*passivos*
liability	*dívida a pagar*
limited (liability) company	*sociedade de responsabilidade limitada (por quotas)*
limited partnership	*sociedade em comandita*
liquid assets	*activos líquidos*
liquidity	*liquidez*
list of assets and liabilities	*inventário*
listed company	*empresa cotada em bolsa*
listed (on the stock exchange)	*cotada*
loan capital	*capital alheio*
loans	*empréstimos*
long-term	*a longo prazo*
long-term liabilities	*passivo de longo prazo*
loss	*perda*
lower of cost or market value	*dos dois o mais baixo (custo ou mercado)*
lower of cost or net realizable value	*dos dois o mais baixo (custo ou valor realizável líquido)*

M

machinery and equipment	*equipamentos e maquinaria*
majority shareholding	*participação maioritária*
make public	*pedir a admissão à cotação*
management	*gestão*
management report	*relatório da administração*
manager	*gestor*
managing director	*director executivo*
market capitalization	*capitalização bolsista*
market value	*valor de mercado*
matching concept	*especialização dos exercícios*
materiality	*materialidade*
materiality concept	*princípio da materialidade*
member of the board (of directors)	*membro do conselho de administração*
merger	*fusão*
merger accounting	*contabilidade das fusões*
Ministry of Finance	Ministério das Finanças
minorities	*interesses minoritários*
minority interest	*interesse minoritário*
minority shareholder	*accionista minoritário*
minutes	*actas*
monetary items	*rubricas monetárias*
money	*dinheiro*
monopoly	*monopólio*
mortgage	*hipoteca*
motor vehicles	*material de transporte*
movable	*mobiliário*
multinational company (MNC)	*companhia multinacional*
multinational enterprise	*empresa multinacional*
municipal tax	*imposto municipal (derrama)*

N

National Audit Bureau	Câmara dos Revisores Oficiais de Contas
National Register of Companies	Registo Nacional de Pessoas Colectivas (RNPC)
National Tax Board	Direcção-Geral das Contribuições e Impostos
negative goodwill	*goodwill negativo*
net	*líquido*
net profit	*resultado líquido*
net profit/loss for the year	*lucro líquido/prejuízo anual*
net realizable value	*valor realizável líquido*
new (share) issue	*acções novas/nova emissão*

nominal	*nominal*
nominal value/par value	*valor nominal/valor ao par*
non-monetary assets	*activos não monetários*
non-restricted reserves	*reservas livres*
notary public	*notário*
notes on the accounts	*anexo ao balanço e à demonstração de resultados*

O

off-balance sheet	*contas de ordem; contas extra-patrimoniais*
office	*escritório*
official auditor	*revisor oficial de contas (ROC)*
operating costs	*custos de exploração*
operating expenses	*despesas de exploração*
operating income	*lucro de exploração*
ordinary share	*acção ordinária*
over-the-counter (OTC) market	*mercado não oficial*
overdraft	*descoberto bancário*
overheads	*gastos gerais*

P

p/e ratio (price–earnings ratio)	*per/rácio cotação/lucro por acção*
paid up/fully paid	*totalmente pago/liquidado*
par	*nominal/par*
par value	*valor nominal/par*
parent company	*sociedade de controlo; sociedade-mãe*
parent–subsidiary relationship	*relações intra-grupo*
partnership	*sociedade em nome colectivo*
patent	*patente*
pay/payable/paid	*pagar; a pagar; pago*
payroll	*remunerações*
pension	*pensão*
pension costs	*pensões de reforma*
pension fund	*fundo de pensões*
pension management company	*sociedade gestora de fundos de pensões*
pension obligation	*prémios (de pensões)*
pension scheme	*contribuições para a previdência*
percentage	*taxa*
percentage of completion method	*método da percentagem de acabamento*
personnel	*pessoal*
physical stocktaking	*inventariação fisica*
plant	*instalações*
pooling of interests method	*método da concentração de capital*

portfolio	*portofólio/carteira*
Portuguese Foreign Trade Institute	Instituto do Comércio Externo de Portugal (ICEP)
Portuguese Institute of Financial Executives	Instituto Português de Executivos Financeiros (IPEF)
Portuguese Patent and Registry Office	Registo Nacional de Marcas e Patentes
Portuguese Society of Accountants	Associação Portuguesa de Contabilistas (APC)
Portuguese Society of Accounting	Sociedade Portuguesa de Contabilidade (SPC)
Portuguese Society of Economists	Associação Portuguesa de Economistas (APE)
Portuguese Society of Financial Analysts	Associação Portuguesa de Analistas Financeiros (APAF)
Portuguese Society of Registered Accountants	Associação Portuguesa de Técnicos de Contas (APOTEC)
Portuguese Workers' General Confederation	Confederação Geral de Trabalhadores Portugueses (CGTP)
pre-acquisition profits	*lucros anteriores à aquisição*
preference shares	*acções preferenciais*
premium	*prémio*
pre-paid expenses	*despesas antecipadas*
pre-paid tax	*impostos antecipados*
pre-payments	*adiantamentos*
price	*preço*
price-level accounting	*contabilidade a preços correntes*
prior period	*exercício anterior*
private company	*sociedade por quotas*
production	*produção*
profit	*lucro*
profit allocation	*aplicação de lucros*
profit and loss account	*demonstração de resultados líquidos*
profit and loss account formats	*modelos de demonstração de resultados*
profit available for distribution	*lucro distribuível*
profit/loss before tax	*resultado antes de imposto*
profit/loss for the year	*lucro/prejuízo anual*
profit-sharing tax	*imposto sobre os dividendos*
profitability	*rendibilidade*
promissory note	*livrança*
promissory note loan	*empréstimo por livranças*
proportional consolidation	*consolidação proporcional*
provision	*provisão*
provision for depreciation	*provisão para depreciação de existências*
provision for doubtful debts/receivables	*provisão para devedores de cobrança duvidosa*

proxy	*procuração*
prudence concept	*princípio da prudência*
public	*cotada na bolsa*
public limited company (PLC)	*sociedade anónima*
purchase	*compra*
purchasing power	*poder de compra*

Q

qualified audit report	*certificação legal de contas*
quoted company	*sociedade cotada em bolsa*
quoted (on stock exchange)	*cotada (em bolsa de valores)*

R

rate	*taxa*
raw materials	*matérias-primas*
real estate, property	*bens imobiliários/imóveis*
realizable	*realizável*
realizable value	*valor realizável*
realization	*realização/liberação/pagamento*
realization concept	*princípio da realização*
receipt	*recibo*
receivables	*dívidas a receber*
recognition	*reconhecimento*
reconciliation of accounts	*reconciliação de contas*
redemption	*reembolso*
registered accountant	*técnico de contas responsável*
registered office	*sede social*
registered (share)	*acçao nominativa*
related company	*sociedade participada*
remaining life	*vida ainda não decorrida*
remuneration	*remuneração*
rent out/let	*arrendar*
replacement cost	*custo de reposição*
replacement price	*preço de reposição*
replacement reserve	*reserva de reposição*
replacement value	*valor de reposição*
report	*relatório*
report and accounts	*relatório e contas*
report of independent auditor	*certificação legal de contas*
report of the auditor(s)	*relatório dos auditores*
research and development costs/expenses	*custos/despesas de investigação e desenvolvimento*
reserve	*reserva*

reserve against consolidated assets	*diferença de consolidação*
results	*resultados*
return on capital employed	*rendibilidade do activo total*
revaluation	*reavaliação*
revaluation reserve	*reserva de reavaliação*
revalue	*reavaliar*
revenue	*proveito(s)/receita(s)*
revenue recognition	*reconhecimento do proveito*
revenue reserve	*lucros retidos/reservas*
royalty	*royalty*

S

salary	*salário*
sales	*vendas*
secret reserves	*reservas ocultas*
secured loan	*empréstimos com garantia*
securities	*acções e/ou obrigações*
securities market	*mercado de títulos*
semi-annual report	*relatório semestral*
share	*acção*
share capital	*capital social (por acções)*
share premium	*prémio de emissão*
share register	*registo de acções*
shareholder	*accionista*
shareholders' equity	*capital próprio*
shareholders' register	*registo de accionistas da sociedade*
shop	*loja*
short-term	*a curto prazo*
social accounting	*contabilidade social*
social audit	*balanço social*
solvency	*solvabilidade*
sources and application of funds statement	*mapa de origens e aplicações de fundos*
special investment reserve	*reserva especial para investimentos*
stamp duty	*imposto de selo*
statutory administration report	*relatório do conselho de administração*
statutory books	*livros selados*
statutory requirements	*exigências/requisitos estatutários*
stock	*capital*
stock exchange	*bolsa de valores*
stock market	*bolsa de valores*
stocks	*título; existências*
stocktaking	*aquisição de capital*
straight-line depreciation	*amortização/depreciação linear/quotas constantes*

subsidiary company   *subsidiária/filial*
sum of the digits method   *método da soma dos dígitos*

T

take-over   *take-over/aquisição*
take-over bid   *oferta de compra*
tangible assets   *activos tangíveis/corpóreos*
tangibles   *tangíveis/corpóreos*
tax   *imposto*
tax assessment value   *base de tributação/matéria colectável*
tax authority   *fisco/administração fiscal*/Direcção-Geral
                                                     das Contribuições e Impostos (DGCI)
tax credit   *crédito de imposto*
tax fraud   *fraude fiscal*
tax rate   *taxa de imposto*
the business community's stock exchange   Comissão do Mercado de Valores
    committee   Mobiliários (CMVM)
the fiscal court appeal   *tribunal tributário*
tools   *ferramentas*
town hall   Câmara Municipal
trade creditors   *fornecedores*
trade debtors   *clientes*
trade mark   *marca comercial*
trade union   *sindicatos*
trading loss   *perda comercial*
trading profit   *ganho comercial*
transaction exposure   *exposição (cambial)/transacção*
transfer price, intra-group   *preço de transferência (no grupo)*
translation (currency)   *conversão*
translation difference   *diferença de tradução/conversão*
translation gains/losses on consolidation   *ganhos de conversão/perdas de conversão*
translation (of currencies)   *conversão (de divisas/moedas)*
true and fair view   *imagem verdadeira e apropriada*
turnover   *volume de negócios*

U

unlimited liability   *responsabilidade ilimitada*
unlisted securities market (USM)   *mercado de listagem/sem cotações*
unqualified opinion   *parecer sem reservas*
unquoted   *não cotada (na bolsa de valores)*
untaxed reserves   *reservas não tributadas*

V

valuation	*avaliação/valorimetria*
valuation basis	*base de avaliação*
valuation method	*método de avaliação*
valuation principle	*princípio de valorimetria*
value	*valor*
value-added tax (VAT)	*imposto sobre o valor acrescentado* (IVA)
variable	*variável*
variance	*desvio/variância*

W

wages	*salários*
withholding tax	*imposto de retenção na fonte*
work-in-progress	*trabalhos em curso/produtos em vias de fabrico*
Workers' General Union	União Geral de Trabalhadores (UGT)
working capital	*fundo de maneio*
working life	*vida útil*

Y

year of assessment	*ano de atribuição*
yield	*rendimento*

Bibliography

BOOKS

Alexander, David, and Archer, Simon (1991) *European Accounting Guide*, London: Academic Press, pp. 457–511.

Arthur Andersen & Co. (1989) *Guide to Investing in Portugal*, Lisbon: Arthur Andersen & Co.

Banco de Portugal (1990) *Relatório do Conselho de Administração/Gerência de 1990*, Lisbon: Bank of Portugal.

BDO Binder Hamlyn (1991) *Financial statements Worldwide*, second edition. London: BDO Binder Hamlyn.

Blum, Patrick (1991) 'Outlook for the Portuguese after five fat years', *Financial Times*, 4 October, p. 3.

Bolsa de Valores do Porto (1990) *Annual Report, 1990*, Oporto: Oporto Stock Exchange.

Caixa Geral de Depositos (1990) *Relatório e Contas 1990*, Lisbon: Caixa Geral.

Calixto, José Gabriel P. (1990) 'O sistema bancário português face à criação do mercado unico communitário', *Estudos* 28, Lisbon: Banco de Fomento e Exterior.

Câmara dos Revisores Oficiais de Contas (1991) *Manual do Revisor de Contas* I–IV, Lisbon: Câmara dos Revisores Oficiais de Contas.

Coopers & Lybrand (1990) *Brief Study on Business Opportunities*, London: Coopers & Lybrand.

Direcção Geral das Contribuições e Impostos (1989) *Código do IRC (comentado e anotado)*, Lisbon: Direcção Geral.

—— (1989) *Código do IRS (comentado e anotado)*, Lisbon: Direcção Geral.

Esteves Pereira, João (1987) *Contabilidade básica* I, Lisbon: Plátano.

—— (1987) *Contabilidade geral* II, Lisbon: Plátano.

Eurostat (1990) *Europe in Figures, 1989–90*. London: Eurostat.

Ferreira, Rogério Fernandes (1977) *Iniciação à técnica contabilística*, second edition, Lisbon: Atica.

—— (1984) *Normalização contabilística*, Lisbon: Arnado.

—— (1991) *Curso de Fiscalidade*, Vol. Ia, IV.

—— (1991) *Il Plano Oficial de Contabilidade (Ensaios e Estudos Críticos)*, Lisbon: Escher.

Gonçalves da Silva, F.V. (1978) *Contabilidade geral* I, fourth edition; II, third edition, Lisbon: Sá da Costa.

—— (1989) *Contabilidade industrial*, ninth edition, rev. Rogério Fernandes Ferreira, Lisbon: Sá da Costa.

Gonçalves da Silva, F.V., and Esteves Pereira, J.M. (1981) *Contabilidade das sociedades*, ninth edition, Lisbon: Plátano.

Gray, Sidney J., Coenenberg, A., and Gordon, P. (eds) (1993) *International Group Accounting: Issues in European Harmonization*, London: Routledge, pp. 191–201.

Instituto do Investimento Estrangeiro and Banco Português do Investimento (1984) *How to do Business in Portugal*, Lisbon: IIE and BPI.

International Accounting Standards Committee (1990) *International Accounting Standards* Nos 1–30, London: IASC.

International Society of Securities Administrators (1990) *ISSA Handbook*, London: ISSA.

Ministério das Finanças (1991) *O livro branco do sistema financeiro*. Lisbon: Ministry of Finance.

Organization for Economic Co-operation and Development (1988–9) *Economic Survey: Portugal*. Paris: OECD.

Silva, António B. da, and Rodrigues, José A. (1989) *Código das sociedades comerciais*, Lisbon: Rei dos Livros.

LEGISLATION

Decreto de 23 de Agosto de 1888.

Portaria n.º 420/76, de 14 de Julho (actualizado).

Decreto-lei n.º 519-L2/79, de 29 de Dezembro.

Decreto-lei n.º 454/80, de Outubro.

Portaria n.º 434/81, de 27 de Maio.

Normas Técnicas de Revisão de Contas, *Diário da República* III Série, n.º 204, de 5 de Setembro de 1983.

Portaria n.º 231/85, de 24 de Abril.

Portaria n.º 270/85, de 10 de Maio.

Portaria n.º 271/85, de 10 de Maio.

Decreto-lei n.º 248/86, de 25 de Agosto.

Decreto-lei n.º 262/86, de 2 de Setembro.

Decreto-lei n.º 410/89, de 21 de Novembro.

Decreto-regulamentar n.º 2/90, de 12 de Janeiro.

Portaria n.º 819/90, de 13 de Outubro.

Portaria n.º 332/91, de 1 de Abril.

Decreto-lei n.º 142-A/91, de 10 de Abril (lei sapateiro).
Decreto-lei n.º 238/91, de 2 de Julho.
Lei n.º 23/91, de 27 de Julho.
Directrizes Contabilísticas da Comissão de Normalização Contabilística.
Normas Interpretativas da Comissão de Normalização Contabilística.

JOURNALS

Jornal do Técnico de Contas e da Empresa.
Jornal de Contabilidade da APOTEC.
Boletim Informativo da Câmara dos Técnicos de Contas.
Revista de Contabilidade e Comércio.

Index

Despite the increasing "digitization" of the technological world, there remain many interactions in mechatronic systems that depend on analog signals. The chapter on analog/digital conversion explores the avenues available for producing analog command signal originating as digital information inside the computer and for gathering information generated by instruments in analog form and converting it to digital information. The basic technology is introduced for digital-to-analog form and converting it to digital information. The basic technology is introduced for digital-to-analog conversion and for flash, successive approximation, integrating, and sigma-delta analog-to-digital conversion. Operating characteristics leading to choice of technology in various situations are discussed as well.

Instrumentation, the counterpart of actuation in mechatronics systems, is the source of ongoing information for the software decision-maker. Because many mechatronic systems utilize mechanical motion, regardless of the final technology of the target system, the discussion of measurement is limited to the most basic quantities of mechanics, velocity and position. Both analog and digital instruments are discussed, including tachometers, resistive measurement, variable reluctance devices, Hall effect, encoders, and resolvers.

The final section is devoted to manipulation of analog electrical signals, both low level for information and at high level for power. Usage of operational amplifiers (op-amps) is explored in both the computing and the follower configurations. General circuit design methods are discussed for a variety of linear and nonlinear applications. Amplifier selection is addressed through a discussion of the specifications of various types and classes of operational amplifiers. While op-amps serve the critical signal processing role for analog information, power amplifiers actually deliver the "goods." That is, the modulated power that allows precise control of mechanical elements. Because all information must go through the electrical medium before reaching the computer, many actuators are of the electro-*something* type, electro-mechanical, electro-thermal, etc. Operation of these elements requires the delivery of large amounts of controlled electrical power. The last chapter of the book is devoted to this subject. Basic operating principles of bipolar junction transistors (BJT) as well as field-effect transistors (FET) are discussed. The crucial factors that come into play when the amplifier has to control large currents at high voltages are brought forward, then configurations found in typical mechatronic applications are explored. Linear (proportioning) amplifiers are discussed as are switching amplifiers for pulse-width modulation (PWM) usage.

In the graduate course taught for mechanical engineers at Berkeley, this material is presented more-or-less in the order in the book. The course is heavily lab oriented and includes a design project for the last third of the semester. The material in each of the major sections, however, is reasonably independent, so the order of study can be varied to meet individual needs.